A PLUME BOOK

THE SECRET POWER OF MIDDLE CHILDREN

CATHERINE SALMON, PH.D., is an associate professor of psychology at the University of Redlands. She lives in Beaumont, California.

KATRIN SCHUMANN is a journalist, freelance editor, and mother of three. She lives in Dedham, Massachusetts.

Praise for *The Secret Power of Middle Children*

"Entertaining and provocative . . . Whether a middleborn or not, the reader will be treated to a fascinating analysis of the ways in which sibling relationships shape people's lives."
—Frank J. Sulloway, author of *Born to Rebel:
Birth Order, Family Dynamics, and Creative Lives*

"A fascinating book about the inner and outer nature of middle children. [It] provides powerful advice that everyone can benefit from."
—David M. Buss, author of *Evolutionary Psychology:
The New Science of the Mind* and *The Evolution of Desire:
Strategies of Human Mating*

The
Secret
Power
of
Middle
Children

How **MIDDLEBORNS** Can
Harness Their **UNEXPECTED**
and **REMARKABLE** Abilities

CATHERINE SALMON, PH.D.,
and **KATRIN SCHUMANN**

A PLUME BOOK

PLUME
Published by the Penguin Group
Penguin Group (USA) Inc., 375 Hudson Street, New York, New York 10014, U.S.A. • Penguin
Group (Canada), 90 Eglinton Avenue East, Suite 700, Toronto, Ontario, Canada M4P 2Y3 (a
division of Pearson Penguin Canada Inc.) • Penguin Books Ltd., 80 Strand, London WC2R 0RL,
England • Penguin Ireland, 25 St. Stephen's Green, Dublin 2, Ireland (a division of Penguin Books
Ltd.) • Penguin Group (Australia), 250 Camberwell Road, Camberwell, Victoria 3124, Australia
(a division of Pearson Australia Group Pty. Ltd.) • Penguin Books India Pvt. Ltd., 11 Community
Centre, Panchsheel Park, New Delhi – 110 017, India • Penguin Group (NZ), 67 Apollo Drive,
Rosedale, Auckland 0632, New Zealand (a division of Pearson New Zealand Ltd.) • Penguin Books
(South Africa) (Pty.) Ltd., 24 Sturdee Avenue, Rosebank, Johannesburg 2196, South Africa

Penguin Books Ltd., Registered Offices: 80 Strand, London WC2R 0RL, England

Published by Plume, a member of Penguin Group (USA) Inc. Previously published in a Hudson
Street Press edition.

First Plume Printing, August 2012
10 9 8 7 6 5 4 3 2 1

(P) REGISTERED TRADEMARK—MARCA REGISTRADA

The Library of Congress has catalogued the Hudson Street Press edition as follows:

Salmon, Catherine.
    The secret power of middle children : how middleborns can harness their unexpected and re-
markable abilities / Catherine Salmon and Katrin Schumann.
        p. cm.
    Includes bibliographical references and index.
    ISBN 978-1-59463-080-4 (hc.)
    ISBN 978-0-452-29793-7 (pbk.)
    1. Birth order. 2. Middle-born children—Psychology. I. Schumann, Katrin. II. Title.
    BF723.B5S25 2011
    155.9'24—dc22

                          2011005023

Printed in the United States of America
Original hardcover design by Catherine Leonardo

PUBLISHER'S NOTE
While the author has made every effort to provide accurate telephone numbers, Internet addresses,
and other contact information at the time of publication, neither the publisher nor the author
assumes any responsibility for errors, or for changes that occur after publication. Further, publisher
does not have any control over and does not assume any responsibility for author or third-party
Web sites or their content.

To Dad:

My middleborn trailblazer and justice seeker.

C.A.S.

To Greta:

We always did say you had special powers.

K.S.S.

Contents

PART TWO

UNLEASHING the SECRET POWER
of the MIDDLE CHILD

ACKNOWLEDGMENTS

Without our agent, Eve Bridburg (now the executive director of Boston's writing center Grub Street), this book wouldn't be in your hands. It took her foresight, imagination, and perseverance to make it happen. Many thanks for bringing us together, Eve.

Caroline Sutton and Meghan Stevenson at Hudson Street Press have given us both excellent guidance *and* free reign. Ever respectful of the writing process, Meghan especially has been approachable and encouraging, while also being the consummate professional.

Thanks to the many researchers, teachers, friends, colleagues, and students who have helped us immeasurably along the way. The dozens of middles who shared their stories with us were generous with their time and ideas. Many thanks to all of you. Now you get your chance to be heard!

We're grateful to those who have shared insights into birth order and parental investment, especially members of the Human Behavior and Evolution Society. A very special thanks also to Frank Sulloway for his innovative and inspiring work on birth order.

Our beta readers helped us find just the right tone: Thank you Lane Zachary, Jennifer Gates, Amy Alkon, Kathleen Buckstaff, and Susan Callahan. The response to our request for input on how middles parent was incredible. To all the Dedham Country Day, Riverdale School, Facebook, and Twitter parents who took the time to fill out our extensive surveys: You've been invaluable. The extended O'Marah clan pulled out all the stops. Thanks also to Christine Duvivier (CEO Positive Leaders) and the *Mothers Need Time Outs, Too* newsletter subscribers for answering our call to action.

Good marketing is such a huge part of being successful, and we're so grateful to the team at Hudson Street and Penguin for their dedication; Ethan McElroy for being our website guru; Kristi Perry for all her inspired P.R. ideas; and Kevin O'Marah for his help with the surveys.

CATHERINE

I owe special thanks to my coauthor, Katrin, who has been so enjoyable to work with, patient with my convoluted academic explanations, and helpful with her own insightful mother-of-a-middle parenting perspective. This has been a great ride.

Another big thanks to Frank Sulloway who helped set me on my own research path, and for being the generous and wonderfully supportive colleague that he is. Special thanks to Martin Daly (and Margo Wilson), my Ph.D. supervisor—the best mentor a graduate student could possibly have. You were always supportive and good at giving me a kick in the pants when necessary. And to Charles Crawford who gave me a place at SFU so I could keep going with my research during the post-doc years.

Thank you to all my friends and family for being so supportive through all the stages of my research and this book. The large Gazeley clan: You are the epitome of what family should be. To Leanne, Maria, Sam, and Bruno: You are a second family to me; thanks for always being there even though I live miles from home. Janice, thank you for bringing me into your family and being such a wonderful and supportive friend. And to the rest of the gang: Carol, Paula, Debbie, Gladys, Robyn, Tamara, Jason, Julie, Tyler, Joseph, David, Terri, Laura, Jessica, Wendy, and Anna. Thanks for putting up with me! Amy Alkon, I am so grateful for all your encouragement and advice. Thank you for being such a cool friend.

And to my own family—my beloved parents who I miss every day and my big brother, David—I thank you for giving me all the love and support this baby of the family needed.

KATRIN

A work of collaboration is only as good as the people you're collaborating with. I couldn't have asked for a more responsive and bright partner than Catherine Salmon. She gave me incredible leeway which made the writing of this book such great fun.

Thank you, Kevin, for putting up with my long days and endless musings. You were so supportive every step of the way. And, my God, you are astonishingly patient. I could not do this work without you.

Peter, Greta, and Svenja: You've been flexible, charming, and truly interested in what I do. You're always ready with feedback and encouragement, and willing to forgive when I'm miles away, whether physically or just in my head. How did I come to deserve such great kids?

I wouldn't be writing books today if it weren't for my parents, Peter and Occu Schumann, and some extraordinary mentors: Penelope Nelson (P.S.8 Brooklyn), Cynthia Hall (S.P.G.S. London),

Dr. Richard Cooper (B.N.C. Oxford), and Marion Lewenstein (Stanford, CA). Teachers *most definitely* have secret powers.

Thanks to my friends from Dedham and London who are always so ready to listen, but especially to Kristi, my running partner, who now knows more about middles than she ever dreamed possible. I am also grateful to the Writers' Room of Boston and the Virginia Center for Creative Arts, sanctuaries that offer writers the space and freedom to find their stories. And, finally, thank you to the vast network of parents and middles—friends and strangers—I tapped into at home and beyond. You made this book come alive.

PART ONE

BUSTING
the MYTH of the
MIDDLE CHILD

CHAPTER ONE

The Myth of the Middle Child

In a family picture that I particularly treasure, there are four people sitting on a couch in a cozy suburban living room. It's Christmas in a steelworkers' town; outside, three-foot-high banks of snow press against the siding, and glacial winds whistle over Lake Ontario. I'm there at the feet of the grown-ups: nine years old, with a halo of white-blonde hair and a grin on my face. As usual, I'm a blur of motion.

Elvis is sitting just behind me. His gleaming teeth are bright against his dark brown skin, and his borrowed winter clothes fit him a little awkwardly. Two more African engineering students are perched next to Elvis, and then, right in the middle, is my Caucasian father—

the middle child who had such a defining impact on my life and my work.

My hometown in Canada was full of mill workers of Anglo-Saxon and Italian descent. Rarely did you see a dark face among the crowd, and most people (including my mother) didn't even think about seeking exposure to other cultures. But my father was different. An engineering professor at the local college, he thought nothing of inviting Elvis and his lonely friends over for Christmas dinner. They were far from home, in a strange, ice-cold land, and my father was kindhearted. He was also fascinated by the unfamiliar.

Not that Dad had grown up that way. He was the third son in a family of four boys and had spent his childhood working on his family's farm in eastern Canada. Yet, as a child who sought to define himself in contrast to his siblings—a middleborn who refused to be lost in the crowd—he became an extraordinary man who embodied so many of the strengths I see in middle children around me. He was a unique person: open-minded, empathetic, patient, driven, loyal, and, frankly, intriguing. I remember him inventing machines, bringing novel characters into the house, and always allowing me to be myself. Since he himself was an independent thinker, he encouraged me to be independent, too. This ended up being critical as both my mother and father passed away before I finished my Ph.D. It was because of him that I— the youngest of two—focused my life's work on middleborns. Because my father was a middle, I just knew there was more to these children than they were being given credit for.

My close friend Leslie is also a middle child. She's one of several in her family of five and is the kind of friend you can always count on. Her positive qualities are legion: She's reliable, generous, kind, and dedicated. But over the years she's made me realize that middles also face certain pitfalls. While Leslie would drive for hours to help someone out, this generosity isn't always reciprocated by friends or even coworkers. She has a terrible time saying no and finds self-advocating challenging. Too often her feelings get hurt.

Leslie is a prime example of how the positive traits of being a middle child can sometimes come back to bite them: Loyalty and generosity can be taken to extremes. I've watched her suffer needlessly, although as she's matured, she's begun to see a pattern emerging in her relationships and has become better at considering her own needs.

These personal experiences set the stage for what would soon become a professional passion of mine. For years I've been perplexed by the fact that the middleborns I've encountered in my own life and middles throughout history seem so capable and accomplished, whereas people's perceptions of them tell a very different story. It became clear to me that middle children are not well understood, and so I turned my attention to them with greater focus.

After more than a decade of research I've come to the conclusion that it's time to shepherd middleborns into the limelight. With this book I'd like to help them not only discover and appreciate their many unheralded positive qualities but also understand how to best put them to use in their daily lives. Middle children are multifaceted and capable, and they face some unique challenges. By highlighting the realities behind the myth, this book will show middles and their parents, friends, and partners how to avoid some of the traps middles can fall into. It will be a practical guide but also full of inspiration and insight. I am the first researcher to take scientific data, historical analysis, profiles of well-known figures as well as real-life anecdotes of ordinary middles, and interpret all this information specifically in respect to middle children. I've spent the past ten years unraveling the myth of the middle child in order to reveal a truer, more complete picture. This book you're holding is the result of that effort.

IT'S ALL ABOUT FAMILY

Ask anyone how family dynamics shapes their vision of themselves, their relationships at work and at home, their hopes for the future, and you're bound to get an earful. Yet, while many books have explored the subject of birth order, not one of them has been specifically aimed at middleborns. There's a distinct lack of good research on middle children, and as a result these false assumptions about them are perpetuated.

Initially, my research in graduate school focused on gender differences, but what I discovered along the way surprised me. In one of my first studies I asked three hundred male and female undergraduate students about the nature of their family relationships, posing such questions as "Who, out of all the people you know, are you closest to?" While 64 percent of firstborns named one of their parents, only 39 percent of lastborns did—and, most surprisingly, only 10 percent of middleborns said they were closest to their parents. The same basic pattern was replicated in a later study of mine as well as in several overseas studies conducted by other researchers.

This was news to me. I was discovering that birth order has a far greater impact on some aspects of family relationships than gender. And middles were proving themselves, yet again, to be different not only from firsts but also from lasts. As I continued my research, I found that middleborns felt less close to their parents, kept in less frequent contact with them once they moved away from home (typically when going to college), were less invested in their own parents (both financially and time-wise), and more attached to their friends. I became fascinated by the seeming paradox in middles' personalities. The middleborns I knew personally and read about were successful, but the research shows that middles are distant from their families, feel less powerful than their siblings, and are overlooked and underappreciated by the general public. How could that be?

While reading reams of psychological literature on birth order, I consistently found very little information focusing on middleborns as a distinctive group. Most often they were thrown into the same category as lastborns, creating the "laterborn" group. In 1982, Jeannie Kidwell wrote cogently about middle children, yet since then much of the work produced has not been backed up by solid theory. But one startling and welcome exception to this was Frank Sulloway's 1996 book, *Born to Rebel*.

Sulloway sat on my thesis defense committee. As a twenty-six-year-old Ph.D. student at McMaster University, I entered the echoing examination room with serious butterflies in my stomach. Already a famous expert back then, Sulloway was more intent on putting me at ease than making me feel like a fool (something many thesis committee members often seem intent on). But it wasn't simply his supportive attitude that inspired me; it was also his groundbreaking work. Here in his book was solid psychological theory on birth order that made predictions and then tested them. And yet, like so many other professionals in the field, Sulloway also focused on firstborns versus laterborns.

Once again, middles were in the shadows. I saw an exciting opportunity and grabbed it. The study of middleborns became my niche.

THE ENDURING MYTHS

Middleborns make up a significant proportion of the population. After all, every family with three or more children has at least one middleborn. While there are around 70 million middles in America (counting adults and children), there's been remarkably little focus on understanding the role that birth order has played in shaping their lives. They're often referred to as "the neglected birth order"—a reference both to the way they've experienced their family growing up *and* the way they've been overlooked by researchers.

But what do people really think about middles? One study from the City College of New York asked participants to list three words that described each birth order position and then rate those words in terms of their positive or negative connotations. The firstborn position was seen as the most favored, with more positively viewed traits than negative ones.

Many traits, such as "ambitious" and "friendly," were listed across several birth orders. Middleborns were the only birth order, however, that did not have the word "spoiled" as a descriptor. Several traits appeared only in relation to the middle position, including "neglected/ overlooked" and "confused." While they actually shared many positive terms with other birth orders (such as "caring," "outgoing," and "responsible"), it's often the traits that make someone *different* that stick in people's heads. Would you remember that middles are "ambitious/ achievers" or only that they are "neglected" and "confused"?

A more recent study explored people's beliefs about which features they attribute to which birth order so researchers could examine how those beliefs influence the way people act. This is important because, for instance, if you believe firstborns are more hardworking or intelligent than others, it could impact which employee you decide to promote. After all, our beliefs about people affect how we behave toward them. Researchers asked Stanford University undergraduates to complete questionnaires that had them rate only children, firstborns, middleborns, lastborns, and themselves on five point scales, including such descriptors as agreeable-disagreeable; bold-timid; and creative-uncreative. Firstborns were seen as most intelligent, obedient, stable, and responsible. Lastborns were the most emotional, extroverted, irresponsible, and talkative.

And middles?

Middle children were perceived as most envious, and least bold and talkative. Not a very good showing for middles in terms of how others perceive them.

And let's take a look at how birth order is portrayed in the media. Dozens and dozens of articles are focused on the so-called "middle child syndrome." According to online, newspaper, and magazine articles, this syndrome is characterized by the following:

- neglect
- resentment
- low creativity
- lack of career focus
- a negative outlook on life
- the feeling that they don't belong

The overall picture is tremendously negative. It portrays middle-borns as unable to find their place in the world, shying away from the spotlight, bitter and resentful, underachievers, and loners. One author of a birth order book remarked that a reader had written to complain about how few pages were devoted to middles compared to other birth orders. The author quipped that only a middle child—neglected and envious—would care about something like that. Considering the lack of attention paid to them in the research literature, I couldn't help but feel for the reader and be annoyed by the author. But it definitely reflects the way middles have been perceived—up until now.

The Secret Power of Middle Children will dismantle these outdated middle child myths and present a fascinating new character sketch. In reality, contrary to expectations, middleborns are agents of change in business, politics, and science—more so than firstborns or lastborns. Middles are self-aware team players with remarkable diplomatic skills. Because they're both outgoing and flexible, they tend to deal well with others—in the workplace and at home. They're more motivated by fairness than money when making life choices, and have a deep sense of family, friends, and loyalty. History shows them to be risk takers and trailblazers, yet they do suffer needlessly from poor self-esteem. Through this book I hope to set the record straight.

THE ROOTS OF OUR FASCINATION WITH BIRTH ORDER

People have been interested in birth order for a long time. Back in 1874, Francis Galton wrote *English Men of Science: Their Nature and Nurture.* He was interested in the relationship between birth order and achievement, and discovered that birth order did in fact influence eminence. You only need to look at how many Nobel Prize winners, classical composers, and prominent psychologists have been firstborns to recognize that there's some truth to this. But did this mean laterborns were less gifted and capable than firsts, or simply that firstborns of his time—males in particular—benefited from more resources than other birth orders?

A few decades later, Alfred Adler, an Austrian doctor, founded the school of individual psychology. Adler is perhaps best known for influencing the disciplines of counseling and psychotherapy, but he was also the first famous birth order researcher. The second of seven children, he was a popular kid, but only an average student. As a boy Adler was extremely competitive with his older brother, Sigmund. In his later writings he emphasized the idea that birth order had long-lasting effects on individual development.

Firstborns, in Adler's view, benefited from being the sole focus of love and nurturing within their families until the birth of a second child. He used the term "dethronement" to describe the firstborns' experience when a sibling comes along. In a three-child family, the oldest was seen as most likely to suffer from neuroticism and substance abuse as they attempt to compensate for excessive responsibility and loss of their pampered position. Adler suggested that firsts would be most likely to end up in jail or suffer from mental affliction (quite the opposite of the kinds of conclusions Galton had arrived at). The youngest was thought to be overindulged, which would lead to poor social empathy.

And middleborns? Since they don't suffer from either dethronement or overindulgence, Adler believed they'd be the most successful of all birth orders. While his attention to middles as an individual group was admirable, his ideas were based exclusively on his own clinical observations and anecdotal evidence.

In more recent history, birth order became a hot topic, leading to a veritable explosion of research in the second half of the twentieth century. But there was no strong theoretical basis for most of these studies and their predictions. In fact, so many hundreds of studies were published that in 1983, Swiss researchers Ernst and Angst conducted a scathing review of all the birth order and personality research published between 1946 and 1980, suggesting birth order effects were minimal at best. This put a serious crimp in further research for years to come.

BUT THEN THE GROUND SHIFTED

All this time no one was asking why. *Why* do specific birth orders reflect certain personality traits and behaviors? Is there a purpose to this? *Why*—rather than *how*—are siblings from the same family so different? *Why* does one child conform and the other rebel? Frank Sulloway, now a visiting scholar at the Institute of Personality and Social Research at the University of California at Berkeley, changed all that.

Because of his attention to detail and the theory-testing orientation of his work, Sulloway started a revolution in the way we think about birth order. He examined all the studies among Ernst and Angst's 1946–1980 sample that controlled for social class and number of siblings. In contrast to their earlier results, he found modest but consistent patterns of birth order effects. In particular he noted that the trends were strongest for the personality traits of *openness to experience* and *conscientiousness*: Laterborns were more unconventional and adventurous, and firstborns were more conscientious than laterborns. This was just as he'd expected.

Sulloway's work supports the notion that personality development has its origins in the family environment, which isn't experienced the same way by each child. In his book *Born to Rebel*, he posits that birth order differences have consequences at a societal level as well, not just among family. His general perspective hasn't gone unchallenged, however. Judith Rich Harris, a scholar with an interest in child development, disagrees strongly with his emphasis on the family environment as a shaper of personality; she argues that the peer group influence is the most crucial. She has written about this at length in her books *The Nurture Assumption* and *No Two Alike: Human Nature and Human Individuality*.

So, just as I was engaging in my own specialized research, the birth order debate was heating up again, and I was right in the thick of it.

WHY BIRTH ORDER MATTERS

Where do I fall in terms of believing in the influence of birth order? While I certainly agree that peers play a significant role in shaping young people's behavior, I think it's a mistake to discount the influence of parents—and particularly parental attention or lack thereof—on young children. Without a doubt younger children whose personalities are just beginning to take form are more influenced by their parents than are teenagers. Children are not passively shaped by their peers; they actively choose their friends. As we'll see later in the book, however, middleborns may indeed be more susceptible to peer influences than their siblings.

Although some psychologists continue to be skeptical about the reality of birth order effects, studies demonstrate substantial differences between firstborns and laterborns in the five basic personality traits:

1. extroversion
2. agreeableness
3. neuroticism
4. openness to experience
5. conscientiousness

These five dimensions surface time after time in personality tests, regardless of the country or the language in which the tests are administered. While the results can be somewhat variable because of the way answers are presented and scored, they reveal strong consistencies that, in my opinion, support the notion that birth order has a tangible impact on the development of an individual's character.

In addition, were researchers to focus more specifically on *individual* birth orders rather than lumping middles with lastborns as they so often do, we'd be able to pinpoint differences with greater clarity and detail. Years ago as I began my own work on birth order and family, it quickly became clear to me that middles deserve to be in their own distinct group: They're radically different from firsts *and* also from lasts. I saw evidence of middle children following a social strategy that was different from their siblings—strategies that reflect the unique challenges of their childhood environment.

I thought often of my own father whose open-mindedness and patience presented an alternative image of middles than the one that is culturally accepted. That's why I'm so fond of that old photo—the one that shows a smiling African Elvis, and a little blonde-haired girl who would grow up to be fascinated by what makes us turn out the way we do.

EVERY CHILD SEARCHES FOR A NICHE

What is it, then, that makes children within a family react so differently to the same basic environment? There's agreement among most researchers that genetic influences account for around 40 percent of the variance in personality and that an almost equal amount of variance (about 35 percent) is due to non-shared environment, in which birth order is key. We call the family environment non-shared as each child experiences it differently.

As we know, if all else is equal on the prenatal and nutritional front, a person's DNA determines how tall he or she will be or whether that person will have curly or straight hair. It even impacts whether the person will favor the left or the right side of the brain—in other words, whether an individual will be interested in avant-garde art or astrophysics. So where does birth order come in? It leads children to pick niches and become specialized: If your older brother is a basketball player and your younger one's a soccer star, there's a greater likelihood that you'll turn to books rather than athletics even if you're six feet two inches tall and love dribbling. It's about the search for a role that allows you to differentiate yourself and grab a little sought-after parental attention.

All families, even animal ones who have multiple offspring at the same time, experience differences in parental allocation of resources. There's always going to be competition among siblings for access to those resources—whether it's parental time, attention, affection, or money. One excellent way to stay competitive for parental investment is to find one's own niche within the family. These niches are shaped by genetic variabilities, differences in sex, and birth order. Each successive child tries to specialize in a unique niche. Conveniently, this results in a division of labor and reduces direct competition. It also makes it harder for parents to compare one child's abilities with another.

Typically, firstborns have the least difficulty in this arena because they're the first to choose their niche and can do so without worrying about their siblings' preferences. (But remember that unless they remain onlies, they *are* eventually dethroned.) If you see personality as a strategy that serves one's interests in the family environment, then it makes sense that the stereotypical firstborn trait of high conscientiousness—being self-disciplined and organized—is designed to please parents and maintain their favor. It's natural that firstborns want to hang on to their special niche and not be dethroned.

Laterborn children, on the other hand, arrive on the scene to find this family role already filled. Their openness to experience makes them more willing to try different roles and develop different abilities in the search for their own niche—one that's different from their older siblings.

THE ART OF DIVERSIFICATION BETWEEN SIBLINGS

Children are notoriously sensitive. All it takes is one negative comparison with a sibling for that child to seek different interests. But even when the comparisons aren't negative, there's still a strong pull toward creating your own special identity.

The boys on the farm during my father's childhood were peas in a pod. They looked fairly similar, were of average height and build, and had baby-smooth faces, dark brown hair, and dark brown eyes (and, later on, receding hairlines!). Yet, as they matured, their paths diverged more and more. The oldest was stalwart, responsible, and serious. The second in line was a bit more of a social animal. When he injured himself and couldn't continue with farm life, he happily turned to the world of real estate.

And then there was my father. Since those above him in the family hierarchy weren't great students and didn't show much interest in the larger world, he chose an academic path. An excellent student, he threw himself into his studies. When he became fascinated by mechanics and began dissecting machines and building contraptions, his parents tolerated his divergent interests. As a middle child he was inclined to march to the tune of his own drum. The youngest, in turn, differentiated himself from my father by remaining to this day working the farm he grew up on.

Had my father's older brothers been better students, my dad might have gravitated more toward athletics or chosen an academic specialty that was markedly different from theirs. The point is that all children in all families seek to diversify their interests in an effort to get more parental attention.

In most social species where there's competition for resources, dominance hierarchies form. Think of the pecking order in birds. Once individuals know their position, there's no need for overt aggression: The dominant one has priority, followed by the next in the pecking order. In dominance hierarchies, the strategies that siblings adopt in order to deal with competition for resources is influenced by differences in size and strength, and these are usually related to age. Older siblings are able to intimidate their younger and smaller brothers and sisters physically. Because of this dynamic, firstborns often become dominant and assertive. And when parents are aware of and discourage these types of physical strategies, firstborns try to express their dominance through status and position in the family. They attempt to do this by meeting parental demands and expectations. As a result, they're often put in a position of authority over their younger sibling(s), a pseudo-parental authority niche unto itself.

Typically, the youngest sibling is best served by low power strategies. Rather than physical force or the threat of it, the baby of the family often appeals directly to the parent in a sibling dispute. We've all experienced the whiny baby sister who runs straight to her parents when the older siblings exclude her or the little boy who throws a tantrum when his siblings won't share.

Where does this leave middleborns? They're typically forced to negotiate on their own, without the parental support given to the youngest. As we'll see, this dynamic leads to the development of numerous abilities that end up greatly benefiting middles in the long run.

Diversifying strategies lets each sibling find his or her own niche in the family, and reduces direct sibling competition. This process is likely to lead to greater differences between siblings who are next to each other in birth order, such as the first and secondborn, as opposed to the first and thirdborn. We can see this at play in my father's family. Despite being a lastborn, his younger brother was actually *less* rebellious and willing to take risks than my father was. And since eldest siblings often occupy the role of surrogate parent with its sense of responsibility and adherence to rules, for laterborns there's no advantage to trying to duplicate that role. Consequently, my father felt less pressure to follow the expected path—the one that led right back to the farmlands of southern Ontario.

BUT WHAT'S SO IMPORTANT ABOUT PARENTAL INVESTMENT?

Many animal species don't engage in parental care at all. On the other hand, human parents provide not only the basic physical means for survival (food, shelter, and protection) but they also invest in fostering the development of skills that are required for their children's success across their entire life span. Think for a moment about parental care in *other* species: Some invest very little, and some invest a lot. Turtles, for example, lay eggs and never even see their babies. Lions and wolves

show their offspring how to catch their own food, and bears are fero-
ciously protective of their cubs for many months after birth.

Humans invest in their offspring for reasons that are often based
on cultural mores. Not all that long ago, primogeniture was the principal system of inheritance. This meant that in a family of four children, in which the first and second child are girls, the third a boy, and
the last another girl, the thirdborn child—or firstborn boy—would
inherit the entire family estate. That child, regardless of his birth order,
would get more attention from the parents than the others. Yet today
we don't feel very comfortable with the idea that parents treat their
children differently. Most modern cultures share an ideal of equal distribution in parenting, though of course this doesn't mean that this
ideal is always realized. In fact, historical evidence, as well as evidence
from contemporary tribal societies, suggests that parental resources are
frequently parceled out unequally.

Biologist Robert Trivers first explained the notion of "parental investment" in an offspring. The more time, money, and/or affection a
parent invests in his or her child, the greater likelihood that child will
survive and later be able to reproduce. But this investment naturally
comes at the cost of the parent's ability to invest in the *other* children,
whether current siblings or future ones. In birds we conceive of this in
terms of feeding and nest protection. In people it covers a wide range
of activities from food and shelter to an education, piano lessons, or
figure skating.

As you can imagine, a child's fitness usually increases with the
amount of parental care he or she receives. Extremely low levels of
parental investment can even result in death since a minimum amount
is required for survival. But at very high levels of investment there's
also a point of diminishing returns, beyond which children are unable
to make use of any further investment. This scenario plays itself out
daily in our family lives. Let's say Johnny, a firstborn, is a decent skater
but doesn't really love the sport and won't ever make his school's var-
sity ice hockey team. In his case, extra practices and hockey camps
cease to be very helpful or fun. In fact, the focus on Johnny's hockey

can begin to backfire if his specific talents and desires aren't considered. Johnny's younger sister, Joan, the middle child, typically gets overlooked (that is, there's very little investment in her) because Sue, the baby, can't survive without constant attention. (Parents must, by necessity, invest highly in an infant.) There's an opportunity for parents here if they can recognize it: At some point parental effort and attention should shift from Johnny to Joan, the middle. Since in this scenario there's likely to be poor return on the investment in the firstborn, and the baby is utterly dependent on parental care, there will be greater overall benefit if the middle gets a share of the investment. There's bound to be an activity that Joan would be delighted to have the chance to pursue if she only had some more of her parents' time and encouragement.

SURVIVAL OF THE "FITTEST"

Of course, it's not just cultural traditions that have an impact on family dynamics. Basic biological impulses play a crucial (if somewhat hidden) role, too. Lying behind so much of our instinctive and learned behavior is the profound and unequivocal desire to survive. Parents who invest highly in children who are unlikely to reach maturity and have babies would soon be out-reproduced by those parents who invest highly in those offspring most likely to provide babies down the road. These children are more valuable in this sense because they are perpetuating parental genetics by providing grandchildren, thereby increasing the genetic representation of their family in the future.

This is called reproductive value. It's a term used to describe the likelihood of future reproduction and plays a role in the "value" of a specific child. Reproductive value increases with age until puberty, so that older, immature kids are actually more valuable than younger ones as a result of infant mortality, etc.

In a way, firsts have a biological lock on their parents' attention.

They then perpetuate this by becoming defenders of parental values and the status quo, while laterborns are more likely to be rebellious.

But the age of the parents is critical, too. As parents grow older, the fitness value of any one child increases while the parents' remaining reproductive value decreases. Because parents' chances of having more babies drop quite dramatically with age, older parents tend to invest more in their children than younger parents. More surviving babies leads to more healthy children, which results in an increased likelihood of healthy adults who can produce their own babies—and ultimately a greater chance that the old parents will be taken care of.

Younger mothers are much more likely than older mothers to kill an infant (controlling for other factors such as marital status and resource availability). This is because younger mothers have a greater likelihood of getting pregnant again, and so they'll have many more future opportunities to reproduce. For older mothers, however, this may be their last chance to have a child.

Let's explore what this means for middles and lasts. While firstborns clearly have an inherent advantage in terms of parental investment, older parents are increasingly willing to invest highly in their lastborn—who represents their last chance, so to speak. In fact, lastborns are the only birth order to receive their parental investment without the competing demands of a younger sibling.

This suggests that middleborns will lose out in terms of parental investment and attention, an important theme that I'll return to in later chapters.

WHEN SIBLINGS BECOME RIVALS

The masked booby is a nesting seabird that breeds on islands in tropical areas. Their nests are shallow indents in the sand, and in each one there are only ever two eggs at a time. When the first egg hatches, all is well—at least, initially.

Within a few days of the second egg's hatching, the older chick forces its sibling out of the warmth and safety of the nest. The smaller chick then dies of exposure or starvation on the sandy beach. Meanwhile, the masked booby parents tolerate this siblicide, either because they can't prevent it or because it's in the best interests of the parents themselves as well as the surviving chick.

But there's a closely related species, the blue-footed booby, which reacts quite differently. When a blue-footed booby chick is placed in a masked booby's nest, the firstborn masked booby will kill the intruder, just as it would kill its sibling. When a masked chick is placed in a blue-footed nest, however, the foster parents prevent the masked booby from killing the other chick. This is presumably because in this species the benefits to parents of having both chicks survive outweigh the cost to the first chick, from a parental fitness perspective.

The comparison is interesting, but obviously humans are nothing like these birds: Our children don't generally try to kill their brothers and sisters. Intense sibling conflict over parental love and attention does occur, though, especially when children are young and close in age. A professor of mine once told a story that made me laugh but also stuck with me over the years. When he was four years old, his seven-year-old sister took him into the backyard and told him to lie down in a hole. Her plan was to shovel enough dirt over her younger brother to put an end to his irritating presence once and for all. He was confused; even when the dirt hit him, he didn't realize what his sister's plan was. The plot was foiled by their mother, and he ended up safe and sound. But the instinctive impulse to grab parental attention was still powerful enough that an idea was hatched whereby his older sister would be able hang on to her coveted spot in the family.

Evolutionary psychologists and biologists, like me, expect mothers and fathers to invest more time and pay more attention to those children who will bring benefits to the parents in the long run. We also expect that offspring will have a different take on the matter. Because biological brothers and sisters share only half of their genes, on average, there's a natural limit to sibling cooperation, and they'll most likely have different views on the allocation of parental resources.

While parents may do their best to encourage equal sharing, children will generally prefer a larger portion of the pie for themselves (sometimes, as we all know, literally). As a result, we shouldn't be surprised when parents and offspring disagree over whether there's been a fair and equal distribution of resources among any particular brood of children. Sibling conflict or rivalry is a frequent occurrence and another major player in birth order differences. This is something middles talk about frequently—and usually with some bitterness. They almost always think of themselves in relation to their siblings, not as freestanding individuals.

Middle children grow up in the shadow of their older sibling and can't help but see themselves as rivals. This may be unwittingly encouraged by the parents and even by the older sibling. Then when the baby of the family is born or the next child comes along, this rivalry is diluted somewhat by the presence of the *new* rival for attention. The middle is no longer the baby and now needs to find his or her place in a new family configuration. Middleborns are not sure how to define their role in the family—the biggest source of frustration and misunderstanding for middle children.

WHAT THIS BOOK SEEKS TO ACHIEVE

It becomes evident rather quickly when reading the literature on birth order that firstborns get the most attention from academics, but you'll soon discover that middleborns have some interesting qualities hidden up their sleeves.

Middles often have little idea of how they use their family experiences to develop strategies that lead them to success later in life. And parents of middles don't often think of their middle children as so distinct and capable. It's my belief that once these unexpected and remarkable abilities are recognized and encouraged, middles—as well as their parents, friends, and lovers—can all benefit immensely. As I began turning my focus on middles a little over a decade ago, I amassed more and more information. I published articles, gathered stories, and then came to realize that the secret powers I was uncovering were almost completely unrecognized by the general public.

This is the book that will help middle children untangle reality from myth. It seeks to shed light on the hidden strengths of middles and show them how to exploit these strengths, while also helping them recognize and overcome their weaknesses. It will help explain the past, the present, and the future with a focus on their own unique experiences.

For parents this research will show them how their child can flourish in a hectic family environment by helping them determine which traits or activities to encourage and which to discourage. In this book I address questions such as these: My first child demands all my attention, and the baby ends up getting all my attention. What can I do to make sure my middle child feels loved? Should I insist on more one-on-one time? What does the future hold for this mysterious and complicated child of mine? This book seeks to provide a support mechanism for mothers and fathers, revealing how the life skills that develop as a consequence of being squeezed in the family hierarchy as a middle child end up turning these youngsters into responsible, gregarious, self-motivated adults. By doing so, surprising lessons for parents may appear on how to raise their other children. Many of the insights that parents can glean from this exploration of middle children lie in the startling realization that parental "neglect" is not always bad.

This book is divided into two parts. In the first part I use historical analysis, academic research, and case studies from celebrities as well as regular folk to throw light on the hidden traits of middles that have previously been overlooked. It's fascinating and empowering to see how many well-known figures from history and modern culture are middleborns and to analyze how their abilities developed as a result of their middle child status.

The second half is prescriptive and practical: I turn the spotlight on middle children *in action*, exploring how their particular characteristics affect their everyday lives in work, play, and love. Here I look at what middleborns need to know to make smart long-term career decisions as well as which personal relationships work best for them and which don't. I analyze how parents are doing raising their middleborns and offer ideas on where to focus their energy. And for the very first time I compile and interpret pioneering research on how middleborns parent their own children.

It's been a fascinating journey of discovery for me, and I hope it will be for you, too.

CHAPTER TWO

How Do You Know
if You're
a Middle Child?

He was named after Richard the Lionheart but left behind a complicated legacy clouded by questions about his character. One of five boys, he was born on a lemon grove in Yorba Linda, California, in a two-bedroom house his father had built from a kit. Richard Nixon was the second child and the oldest of the three Nixon middles.

When Nixon was twelve years old, his baby brother, Arthur, fell ill. Arthur, curly haired and mischievous, had been the family favorite. "I recall so well, oh, the days before he died," Nixon said in a 1983 radio interview. "After they'd made a spinal tap and found that it was tubercular meningitis and said that there was no hope, he [Father] came down the stairs and . . . said, 'They say'—he was crying uncontrollably. He says, 'They say the little darling's going to die.' "

Just a few years later Nixon's beloved older brother, Harold, began to waste away. The firstborn of the Nixon boys, Harold was tall, blond, and handsome, a ladies' man with intelligence and charisma. After their lemon orchard failed, the family moved to Whittier, where they opened a gas station and grocery store. Money was very short. In a desperate attempt to save his life, Harold and his mother moved four hundred miles away to a sanatorium in Prescott, Arizona, where the air was drier. The boy hung on for five years and then died of tuberculosis. "And when Harold died, it was sort of—sort of the end of everything," Nixon said.

For much of Nixon's youth he was the secondborn of four boys. Then, he suddenly became the secondborn of *three* boys. In his early teen years, when Harold and his mother moved away, Nixon became the nominal first child in the house. During that time another boy was born to the family, so Nixon became the second of *four* again. Finally, when the eldest, Harold, passed away, he officially became the oldest living Nixon boy.

Does this make him a "real" middleborn? One of multiple middleborns? His older brother and one of his younger brothers both died before Richard Nixon turned twenty-one. Did he then become technically a first child? Was his tricky personality—that unnerving combination of astute perception and devastating self-delusion—a result of his birth order and the circumstances of his upbringing, or was it simply an inherent part of his personality?

UNTANGLING REAL AND PERCEIVED BIRTH ORDER

People tend to jump to conclusions about birth order based on a simple assessment of basic family hierarchy, without realizing that numerous factors come into play when determining *real* birth order. For instance, what about families with more than three children (such as Nixon's) or stepfamilies—such as the infamous TV brood, the Brady Bunch? Are you always a middle child if you have an older sibling and a younger one? Can you exhibit the personality of a middle child if you're in fact a lastborn or a firstborn? What if there's a big age gap between children? How does that affect a child's birth order? And how do divorce, death, or disability affect birth order? In the past, older sisters weren't even counted as significant offspring, and it was only the males in the family whose birth order was considered important. Is this still the case in certain communities today?

In the previous chapter I introduced the concept of parental investment and its effect on children. The crux of birth order theory lies in how much investment—time, attention, and money—each child in any given family is accorded by his or her parents. Every child experiences family life differently depending on whether the child is born first, last, or in between.

But, of course, other factors come into play as well. In Richard Nixon's case, both the death of his baby brother and then, not long after, the slow and agonizing demise of his oldest brother had a profound effect on his life. The attention he was given was compromised not only by his position in the hierarchy but also by extraordinary family circumstances. He developed middle child characteristics, but then, as an adult—after he had become the oldest living Nixon child—he assumed the mantle of the firstborn, thereby shifting his role in the family. But as we'll see, the complexities of birth order don't end there. What if the oldest Nixon child had been a girl? Would Nixon, as the first *boy*, have always been treated as a firstborn and absorbed the responsibilities and pressures that the eldest experiences? And what if Nixon had been born *ten years* after his older brother, and Harold had died once Nixon was already a grown man?

Let's dive in and explore the nuances.

1. THERE CAN BE MORE THAN ONE MIDDLE IN A FAMILY

When the Bush clan gets together for reunions in Texas, they need a photographer with a wide-angle lens to capture all the family members. Among the smiling multiracial faces are adopted children, birth children, grandchildren, old spouses, and new spouses. The forty-first president himself, George Herbert Walker Bush, has six children and fourteen grandchildren. Of Bush's six children, who is the middle? The forty-third president, George Bush Jr., came first, followed by Robin, Jeb, Neil, Marvin, and Dorothy. Robin died of leukemia before Jeb Bush was born, leaving five children. Does that make Neil, a businessman and education reform proponent—who then fell right in the middle between the two oldest and the two youngest—the real and only middle child of the family?

Consider this: Although it seems counterintuitive, there can be more than one firstborn or lastborn in any given family. Let's say a couple has one child, and that child passes away. Two years later they have another baby. That baby will be treated as a firstborn child even though technically it is the secondborn (or even middle if they then have another baby). Equally, if a family with three children has an eight-year gap between the lastborn and a surprise fourth baby, the youngest child is a mixture of firstborn and lastborn.

There can also be multiple middleborns in a family, and this position can also shift due to family circumstance. In the Bush family, Jeb, Neil, and Marvin are all middleborns. None of those children ever benefited from being the first and only child in the house. Nor were they ever the baby after whom no additional infant arrives on the scene to be cooed over and coddled. Thus, every child born between the first and last is a middle child.

But just because these three Bush children are all middles does not mean, of course, that they are all the same. Within their group of three, each middle child fights for his or her own piece of the pie. The younger middle will always develop in response to the chosen direction of the older middle. They may share certain personality traits—

such as a talent for negotiation or the propensity to think outside the box—but they will most likely seek to differentiate themselves from the others by picking unique areas of interest.

2. IT MAKES A DIFFERENCE IF YOU'RE A BOY OR A GIRL

Tracy, a sweet-natured, curly haired girl, is the oldest of four children in her Midwestern family. Julie is the second child, and her brother, John, a towhead, is the third. They're the two middleborns in the family. Little brother David, a dynamo of destructive energy, came along a few years later. Each was born within two years of the previous child.

The family is very close to the children's paternal grandparents and to Dad's younger siblings. They all live within ten miles of one another in the same small town. Most weekends—before the kids graduated and headed off to college—you could find them all piled into an aunt or uncle's house, playing with cousins and scarfing down tons of barbecue. As the oldest child (and oldest cousin) Tracy was often in charge of the younger kids. As one new child after another became part of the clan, she took care of them all.

Things changed significantly for Tracy when John was born. Her grandfather beamed with pride as though he himself had given birth to this robust baby. Tracy's dad would hold John up to family and friends and say, grinning, "Here he is, the venerable John the fifth!" Although Tracy didn't know what "venerable" meant, she knew what the fawning was all about: Finally there was a boy who could be named after her great-grandfather.

John O'Donnell the first had been a soldier in the Great War, World War I, and died heroically on the battlefields. He left behind his son, John O'Donnell II, and six other children. John O'Donnell III is Tracy's beloved grandpa; her dad is John O'Donnell IV, so the new baby, the only boy, became John O'Donnell V. From the day he was born he was expected to carry on the family name and do them all proud.

Although baby John was clearly a middle child, the family treated him more like a first. He was accorded much more attention than if he'd been a girl. If gender wasn't relevant, one would have expected Tracy to be assertive, conscientious, reliable, conventional, and a perfectionist, and one might have predicted that John would be more laid-back, friendly, and patient. But while Tracy was always nurturing toward her younger siblings (evidence of her hardworking, reliable nature), John is pushier and more of a perfectionist than his older sister.

In John's case, gender was a better predictor of parental investment, attention, and expectations than strict birth order. What mattered more than Tracy being firstborn was that John was the firstborn boy. As such, his personality is a mix of first and middleborn traits.

Different cultures, different customs

Attitudes toward gender vary from one culture to another and one family to another. Anthropologist Mildred Dickemann reviewed historical data on infanticide within the Indian caste system and discovered that killing infants was very common among the highest castes before the twentieth century—and that female infants were usually the victims. In those castes the daughters had very few marriage options since they could marry only within their own caste, not a lower one. Among high-caste Indian families, investment in males (who could marry females from their own or lower castes) paid larger dividends in terms of grandchildren, and so, accordingly, parents heavily biased their investment toward males.

Lower on the social scale, however, the tendency toward males marrying down meant that daughters out-reproduced sons in terms of offspring, and so parents biased their investment toward daughters, resulting in a much lower rate of female infanticide.

In societies where having money has a significant impact on male reproductive success, a preference for sons (or for investing highly in them) is seen among the affluent. There's a reason that England's Prince William has often been referred to as "the heir" and his younger brother Harry "the spare."

Tom Cruise, an actor who the public knows as intense, driven, and phenomenally successful, was a middle child who grew up being bullied by his father. His mother divorced and moved out of the house with her children. Cruise suffered from dyslexia, attended eight elementary schools and three high schools, and never went to college. But none of this seems to have held him back. Tom Cruise has the focus and competitiveness we think of as typical for a firstborn. And in some ways, despite being child number three of four, he is a firstborn—because he's the first boy.

When girls have the upper hand

Where one society prefers male offspring to females, others have the opposite preference. Studies of Hungarian Gypsy populations actually show a female-biased sex ratio. Compared to the native Hungarian population, Gypsies have many more daughters than sons and, like the lower caste Indians, are considered to be of low social status. Gypsy women are consequently much more likely to marry up the social scale—and outside the Gypsy clan—than men. In doing so, they tend to produce more offspring than their brothers. They also tend to have healthier babies than Gypsy women who marry within their own group.

It's not surprising, then, that Gypsy parents invest more heavily in their daughters than in their sons. The researchers also found that compared to native Hungarians, Gypsy women spent more time nursing their firstborn daughters than their sons and provided more education for their daughters. This is significant because education was not free, and so there was a substantial cost to the parents.

Also consider this twist. Let's take Tracy's family as an example again. One could argue that if most of the children had been boys and the third child was the only girl in the family, it could have shifted dynamics enough to impact the perceived birth order. Rather than being treated as a firstborn, perhaps that female child would have been coddled like a lastborn—even though there was another baby born after her. Had family expectations remained traditional, and the boys were expected to take over the family landscaping business, that girl would likely have been even more babied, making her less of a typical middle.

When one sex is likely to be more successful (that is, leave behind more "high-quality" offspring), parents will invest more in children of that sex: It's a bigger payoff in terms of quality grandchildren. Generally, females are a less risky investment. In the absence of modern birth control, most females have about the same number of surviving offspring. In contrast, the number of children that a male has can vary greatly over a lifetime, particularly in some populations where they have multiple wives either at the same time or serially. Some males have lots of offspring, while some have none. Getting a female to mate with them is the key: High-status males have no problem with this, whereas the homeless guy on the street corner might have more trouble.

The core question is: Which gender should the parent invest in? If male reproductive success depends on the individual's condition—the ability to acquire resources, for example—then mothers who are in good condition and can invest heavily will be able to influence the reproductive success of their sons more successfully than mothers in poor condition or with access to few resources. They would therefore prefer to have sons or to invest more in the sons they have.

Mothers in poor condition, however, would prefer investing in daughters because they are reproductively less risky. This can be seen in the results of a recent study completed in the United States that concluded that female infants from low-income families are nursed more than infant boys.

As we can see, in some cultures what's important in terms of first-born status is not being the first child born in the family but being the firstborn of a certain gender. In Western culture and many others, the firstborn daughter may be given responsibilities in terms of looking after her younger siblings, but a greater degree of parental investment and expectations for success typically fall to the first son. In such a situation, the middleborn son, first of his gender, may take on more of the characteristic traits of the firstborn.

3. AGE GAPS CAN LEAD TO TRADING PLACES

Britney Spears, by definition a middleborn, is a great example of how age gaps can affect real birth order. Her brother, Bryan, was born in Tennessee in 1977, and Britney came along four years later. Having started her singing and acting career early, by the time she was ten years old she and her mother—and the new baby in the family, Jamie Lynn—moved to New York City to pursue dreams of fame and fortune. In the early years of her life, Spears was effectively a lastborn. While living apart from her older brother for a few years (and welcoming a baby sister to the family), she likely felt some of the responsibility of a firstborn, especially since she was the major breadwinner for the family. Once the Disney show she was acting in was canceled, she returned to Knoxville and became, once again, a middle, sandwiched between the older brother and baby sister.

Because of the ten-year age difference between Spears and her little sister, however, I would argue that by personality she is more of a lastborn than a middle. This is reflected in some of her behavior: Like many lasts, Spears craves attention and adulation, and is unhappy being relegated to the sidelines. Unlike most middle children, she's not an especially good negotiator, seeming to lack the skills necessary to assess the character of those around her and form her own independent judgments. In addition, her desire for risk taking and her tendency to act out are uncharacteristic of more levelheaded middles.

It's about how much each child steps on the other's turf

The impact of birth order is increased when children are born in quick succession because the siblings have the same basic needs at the same time, and so are in immediate competition with each other. In some societies having a second child too close to a first means the mother must abandon the second in order to better care for the first one. When the interval between births is very large, the children aren't really competing for the same resources from parents. For example, a middleborn with a sibling seven years older and another sibling one year younger may have a personality more representative of a firstborn than a typical middleborn.

Parents invest in their offspring based on many different factors. To some extent there's a cost-benefit analysis going on. For siblings, their brothers and sisters also entail costs and benefits, and these vary in proportion to the length of time between each birth. Obviously, substantially older offspring who are no longer dependent on parental care experience minimal costs from additional siblings; typically, they tend to be protective rather than competitive. Close age spacing, however, increases competition for parental investment and promotes greater parent-offspring conflict as well as increased sibling rivalry.

You might wonder what happens with twins. Fraternal twins tend to experience high levels of sibling rivalry; in ancestral times one of the twins was usually abandoned to die as mothers could care for only one infant at a time. It's a different story, however, for identical twins; because they are genetically identical, they typically do not compete in the same way. Saving your sibling is, in a sense, saving yourself. When the "middle child" is a set of twins—particularly identical twins— they are most often not very typical of middleborns. This is because they have a unique role to play in the family simply by virtue of being twins, whereas a regular middleborn does not have a special role. While each twin will probably engage in the typical effort to distinguish itself from its co-twin, the twin middles will always be the recipients of extra attention (and even adoration) because they are remarkable just for being twins.

The influence of birth order on sibling strategies is greatest for children who are born within five years of each other. Under these circumstances, older brothers or sisters tend to highlight their own worth and run down the value of their younger siblings. In turn, younger children respond by trying to minimize direct comparisons with older siblings, diverging in their interests, and perhaps searching out nonparental sources of attention as they get older. Over most of our evolutionary history, small children were extremely dependent on their parents (the mother in particular) for their survival. The larger the birth spacing, the less similar their needs.

The Spears family is a case in point. Bryan Spears was still under five years old when his little sister Britney was born. He was not yet in school, and as such the mother tended to the two young children simultaneously. If baby Britney had to be fed or comforted when Bryan was expected at a playdate, Bryan had to wait. When Jamie Lynn was born, on the other hand, Britney was already ten years old. There was much less conflict between her interests and those of the baby's. Britney was already launched in her singing and dancing career, and the infant's need for feeding and protection did not clash directly with Britney's needs.

What does this mean for middleborns? When a child is born within a couple of years of their older and younger siblings, this makes them the most middleborn in nature. When there's a large gap between the first and middle child, direct parental comparisons are less frequent, and so there's less pressure for middleborns to differentiate themselves in order to stand out. They will have less strongly defined middleborn traits as a consequence. Finally, when there's a large gap between the middle child and the lastborn, the middle child may spend quite a few years as a lastborn and so may have more lastborn traits than one would otherwise expect. This is the case with Britney Spears and makes some of her impulsive behavior seem less puzzling.

4. THE IMPACT OF DISABILITY OR DEATH

Russell was an easygoing baby. Born at nine pounds, five ounces by cesarean section, he grew up in a large family—born and bred New Yorkers who could trace their heritage back to a medieval Jewish community along the Rhine in Germany. His father is an oncologist and his mother a librarian. Two years later, Sydney arrived, and then three years after that, Sophia.

All was well until Russell began to stumble at age six. Within a year he had lost most of his eyesight and almost all of his ability to grasp objects or move around. His parents spent weeks on end at a large hospital in Manhattan trying to figure out what was happening to their son. They discovered that, as Ashkenazi Jews, both parents were carriers of a deadly gene they had unknowingly transmitted to their child. Russell had inherited sub-acute Tay-Sachs disease, and over time his brain became clogged with fatty tissue that would eventually destroy his central nervous system. Neither Sydney nor Sophia had inherited the gene.

For many years Sydney had played happily with her older brother, and when the new baby arrived, she was glad to have a playmate who would prefer baby dolls over cars. But family dynamics changed dramatically when Russell became ill. Sydney lost her original playmate and, for a time, her parents as well (when they became consumed with helping her brother). Just three years later, Russell had to be moved into a special home where he could be properly cared for.

In Sydney's case, she felt the transference of parental expectations acutely even though Russell survived into adulthood. "I don't remember ever thinking about what my dad did for a living, at least until my brother became so sick," she explains. "Then, eventually, it just became obvious to me that I should become a doctor." Although her parents still did not spend all that much time with her, she came to feel that more than anything, her father wanted her to go to medical school. She had become the de facto first child.

When natural selection plays a role

A spider's web is an amazingly mathematical structural marvel, yet no one believes the spider does complex math in its head while it's spinning. Likewise, people are often not conscious of the motivations that underlie their actions. The psychological mechanisms at play in how we take care of our offspring are ultimately intended to help both us *and* our children be healthier and safer—thereby living longer. Seen this way, future survival and reproductive success influence how much a child does or does not benefit his or her parents. If parents are unlikely to see a return on their investment in terms of their child's health and potential for procreation, natural selection would suggest the parents are less likely to invest in such children. Parents will thus be more "attached" to their "better" offspring, though of course they are not conscious of this. As discussed earlier, gender can factor into this equation, too. In addition, children who are disabled in some way are less likely to have future reproductive success than children who are healthy, and so their parents would tend to invest less in those children.

Poor infant health clearly has an impact on parental investment. Offspring born with a severe physical deformity are more likely to be the victims of infanticide, especially in traditional societies where institutional care of the handicapped is not available. The increased level of care that such children require for a low evolutionary payoff (they're unlikely to reproduce even if they do survive) means that parents are better off if they terminate investment early on and begin to invest in new offspring. Even in North America, handicapped children are at greater risk of abuse at the hands of their parents than healthy children and are more likely to suffer injuries requiring a visit to a hospital. It must be noted, however, that many parents in resource-rich societies do invest substantially in children with disabilities, and help them minimize the long-term negative effects of their disability.

As we've already seen, death can alter birth order influences, depending on what age the sibling dies. Richard Nixon's experience of losing his older brother was similar to Sydney's in that he assumed more of a firstborn role once he became the oldest child in the family. If the death occurs before age five or six, it's much more likely that the middle child's personality will be more firstborn in nature. Why? Because that second child becomes the oldest child in the household during important personality-forming years. Thus, these children inherit the parental investment benefits and responsibilities of a firstborn child.

If death occurs when the child is older (such as Nixon, who was fourteen when Harold got sick and twenty when he died), it's likely that many of his or her personality traits will remain more typically middleborn because they were largely shaped when the oldest child was still alive. Still, when the older sibling dies, the middle child may end up as the new vessel of the parents' hopes and dreams. This is liable to change the way he or she views the world.

In Nixon's case, his exceptional drive—the *success at all costs* philosophy—was likely born of his desire to make up for the loss of two children in their very poor family. "He clung to the idea of being 'tough.' He thought that that was what had brought him to the edge of greatness," wrote his biographer, Richard Reeves. "But that was what betrayed him." This toughness, the destructive blend of secrecy and drive, may not have been as pronounced if Richard Nixon had grown up as the younger brother of a successful and powerful older sibling.

5. THE MODERN FAMILY: MERGERS AND ACQUISITIONS

Do the names Greg, Peter, Bobby, Marcia, Jan, and Cindy ring a bell? Then you've seen *The Brady Bunch*, a popular American television series from the late 1960s and early 1970s that has lived on for decades in syndication. About the merging of two families with three children each, the series tapped into the zeitgeist: At the time, 40 percent of marriages in the United States included a child or children from a previous union.

Although the character Jan is famous in the show for being a whiny and difficult middle child, other birth-order-related frictions abounded in this blended family. Marcia, the oldest girl, was dethroned by Greg, the oldest boy from the father's first marriage. Bobby,

the youngest boy, was no longer the lastborn because Cindy, the insuf-
ferably cute baby of the bunch, took his place. And instead of each
family having one middleborn, suddenly there were multiple middles
of both genders. Talk about a mix-up.

Divorce and/or remarriage can really muddy the waters of birth
order, although the impact depends largely on the age of a child when
the parent he or she lives with remarries. As one might predict, the
younger the child, the greater the impact (unless the child is still an
infant). In a situation such as the Bradys' and in many stepfamilies, the
birth order is then shuffled around. And in a situation where parents
remarry and produce *new* offspring together—that is, there are two
consecutive sets of children—the lastborn of the previous union becomes a middle child. Not only that, but the child who's been accustomed to the coddling of a lastborn is actually displaced by a *firstborn*
(the first child of this new partnership), thereby adding insult to injury.
That lastborn-turned-middleborn will be more likely to exhibit negative middleborn tendencies than the positive ones. We'll be exploring
these negatives in greater detail later.

When parents divorce, the interests of the child and the parent
often begin to diverge quite dramatically. When I was eleven years old,
my friend Sarah's parents got divorced. Over time, her father turned
his attention away from the children from his first marriage and began
spending more time (and money) socializing. In a biological sense, he
shifted gears in order to attract a new partner and secure the prospect
of another union which would enhance rather than diminish his own
fitness.

Genetically speaking, what makes our children stronger also
makes us stronger. But as we all know, social behavior isn't quite so
straightforward: The interests of interacting individuals invariably
conflict at one time or another. Even when there's cooperation, there's
almost always competition, too. So while parents and children both
share the objective of enhancing offspring success, they can also disagree on how important individual offspring are relative to other options. In Sarah's case, her father chose to allocate his resources

differently after the divorce; while his ex-wife, his daughter Sarah, and the other siblings wanted him to continue investing in the children from his first union, his attention was shifting toward the possibility of a new relationship. These kinds of complications impact all birth orders—and middle children, whether by birth or circumstance, in particular. Since middles are already at a disadvantage in the investment game, this type of dynamic only increases this disadvantage further. It makes you feel sympathy for all those middles in the Brady Bunch!

But it's not only modern families that show evidence of this kind of birth order jumble. The first president of the United States is widely credited with being a middleborn, and in some ways he is. George Washington was actually the first child born of the union between his father and his second wife, Mary Ball Washington. He had two older half brothers (and a half sister who died) as well as five younger siblings. The question that becomes all important here is how much the older siblings influenced Washington when he was still a boy. His father died when he was eleven, at which point he assumed many of the responsibilities of the man of the house, helping his mother manage the Rappahannock River Plantation where they lived. He worked exceptionally hard and did not have the benefit of a private education. So was this man more a firstborn by nature or in fact a true middleborn? I would argue he was a perfect blend of both despite technically being a middle.

6. WHEN THE FIRSTBORN DOESN'T FIT THE MOLD

Marissa is a serious, dark-haired woman in her midforties who works sixty hours a week as a partner in a downtown Miami law firm. She often works weekends and, by her own admission, has no social life. "I don't remember the last time I had fun," she says. "I'm just not wired that way."

But it wasn't always like that. Marissa's mother remembers her as a carefree child, playing on the streets with the neighborhood kids and coming home every day from school with ice cream dripping down her chin. When she was a preteen, her older sister, Josephina, got in with a fast crowd and stopped making her curfew. Things went from bad to worse. By the time Marissa was thirteen, Josie—only two years older—started skipping school altogether and turning up at home drunk early in the morning. A year later she moved out.

As a young girl Marissa had been jealous of Josie's artistic talents. "I felt like I was always in her shadow," she admits, "and so I turned away from anything creative." Later, once they discovered that Josie was living on the streets and had developed a drug problem, Marissa actually felt as though the shadow cast over her had deepened and become even less bearable. Her parents had fled from Cuba two decades earlier and made very little money. They both worked exceptionally hard and strived to show their four children how to be independent and successful in their adopted country. But Josie refused to fit the mold. As a consequence, Marissa was driven by the desire to please her parents—perhaps to make up for the disappointment they felt in their oldest daughter. "It's shameful to them," Marissa says. "And I can't bear for them to be disappointed or worried about me."

For middleborns, what affects the development of their personalities is not so much their own conflict with their parents but that of their older sibling (or siblings). It's not surprising that high levels of conflict between parent and child increases the likelihood that children will reject authority. If this kind of friction occurs between a middleborn and a parent, it may not make much difference other than encouraging some increased rebelliousness (although, as we'll see, this is characteristic of laterborns anyway). But for firstborns, their typical role is to uphold parental authority and the status quo, and in turn they are most often the recipients of parental favor. As birth order researcher Frank Sulloway has documented, conflict between firstborns and parents can lead them to abdicate their usual role and take on more typical laterborn rebelliousness, receiving less favor in turn. Under such circumstances, middleborns may be inclined to move into a more firstborn-like role and thereby receive the parental favor that goes along with it.

WHAT DOES ALL THIS MEAN FOR YOU?

There are some societies in which birth order is all important in terms of establishing a clear hierarchy within families and larger communities. In Bali, for example, all children are named according to their birth order, and their gender. Firstborns are all called Wayan, Putuh, or Nengah; seconds are Made or Kadek; thirds are Nyoman or Komang; fourths are Ketut; and then with the fifth child it begins all over again. The prefix "I" connotes males and "Ni" connotes females. In their culture there is no expression for middleborn or lastborn. The numerical order of birth is the distinguishing feature, although there is no preference given to firstborn males over other males in the family: All males inherit equally upon death of the parents.

Yet no matter what name you might give your children or however important or irrelevant you find birth order to be, the fact remains that children in the middle of a family have a unique set of circumstances to deal with as they grow up. Life will never be quite the same for a child in the middle as it is for either the firstborn or the lastborn.

But what you will come to appreciate, I hope, is that middle children develop strategies as a result of their position in the family that can serve them extremely well later in life. Every family with three or more children has at least one middleborn, and I'll show you how these children have underappreciated and surprising talents that are a direct result of being squeezed between the firstborn and the lastborn.

FACTORS THAT DETERMINE YOUR "REAL" BIRTH ORDER

1. **It's not about your biological order of birth.**
    Birth order is an environmental factor, not a biological one. Your birth order depends on how your parents raised

you. If you're very young, being introduced into a family by adoption or remarriage means you're likely to develop according to your birth position in this new family.

2. **There can be more than one middle in a family.**
Any child born between the firstborn and the lastborn is a middle child. But that doesn't mean all the middles in any given family are exactly alike. Each middle still searches for his or her own distinguishing niche.

3. **Birth order is not fixed.**
Birth order can be jumbled up if family circumstances change. When an older sibling is compromised or two families merge, children's biological birth order can be rendered meaningless. A middleborn can become more like a firstborn or like a lastborn.

4. **Boys and girls are different.**
In many cultures what makes the difference in terms of parental investment is not being the firstborn but being the firstborn boy. Under these circumstances a firstborn girl may end up in the middleborn role, and a middleborn or lastborn boy can end up in the privileged firstborn position, in terms of parental attention and investment.

5. **There's a cost-benefit analysis at play.**
Biologically speaking, parents are motivated to give more time and money to children who will benefit them in the long run. This usually means healthy firstborns because they're more likely to generate offspring and take care of elders.

6. **When the first isn't typical, it affects the middle(s).**
High levels of conflict between a firstborn and a parent (or

parents) is likely to cause firstborns to rebel. This leaves the conforming traditional firstborn role open to be occupied by a middleborn sibling. Since siblings seek to differentiate themselves from their next oldest sibling, a rebellious firstborn tends to make for a more conforming middleborn.

CHAPTER THREE

Middle Children Are Brilliant Negotiators

The trim, fine-boned Egyptian stood confidently in front of the Israeli Parliament in November 1977. As he looked up from his papers, his square glasses reflected a room packed with people filled with both skepticism and hope. The crowd hung on his every word. This was the first time in modern history that the leader of a nation at war had set foot on enemy soil to calmly make the case for peace.

This moment, broadcast live around the world, proved to be a defining moment for the Arab world. The Arabs and the Israelis had been at odds for decades, culminating in the Six-Day War in 1967. Six years later the Egyptians launched the October War. These two nations regarded each other with fear and hatred. Yet now the presi-

dent of Egypt, Mohammed Anwar el-Sadat, stood on enemy
territory.

Sadat was the middle child in a pack of thirteen children born to
an Egyptian father and Sudanese mother. They lived in a tiny village
tucked far away in the countryside of the Nile Delta. He and his siblings were brought up mainly by his grandmother, and under her influence Sadat became an avid anticolonialist. A desire to change the
inequities he saw around him and a compulsion to question the status
quo was ingrained in him at an early age. His role as just one of a multitude of children led him to understand the realities and complexities
of life, while also learning how to negotiate consent among groups of
individuals with divergent goals.

As an adult, this middle child took the risk of appearing before the
enemy in an attempt to advance peace negotiations. Early in the speech
to the Knesset, Sadat tried to break down defenses by insisting, "In all
sincerity, I tell you, we welcome you among us . . . This, in itself, is a
tremendous turning point; one of the landmarks of a decisive historical change." He acknowledged the small yet continuous humiliations
heaped upon the Jewish people since the creation of Israel. He asked,
"Why should we bequeath to the coming generations the plight of
bloodshed, death, orphans, widowhood, family disintegration, and the
wailing of victims?"

Once Sadat conceded the unfairness of the Arabs' past treatment
of the Jews and requested that they join together to broker peace, he
asserted in straightforward terms the bottom line of his argument: The
Israelis must leave the occupied territories and recognize the Palestin-
ians. He offered hope and conciliation and yet was not flexible on the
terms of peace. He was respectful yet forceful, drawing upon common
proverbs and psalms to lend his words gravitas.

The most successful politicians have the ability to persuade not
only their constituents but also their doubters of the integrity of their
message and their goals. To achieve this they must be excellent negotiators. Over the centuries countless political figures have achieved
power by bullying and misrepresentation. But those with the most

enduring positive legacies have found a way to bring people along with them, making them feel they have a personal stake in a political issue and convincing them of their sincere desire for the good of all mankind, not just their own people.

Although ultimately Anwar Sadat was not able to bring lasting peace to his region, his audacious visit is a prime example of a middle child's uncanny ability to assess his role in a complex negotiation. Accustomed to a life in which they are rarely the center of attention, middle children develop skills they can put to direct use later in life when attempting to bridge the gap between adversaries with reasoning, patience, and passion.

BEING A GREAT NEGOTIATOR IS PRICELESS

Not everyone is born with the skills required to be a good negotiator, let alone a brilliant one—and yet a talent for reaching consensus is one of the most valuable skills one can possess. Negotiating well helps us solve problems, achieve compromise, and avoid serious conflict. Since much of this can be learned, it's valuable to analyze the skills that go into being a killer deal maker. Awareness breeds practice; practice breeds confidence, and confidence combined with patience breeds success. This is an arena in which middles, by dint of their unique role in the family, excel.

Negotiation skills are critical to every aspect of our lives. Just think of the variety of situations we're faced with that require give-and-take, whether it's dealing with a landlord, asking for a raise, navigating a divorce, closing multimillion-dollar business deals, parceling out a parent's inheritance, bringing peace to a war-torn region, or simply getting the best deal for an antique at a flea market.

Families are involved in negotiations on a daily basis. What should your teen's curfew be? How much homework before TV? Who takes care of elderly parents when they're in the hospital? Similarly, work life requires the constant ability to achieve compromise and understanding: Can this report really be finished by the deadline? How many items can we deliver by what time? What rates do we negotiate for shipping?

Politicians and big businesses engage in negotiations that can have enormous impact on the world as we know it, especially if those negotiations go wrong or are never successfully concluded. For instance, numerous politicos—such as Ian Paisley, Margaret Thatcher, and Bill Clinton, to name just a few—tried and failed for decades to achieve consensus on peace in Northern Ireland. And as we have seen, countless negotiations on the Middle East have run aground, perpetuating bloodshed and misery. When business negotiations fail, the results can be disastrous, too, such as when the United Auto Workers Union fought with the big three automakers in the 1970s. They could not reach an agreement and went on strike, creating a ripple effect that eventually contributed to the precipitous downward slide of American car manufacturers.

KEY NEGOTIATION STRATEGIES THAT MIDDLES USE

Dozens of books about negotiation have been written by academics such as Daniel Shapiro, associate director of the Harvard Negotiation Project, as well as others, such as Donald Trump, one of the most famous middleborn businessmen in the world and author of the bestselling *The Art of the Deal*. Another important treatment of negotiation was written by Chester Karrass. He interviewed successful negotiators about the traits they considered crucial to their success. In his book *The Negotiating Game*, Karrass provided an insight from the doers themselves, rather than an analysis by academically oriented authorities looking from the outside in. Most of the experts agree that autonomy, appreciation, affiliation, status, and respect are key elements to successful negotiating.

In my opinion, and taking into consideration the opinions of these various experts, the following five characteristics are the most crucial when it comes to being an excellent negotiator:

1. Honesty and integrity
2. Empathy and tact
3. Openness and flexibility
4. Emotional stability
5. Self-esteem

Anwar Sadat's behavior in reaching out to the Israeli people shows many of the above middle child characteristics at work. Ultimately, by choosing compromise over pan-Arabism, he paved the way for the Camp David Accords and the Israel-Egypt Peace Treaty. In 1978, Sadat and Israeli prime minister Menachem Begin were awarded the Nobel Peace Prize. Although peace in that region has remained elusive, Sadat's relentless pursuit of a dialogue with the "enemies" makes this middle child one of the most renowned negotiators of our time.

In Sadat's historic speech to the Knesset, he showed respect and compassion while also taking a firm position and making his goals clear: "The first fact," he said, "is no one can build his happiness at the expense of the misery of others." Second, he emphasized his frankness: "I never deal with anyone except in one language, one policy, and with one face." And, finally, he appealed to his enemy's sense of fairness and logic. "Direct confrontation and a straight line," he said, "are the nearest and most successful methods to reach a clear objective." Through drawing on universal points of reference he emphasized that, in this most tense and complicated negotiation, everyone shared the exact same goal: peace.

1. HONESTY AND INTEGRITY

One refreshing finding I've encountered is that middle children tend to be honest and typically operate with integrity in all areas of their lives. This is borne out by a 2009 study of undergraduates in France that looked at how selfish or cooperative different birth orders were. In it, participants were asked to play an investment game, and researchers then analyzed the different strategies they had used to win.

Two players, A and B, are each given thirty "dollars." Player A has to decide how much money, if any, to share with player B. This amount is then tripled by the experimenter and given to player B. Player B then has to decide how much, if any, of his total to send back to player A.

The logical choice for a player who lacks trust is to hold on to the money for fear he won't get it back from player B—just as the logical choice for player B is to take the money, pocket the triple profit, and stop the game (that is, not show reciprocity to player A). A surprising number of experimental studies have shown, however, that not everyone makes logical choices even if these choices would appear to be in their best interests. This kind of "irrational" choice is indicative of unselfish behavior and cooperation with unrelated individuals (i.e., non-family).

In this instance, middleborns more frequently trust they'll get the money back, and so they consistently gave more of their money to player B. Middles also demonstrated greater reciprocity as player B by giving money back to player A more frequently than other birth orders. In contrast, firstborns were significantly less trustful toward non-family and reciprocated less than middleborns, lastborns, and onlies. As has been well documented, firsts tend to be prudent and more concerned with advancement of self than other birth orders.

Middle children, on the other hand, operate cooperatively. It's relevant to us here because cooperative behavior is one of the keys to successful negotiating. Their behavior in dealing with complex interpersonal negotiations exploits this tendency toward trust and reciprocity, and is a dynamic we can see at play whether in high-powered examples like Sadat or in regular family squabbles about inheritance, for example.

A few years ago when the matriarch of the Logan family died, the three surviving children found themselves locked in a dispute over their Ohio farm. At one time, the farm had comprised hundreds of acres along the banks of the Ohio River. Apple and peach trees dotted the land as far as the eye could see. Each successive generation sold off more and more land until the original farmhouse was surrounded by a few dozen acres and a bunch of suburban developments. By the time Maura Logan passed away at age eighty-seven, none of the heirs wanted to live in the farmhouse even though each child felt drawn to the land and the old house.

The Logan kids had been born in rapid-fire succession: first Timothy, the only boy; then eleven months later, Jane; and finally Susannah after just one year. As children they were often busy with chores and spent a lot of time together working to help their parents. They spent countless nights putting together puzzles in the kitchen and playing board games by the huge fireplace in the living room. They would later characterize their relationships as very close and compatible.

Jane, the middle child, was often the referee when the siblings played or worked together. If one complained the other didn't have as many chores to do, it was Jane who figured out who was right. When playing games, if Tim got impatient with Susannah's dramatics or Susannah tired of Tim's bossiness, they'd inevitably turn to Jane to play the peacemaker. As soon as she told a lie, Jane's face would flush bright red, and she'd immediately be caught out. Jane had a reputation in home and at school as a reliable straight shooter.

In all financial dealings with the house and with their mother, Tim—who'd become a lawyer—took the reins. He was organized and quick to make decisions, and that suited the family fine, at least until Maura died.

Tim and Susannah both insisted that they could pool their resources and hold on to the farm. Everyone knew that as an artist Susannah didn't have the resources and that Tim would end up bearing the brunt of the costs. But Jane also knew they weren't ready to face reality and hash out all the details. The third time they got together after their mother's death, the three siblings had a huge fight. Their relationship became so tense that they decided to put all discussions on hold for six months to think things through.

Jane was literally stuck in the middle. Her mother, Maura, would turn in her grave if she knew about the siblings' gridlock. And Jane particularly resented Tim's brusque way of taking control of all conversations and then making pronouncements as though they'd all agreed with what he had proposed.

The power of truth telling

It makes sense that when involved in contentious negotiations, the party considered to be the most honest would have the upper hand in terms of swaying others. An element of distrust on either side undermines dealings. Often, feelings of wariness arise simply because one party doesn't fully understand what the other party wants. Being truthful and clear, and letting others know there are no hidden motives, mitigates this.

As we saw with Sadat, he worked exceptionally hard to persuade the Knesset—and the wider world—of his integrity, using variations on the words "frank" and "sincerely" fifteen times in his speech. And in the case of the Logan family, Jane's reputation as excruciatingly honest eventually helped her take over the failed sibling negotiations from her older brother and reach an agreement that everyone could live with.

Jane called her siblings and suggested they meet again. She was open about her financial situation and detailed the trajectory of her expected income over the next decade, admitting that there was no possibility of her underwriting the property. This unsentimental disclosure encouraged the siblings to lay aside emotions and be honest about their intentions and their own financial situations.

After significant back and forth, they agreed that Tim would buy the house and shoulder the burden of maintaining and renting it. While they all realized that practicality had to trump emotional considerations, they would not have been able to reach this conclusion had Jane not recognized the unique role she could play in helping her brother and sister face reality. Her siblings appreciated her integrity and were more comfortable with a deal that would have been hard to swallow if it had been introduced to them by the either of the other siblings.

There are pitfalls to being a truth teller

We're familiar with the image of a deeply chiseled face, a shock of dark hair, and a gangly body with oversize hands and feet. "Honest Abe," as Abraham Lincoln was known, was a striking man not only for his homely face and awkward physical bearing but for his intractable truthfulness and integrity. "He was deeply and sincerely honest himself, and assumed that others were so," wrote a lawyer friend of his. "He never suspected men; and hence in dealing with them he was easily imposed upon."

Lincoln, the second child in his family, was born in 1809 in a rustic cabin in Rock Spring Farm, Kentucky. His mother died when the boy was seven, and his father soon remarried, adding three young children to the family. Working the fields with his siblings, Lincoln had little time for education, learning only rudimentary reading and arithmetic. His was a life of backbreaking hard work, but he remained a cheerful and generous child.

When considering the chaotic and contentious political life that Lincoln led as sixteenth president of the United States—holding the Union together despite the devastating Civil War and abolishing slavery—it is perhaps surprising that this stern-looking yet amiable man was honest to a fault. Political machinations of the complexity Lincoln dealt with would require considerable finesse, and yet Lincoln was reportedly utterly direct and honest at all times, occasionally to his detriment. Some people found him to be too frank, and others thought him too quiet and contemplative. He was accused of being prideful, being a sloppy administrator (perhaps because he was too enamored of spending time listening to the ordinary folk), and having trouble managing his cabinet effectively. When dealing with political complexity, truth telling can sometimes be a double-edged sword.

What kind of impact does birth order have on trust and cooperative behaviors? As we saw from the investment game, middleborns engage in more cooperative strategies than other birth orders. They also score higher than firsts on altruism and tender-mindedness, both of which are components of agreeableness. When someone is altruistic, agreeable, and tender-minded, it increases their willingness to give others the benefit of the doubt and engage in activities that are to everybody's benefit, as Lincoln often did. Yet, as we see with Lincoln, this can prove to be a trap for some middle children. As advantageous as it is to be candid and to be perceived as sincere when negotiating, it is also possible for this truth telling to come across as a rather blunt instrument. Equally, it opens middles up to being taken advantage of. When Jane (the middleborn from Ohio) was a child, she sometimes found herself subjected to the machinations of her friends and siblings. "They knew I could never tell a lie, and they'd wrangle information from me or even take advantage of my trust in them," she admits.

Most often, as middles mature and learn to navigate life outside the home, they develop the ability to use this truth telling to their advantage. In Jane's case, she learned to toughen up and become more circumspect about the information she was willing to share. This, combined with her instinctive openness, served her well when it came time to manage the contentious discussion about her family's inheritance—just as, ultimately, President Lincoln's inability to be insincere ended up helping rather than hindering him. Most people perceived him as infinitely patient and honest, and this helped him enormously when he was called upon to make unpopular decisions. While he listened and showed respect to his opponents, he formed opinions on his own, often without consulting his cabinet. Rather than lie, he evaded through silence—eventually becoming a spectacularly good manipulator and conciliator.

2. EMPATHY AND TACT

Middleborns are unique in the family because of their empathy. While firstborns specialize in strategies designed to establish authority over their rivals, laterborns adopt entirely different strategies. As many of us know from experience, lastborns often appeal to our sympathy by playing the little one who needs protection. Rather impatient, they don't tend to spend much time listening to others or parsing their words when communicating. Middles, in contrast, choose another route.

Middle children become great listeners. They understand the value of acknowledging others' positions and feelings, and use this information as ammunition to help them get what they want. "People thought I was quiet as a kid," says Michael, a magazine writer in his fifties. "But what no one realized is, I was busy listening. It's not that I have nothing to say—I just want to talk knowing the real context."

Michael is an excellent example because he recognized his skills early on and parlayed them into a profession he finds satisfying and worthwhile. One scenario he shared with me is especially revealing. As a cub reporter for a small local newspaper in Florida, he was asked to try to get an interview with a major real estate developer whose deals had recently been going sour. Engaged in a vigorous back and forth with the businessman's public relations firm, Michael was encountering firm resistance.

A scandal had broken just the previous week about some shady dealings involving the developer and a large mall in suburban Miami. Michael found he had the most success persuading people to grant him an interview when he approached tricky topics in a direct yet tactful manner. "I developed a reputation as someone who really saw all sides of the story," he explained, "and I fostered this by choosing my words very carefully."

In this case, he talked about the incident in a nonconfrontational yet fully engaged manner with the PR director, making the point that he would be the perfect reporter to relay the nuances of development dealings. The developer had already been aggressively courted by other reporters, who were blunt rather than diplomatic or tactful. "But the guy knew I wasn't on a crusade to crucify anyone," Michael said. He got the interview.

Hidden personality traits

What is fascinating and goes against expectations is that middles are often actually extroverts who—rather than being brash and attention-seeking—are sociable individuals who also *listen to others*. This combination of characteristics helps middle children deal especially well with a variety of different people; since they're able to empathize with others, they tend to be tactful and courteous.

Real estate mogul Donald Trump, a middle child, has some very obvious firstborn tendencies: He is aggressively attention-seeking and appears to have unshakable self-confidence. What we don't often recognize, however, are the elements at play behind the scenes. Certainly, he's an extrovert, but he also understands the importance of listening. In any given day Trump manages between fifty and a hundred telephone calls and a dozen meetings. He's constantly called upon to come to agreement with people from all ranks of life: construction managers, billionaires, politicians, media moguls, city supervisors, lawyers— but also the everyday people who make his hotels and casinos run smoothly. His family pastor said of him in a *New York Times* article, "He's kindly and courteous in certain business negotiations and has a profound streak of honest humility."

Trump is well known for his loyalty to friends and employees. He may not always be the most discreet or sensitive middle child, but he can be charming when he wants or needs to be. He can make peace just as easily as he can make war: After two bitterly contested real estate deals when he went head-to-head with Preston Robert Tisch of Loews Corporation, the two men became friends. Even when in deep disagreement, Trump considers courtesy imperative.

Perhaps Donald Trump's actions in his public and private life don't seem at first blush to be typical middle child behavior, but his business successes reveal how much he benefits from a mixture of birth order traits. One of the most important of those traits, when it comes to being a brilliant negotiator, is the ability to put yourself in someone else's shoes. This relative empathy—combined with Trump's larger-than-life persona—has stood this middle child in good stead when it comes to making deals.

Shaking off preconceptions

Sometimes we need to dig a little deeper to get the inside scoop. Personality tests can be helpful in this regard—particularly the NEO PI-R test, which reveals elements of middles' characters that we don't always appreciate.

While we often write middles off as being wallflowers, the NEO PI-R test tells us a different story. In order to gauge how middles' personalities measure up, throughout this book, I'll frequently make reference to the five traits examined in this particular test. These traits are agreeableness, extroversion, openness to experience, conscientiousness, and neuroticism. We've already looked at agreeableness in relation to negotiating skills; now let's take a closer look at extroversion.

Extroversion is characterized by a positive, enthusiastic, and energetic attitude, and a desire to be in the company of others. Extroverts like being with people and engaging with the world, whereas introverts tend to be shy and less energetic. Overall, laterborns score higher on extroversion than firsts. (Trump is clearly an extrovert.) In personality tests, extroversion is calibrated by assessing a respondent's dominance and sociability, but in the case of middles, this can cause misleading results. Why? Because middles are sociable without being dominant.

A recent study looked at these two aspects separately, asking ninety-six undergraduate participants to rate themselves and their siblings on the twelve-item extroversion scale from the personality test. These were divided into two groups:

- five *dominance* items concerning assertiveness, activity, and excitement
- seven *sociability* items related to warmth, gregariousness, and positive emotions.

As researchers predicted, firstborns rated significantly higher than laterborns on dominance, while laterborns rated significantly higher on sociability. In addition, a number of studies have demonstrated that middles and lastborns score higher than firstborns on agreeableness. So we see that, contrary to our assumptions, middles are actually quite extroverted: They're able to get along well with others without being overpowering.

Another personality study asked individuals to rank themselves and their siblings on a series of slightly different variables including rebelliousness, social confidence, agreeableness, and conscientiousness. Middles were asked to agree or disagree with statements such as *I feel others' emotions* and *I make people feel at ease*. When respondents agreed with such statements, they were reflecting an image of themselves as being highly empathetic individuals—likely an image they project to others through their actions as well. In this case, laterborns were also significantly more likely to be the most agreeable when compared to firstborns. As we'll explore in greater detail in chapter 5, "Middles Are Justice Seekers," this trait manifests itself in a strong concern for social harmony and highlights the value that middles place on getting along with others.

Why sociability matters

Middles' lack of dominance can be seen in their ability to listen and be tactful, and this makes them attractive friends. In many ways, middles are friendship specialists. They gravitate toward socializing with people outside their own families.

Let's look at Miriam, the second child in a family of four. Her older brother, John, was a star baseball player, and her younger sister, Dana, was born with Down's syndrome. The baby of the bunch was Wes, who excelled at singing. Miriam grew up feeling she was ordinary. "Everybody had something that drew attention to them, even Dana," she says. "But me, I was just plain Miriam."

They moved to a larger city in Massachusetts when Miriam was fourteen years old, and she entered a big local public school. "I knew this move gave me a chance to reinvent myself," she explained, "and I did that by using my ordinariness to my advantage."

But how? Miriam capitalized on the fact that she was easygoing and spent a lot of time being the sounding board for the other girls in her class. They always came to her because they felt safe telling her their secrets. She was eternally patient, listened to their problems, and always offered gentle but pointed advice.

Feeling like a small fry at home helped this middle child develop empathy, and she never minimized other people's concerns or made snap judgments. She made lots of new friends and quickly found her special niche in that unfamiliar social group. On a small scale, Miriam was a great negotiator.

But beware the motormouths

Showing sensitivity to what others are feeling and exuding empathy are not typically considered problematic characters traits, but middles can be drawn into relationships, both at home and at work, in which they are taken for granted.

Let's look at Jane in Ohio again. While she managed to broker a deal between her siblings, for almost a decade before that she had tired of her role in the family. During and after college she avoided going back home when her siblings would be there. Either Tim would complain about his wife, or Susannah would chatter on at length about how hard being a musician was. While Jane liked the fact that her siblings felt they could confide in her, she was frustrated that they so infrequently asked her about herself.

Similarly, agreeable people assume others are as trustworthy and decent as they are, and can be taken advantage of more easily than those who are more wary. When Michael, the journalist, began writing for national papers, he realized that while his instinct was to be courteous and empathetic, in order to do his job properly he needed to work harder at also being skeptical. After publishing a story using quotes from a source that was later discredited, he understood that his tendency to be trustful did not always stand him in good stead. Now he tries to balance these instincts out so that he can remain true to his personality while also investigating stories with the thoroughness and detachment necessary for a journalist.

3. OPENNESS AND FLEXIBILITY

It's a myth that lastborns are the rebels of the family; in reality, it's the middles. They just don't make as much fuss about it. Even researchers tend to underestimate the social and rebellious personality of middle children, mainly because of the way past studies have been designed.

When you are open to experience, it means you're intellectually curious. These individuals tend to appreciate art, imagination, and beauty, and enjoy a variety of experiences. This naturally also reflects a person's ability to put themselves in another's shoes, as middles do. Middles are less judgmental than other birth orders, and are more willing to entertain the possibilities inherent in new concepts rather than simply sticking with the old way of doing things.

One particularly illuminating study from Belgium confirms that middles are frequently more rebellious and open-minded than other birth orders. Researchers asked 122 young adults (all from three-child families) to complete the NEO-PI R test and answer some additional questions about religion and school performance. Also included were assessments of the participants made by their mothers. Using a seven-point scale, respondents were asked to indicate how much they agreed with certain statements, such as the following:

- *Once I find the right way to do something, I stick to it.* A high score on this means low openness and low rebelliousness.
- *I enjoy hearing new ideas.* A high score means high openness and moderate rebelliousness.

Here the middleborns were revealed to be the more rebellious (and also *less* conscientious and religious). The openness to experience associated with rebelliousness is also often seen as being part of risk-taking. In fact, the authors described middles as being the "true rebels of the family."

But the results are more nuanced than these terms might at first suggest. Middles do not seek novelty or risk for its own sake. Because they're inquisitive and are interested in others' stories and feelings, they have a nonjudgmental approach to life. As this study also noted, middles are more prone to fantasy than other birth orders. This tendency toward an active imagination speaks to their open-mindedness but doesn't mean they're necessarily going to be daring or rash. It does suggest, however, that they are more flexible in their thinking and their approach—and flexibility is a key component to good negotiation.

Cutting to the chase

In the early 1990s, RJR Nabisco had just gone through a massive leveraged buyout worth $25 billion. The corporate culture was considered too freewheeling and out of control, and Louis Gerstner was brought in to steer the company in a different direction. This required a mixture of management styles: a steady, authoritative approach combined with a degree of flexibility that allowed colleagues and subordinates to be guided toward change while not feeling bullied.

Gerstner is a middleborn, the second of four sons. Born in Mineola, New York, he was driven to work hard at his private Catholic school and, as an adult, quickly made his mark on business. He started out at McKinsey & Co., then worked at American Express, RJR Nabisco, IBM, and the Carlyle Group. His successful tenure at RJR Nabisco ended when he was recruited—after only four years—to work his magic at IBM. Gerstner was not a micromanager but was excellent at seeing the big picture and then implementing the necessary changes. He was credited with putting IBM back on solid financial ground.

While Gerstner's management style was not particularly congenial, his successes at turning around businesses that needed to be steered in opposite directions speaks to this middle child's ability to think outside the box—in other words, to be open and flexible. In 1993, when he was hired away from RJR Nabisco to become the CEO and chairman of the board at IBM, the company was on the verge of breakdown. Once there, he initiated a full-fledged cultural revolution, freeing up the bureaucratic structure and reinstituting a focus on the customer that had been sorely lacking in the past. "The company stopped listening to the outside world," Gerstner said in a *Sunday Times* interview. "It lived inside a cocoon." He recognized the need to rethink the company's mandate and make customers a priority again. Many people have credited him with saving the company from disaster.

His experience as a middle likely impacted the development of vital skills needed to negotiate such drastic change. Middle children quickly learn that to achieve their goals in a busy household, it's most effective to openly consider all the various alternative approaches and then cut to the chase once clearly defined goals have been developed. When they adapt these strategies to other areas in their lives, middles are often quite successful.

In *The Art of the Deal*, Trump writes, "I also protect myself by being flexible. I never get too attached to one deal or one approach." This middle has the ability to mold himself to fit different circumstances, which firsts have trouble with. When the middle child is embroiled in a tricky negotiation, he's less likely to dig in his heels and more likely to listen and assess, keeping an open mind. Then his position is informed by circumstance, and he can tailor his arguments to the particular situation. This is crucial in making the people with whom one is negotiating feel that they are being heard and understood, which in turn encourages them to reciprocate with an equally flexible attitude.

The danger of being wishy-washy

As long as you know what you need to achieve, being flexible in negotiations is rarely problematic. But it's never advantageous to appear to be so flexible as not to have a defined point of view. Sometimes middles err on the side of being too solicitous. This can draw negotiations out longer than necessary, which makes participants impatient and less open to change. It can also sometimes confuse those involved in the process as they become unclear about what their adversary is trying to achieve.

Middles should be sure to determine their goals *before* entering a negotiation. During the process they can make their arguments more sophisticated by listening to others and taking into consideration their needs and desires, but they will have a strong basis from which to build their own case.

4. EMOTIONAL STABILITY

When a negotiating partner is excitable or neurotic, with noticeable highs and lows in tone or affect, this creates a volatile atmosphere that is not conducive to reaching consensus. To manage negotiation well, it's important to give the impression of calmness and control. Although studies offer us no conclusive affirmation of middles' stability or patience—mainly because there are so few that look directly at emotional stability in relation to birth order—one useful approach in the face of lack of positive statistical evidence is to investigate what middles are *not*. In this instance, drawing a comparison between middles and firsts in terms of their neuroticism scores on personality tests is enlightening.

A neurotic individual is more likely to be impatient, easily angered, or tense. Life is full of challenges, and emotional stability or instability reflects the way people deal with such stressful events. Those who are emotionally stable weather the storms of life; they may react, but not disproportionately. Those who score high on neuroticism, on the other hand, are rocked by challenges; these disrupt their lives frequently, and they can become emotionally unbalanced. They're often perceived as moody or unpredictable. Additionally, they're more likely to have high levels of anxiety, and to develop posttraumatic stress disorder in response to highly emotional and negative events.

One 2004 study looked at differences in the big five personality dimensions within three-child families, with a special emphasis on studying the degree of neuroticism of the participants. Middleborns scored *lowest* on the neuroticism scale, lastborns had intermediate scores, and firstborns scored the highest. In families with four children, the secondborn scored lowest. In five-child families, *both* the second and third child scored lowest on the scale. The relationship between neuroticism and birth order was not linear but more u-shaped, with children in the middle of families having the lowest levels of neuroticism.

As you might imagine, being neurotic can put a strain on personal and professional relationships. Faced with an open-ended discussion in which a neurotic person has a stake in the outcome, more than likely that person will find the situation threatening or hopeless. Naturally, in a negotiation, these are powerfully negative emotions to convey when trying to persuade someone of the validity of a particular point of view. Since middles score so low on neuroticism, of all the birth orders they will suffer least from this problem.

Learning to wait

"In temper he was Earnest, yet controlled, frank, yet sufficiently guarded, patient, yet energetic, forgiving, yet just to himself; generous yet firm," wrote J. T. Duryea about Abraham Lincoln. This intriguing combination of traits is not uncommon for middles.

In the 1860s when Lincoln was in the White House, the presidential residence had no greeting or press room. There was one large reception area on the second level and a few additional adjoining rooms for Lincoln's subordinates. The reception room was often packed: You could find tear-streaked mothers begging for pardons for their sons who had committed military offenses; members of Congress seeking to discuss a political issue; old men in heavy work boots asking permission to travel to the front lines to haul their dead back home. The level of noise was intense; it was a daily rabble that wanted the president's ear. Yet Lincoln insistently and patiently made himself available to ordinary folks and politicians alike.

His face was often stern and melancholic, but when he'd hear a story or listen to an argument, his features would soften, his eyes expressing amusement or sympathy. Though these sessions could be long and tedious, Lincoln loved them. Preoccupied as he was with several fronts in the Civil War, an often hostile Cabinet, and conniving opponents, he nonetheless listened with extraordinary equanimity to these various pleas. This not only helped improve his reputation as a man of the people (and certainly helped secure his reelection in 1864), but also reminded him constantly of the circumstances of real people in the real world.

As children, middles have to wait a lot. Modern middles wait while their younger sibling is loaded into the car seat. They wait while the firstborn performs in the recital. They wait to be served at the dinner table and to be complimented for their hard work in school. Middles are accustomed to not getting what they want right away. They learn the art of delayed gratification—and this helps them immeasurably later in life.

5. SELF-ESTEEM

Unless you enjoy a position of strength or authority—or at the very least *project an image* of strength or authority—it's hard to be taken very seriously. It is argued that in order to be a good negotiator, you must appear to be firm and confident, as Anwar Sadat, Abe Lincoln, and Donald Trump have been. A nervous or indecisive person is unlikely to inspire confidence in his or her abilities to help resolve a conflict or negotiate a deal.

Yet one birth order effect that shows up from time to time is that middleborns score lower in self-esteem than their siblings. This lower self-esteem comes from the lower levels of parental investment that middles receive, in combination with their unclear role in terms of family structure and parental expectations. Middles don't know quite where they fit in, and this anxiety contributes to their rather complex relationship with self-esteem.

In 1982 one of the first academics to study birth order with specific emphasis on middles, Jeannie Kidwell, published a paper called *The Neglected Birth Order: Middleborns.* Taking a sample from a national study on male adolescents, she examined the self-esteem of middles compared to firsts and lasts in over two thousand teens. Based on a self-report measure of self-esteem that was one part of the study, Kidwell discovered that middleborns have significantly lower self-esteem than firsts and lasts. Middles viewed their parents as more punitive, less reasonable, and less supportive than did firsts or lasts, and suffered from a sense of being "pushed around." This was presumed to affect their confidence adversely.

In addition, a 2002 master's thesis investigated whether being the only male or only female child in a family with three or more children led to higher self-esteem than being a middle of the same gender as another sibling. The author found that those middles who were the only ones of their sex had higher mean self-esteem than those who shared the same gender as their other siblings. How should we interpret this? For these middles, being the only one of their gender gave them a unique position and role in the family—and for a middleborn who is one of several of their same gender, this doesn't happen. This is one reason that birth order effects (especially in terms of middle child differences) are often strongest in families where all the children are of the same gender. The implication here is that middles, with no preset, unique family role, usually suffer from lower self-esteem than their siblings unless they are the only boy or girl in the family.

But the real question here is this: How much does this supposed lower self-esteem impact the likelihood of success in negotiations, given that negotiators are supposed to appear confident and authoritative? I argue that not only do we have to do a double take on these findings, but the connections drawn between self-esteem and success are often exaggerated.

Hold your horses

First, it's important to remember that most of these types of studies are conducted on adolescents and university undergraduates, where the participants are usually under twenty-four years of age. While at this age it's not uncommon to carry some childhood grievances, as individuals mature, they typically outgrow the old grudges they may have held against their parents or siblings when they were children.

Take the case of Jack, an investment manager from New York. The third of five children, he had grown up in suburban New Jersey. Throughout high school, he always had odd jobs at a pizzeria or the local movie theater to help make ends meet. Work was relentless, and he sometimes felt the weight of the world on his shoulders. When he was in college, he rebelled against authority and his parents, often skipping classes and not turning papers in on time. He was put on academic probation, and his parents threatened to cut him off if he didn't get his act together.

"For a while I really felt they were treating me differently from the others," he explained. "And that made me feel unsure of myself—kind of like I wasn't worthy." Then, late one night while sitting in the kitchen with his father, he had a sudden turning point. His dad looked him in the eyes and told him it was time for him to embrace his opportunities. "He told me how proud he was that I'd always held a job, that I had taken care of myself, and that he'd never realized I didn't think of myself as independent and capable."

For Jack it took some growing up to understand that he was transferring the way he had felt while in the home to the way he navigated life in the real world. It was the realization that he needed to look forward instead of backward that helped him acknowledge his innate strengths—in particular his ability to convince others of his point of view. He uses this skill daily in his job in the financial industry.

Second, as middles begin to navigate life on their own, in college and then in the workplace, they gain a sense of accomplishment. Our sense of self-worth is shaped not only by our own opinions but by the opinions of others around us. For each milestone, each achievement, and each challenge that is met, our self-esteem is strengthened. And so the social approval and reinforcement that middleborns receive from friends and colleagues in turn reinforces their own self-esteem over time. It is these kinds of nuances that are missed by self-esteem tests in which participants are barely out of high school.

Being *too* confident puts people off

Sadat famously said that his hardscrabble life in a small village prepared him for the city by deepening his "feeling of inner superiority, which has never left me." That feeling of confidence expressed itself first against British colonialism over Egypt and then against the Israeli incursion into Lebanon. And although Lincoln appeared placid and even unnervingly severe, on occasion, he, too, had an inner confidence that was evident in his decision-making process. As many observers of his day noted, although he allowed everyone to plead their case, when it came time to make decisions, he neither asked for opinions nor wavered in his judgment. But there's a difference between confidence and overconfidence and the impression it makes on others.

Remember Jack, the New York investment manager? A few years ago he was partnering with a younger associate on the investment of a very large portfolio, and they were trying to come to an agreement on their terms. The younger man, Kyle, was tall and lean, and carried himself in a self-assured manner that made most people assume that he was older than he actually was. At thirty-two he was still a bachelor.

In contrast, Jack had developed a rather laid-back personality. He was well liked by everyone in the firm and was considered solid and trustworthy. Every now and then he would unleash a wicked sense of humor that was disarming. The impression he made in company meetings was very different from Kyle's; he appeared to be somewhat detached, while Kyle tended to throw his weight around. But this eventually backfired for Kyle. People started resisting his ideas. "He oversold himself," said Jack, "and even though I wasn't in-your-face, they somehow trusted me more."

Sometimes people who are overly confident will also promise more than they can produce. This is something middles are unlikely to do. They tend to be more measured and realistic, with a core of humility that serves them well.

MIDDLES: MANIPULATION AND MASTERY

We know middles don't like conflict. They learn to be good at negotiating, often by using a bit of manipulation rather than facing someone head-on. The downside is that they sometimes hesitate to bring attention to issues in the first place so they can avoid getting embroiled in conflict.

But in negotiations, the manipulative side of middle children—their savviness, combined with empathy and openness—is the very key to their success. In seeking to evade conflict, they're much more likely to finesse a situation, avoiding extremes of emotion and focusing instead on getting the deal done in whatever way seems most effective.

Their honesty and integrity makes adversaries relax and encourages an open mind in others. Middles' sense of tact, largely a result of their overshadowed position in the family, helps them appreciate all sides of an argument and makes them appear willing to compromise. A tendency toward openness, combined with this flexible attitude, helps middle children navigate their way around and through tricky discussions involving diverse sets of interests. This is a truly valuable skill.

As the parent of a middle, it's wise to brace yourself for a protracted series of negotiations with your clever and calculating child. Respect the middle's tenacity and logic, and that child will likely respect yours. As a middle yourself, rest assured you have the inherent skills necessary to broker a tough deal with your boss, to placate or help your grown siblings and friends, or to negotiate that killer transaction that will rock the world.

THE LOWDOWN ON MIDDLES' NEGOTIATING SKILLS

1. **Middles are experienced umpires.**
   As the frequent middleman in disputes among siblings, friends, and coworkers, middle children know how to best handle disagreements: with honesty, tact, openness, confidence, and stability.

2. **They grow up to be excellent listeners.**
   Middleborns may seem quiet, but they're probably listening rather than talking. The perception of being passive or disinterested can be avoided by speaking up every so often in any conversation even if it's simply to ask a question.

3. **Sometimes middles just need to walk away.**
   As the most trustful and giving of the birth orders, middles can benefit from learning when to gracefully bow out and say, "Look, sort it out for yourselves."

4. **And sometimes they need to step up.**
   When the need calls for it, middle children should stand up for themselves, face confrontation, and play a more aggressive role in interpersonal interactions to avoid seeming wishy-washy or disinterested.

5. Middleborns carry themselves well.

Middle children may have lower self-esteem than other birth orders, but this actually works in their favor: Being overly self-confident (like a firstborn) can put people off.

CHAPTER FOUR

Middle Children
Are Trailblazers

"You will be a disgrace to yourself and your family!" the middle-age doctor complained to his son. Even though the boy knew his father thought he was lazy and unfocused, he couldn't seem to change his ways. The child was pleasant enough—mild-mannered and polite—but he could also be pig-headed. It was the early 1800s, and he had been born into privilege, the second son and middle child of a wealthy English family. His father had assumed he would follow in his footsteps when he grew up, becoming a country doctor, but Charles had other ideas.

As a student, the boy didn't do well. He dropped out of university after only two years. Medicine bored him, and the sight of blood made his stomach turn. Instead, he dedicated himself to such esoteric pursuits as collecting beetles and preserving dead animals. In desperation, his father sent him off to Cambridge to become a parson.

Yet even that didn't work out as expected. At age twenty-two, when Charles begged to be allowed to accompany a team of researchers on a mission halfway across the world, his father refused permission. An uncle intervened, and Charles was eventually given his family's blessing. In 1831 he began his epic voyage, sailing on the HMS *Beagle* around South America, across the Pacific Ocean to the distant Galápagos Islands, and then back via the Indian Ocean and around the horn of Africa. It would be five years before he returned home to England.

While on the islands, Charles Darwin was extraordinarily productive. Although his previous academic work had been undistinguished, once he found his focus, he was extremely thorough and insightful. His studies of the native animals, in particular the thirteen different species of birds that became known as Darwin's finches, led him to develop his theory of the origin of species by natural selection. Modern biology would not exist today without the synthesis of Charles Darwin's theory of evolution with modern genetics.

Darwin had been an unpretentious, mild-mannered middle child. While he had displayed only average intelligence in his scholastic efforts, he showed above-average drive and passion for those things he *did* find interesting (a trait shared by many middles). Against all expectations, this drive and passion eventually led him to blaze a trail through the scientific community that remains as relevant today—almost two hundred years later—as it was revolutionary then.

WHO ARE THE SECRET POWER BROKERS?

When asked to name a middle child who has achieved lasting and far-reaching change in society, most people draw a blank. But when people are asked more generally about the birth order of successful people, they typically assume them to be firstborns. What few people realize is that middle children are actually *more likely* to successfully effect change in the world than any other birth order. As is so often the case with middles, they're perennially underestimated. For instance, while it's often pointed out that 36 percent of United States presidents have been firstborns, it is overlooked that 52 percent of them have been middleborns. (The main reason for this is that older sisters weren't counted in terms of birth order. This led to an overcounting of male presidents as firstborns when they were actually middles with older sisters.)

When it comes to politics, business, science, and the arts, in many ways middle children secretly rule the world. Consider presidents Theodore Roosevelt and John F. Kennedy (to name just two heads of state); business tycoons Bill Gates and Michael Dell; inventor extraordinaire Benjamin Franklin; and the creative visionaries Madonna and Jane Austen. What do these vastly different personalities, living in radically different times and facing different challenges, have in common? They have the middleborn capacity to use their birth order to their advantage to get the most out of their chosen fields of interest.

In looking at what qualities lead middles to become trailblazers, it's helpful to examine three core issues:

1. the debate on intelligence and the role that education plays in the development of an individual's potential;
2. family dynamics and how this affects the choices that middle children make about where to direct their focus;
3. which specific personality traits influence middles' ability to carve out new paths for themselves and to see change through.

In Darwin's case, he stumbled into a role that led him to become world famous and controversial despite not having an especially charismatic personality. Methodically and with great patience, he followed his interests and stood up for his beliefs. Although surely unnerved by his family's disapproval and his culture's inflexibility, Darwin ultimately refused to bend to the demands of nineteenth-century English society. And, like many middles, he pursued his passions without necessarily intending to create such divisiveness.

THE DEBATE ON INTELLIGENCE

To what extent are middle children's qualities—including their tendency to become trailblazers—a result of the talents, inclinations, or intelligence they're born with? In our society we're conditioned to believe that high IQ scores or good grades in school correlate with success in life. Yet for decades there's been an ongoing debate in academic circles regarding the relationship between intelligence as measured by IQ tests and an individual's potential for success and happiness.

Almost from the development of the very first intelligence test there has been significant disagreement over what exactly the tests are measuring. Alfred Binet developed the Binet-Simon intelligence scale in the early 1900s to identify students in need of special assistance in the classroom. He argued that intelligence is not fixed and believed that classroom performance could be greatly improved with time and extra attention. So in reality the test was designed to advocate for more education for all children.

Over the next few years the test was picked up by others, including those in the eugenics movement who were focused on using it for such purposes as curtailing the reproduction of those who were "feebleminded" or of criminal disposition. In more recent years, there has been heated debate over the topic of IQ and race and the cultural relevance of some of the questions. Instead of focusing so much on traditional concepts of intelligence as measured by standard IQ tests, some researchers have turned to other measures and constructs. Later we'll look in greater detail at how this relates specifically to middle children.

True or false: middles aren't as smart as firsts

A few years ago news about intelligence and its relationship to birth order made international headlines. Everywhere people heard about what a great disadvantage it was to be anything but a firstborn. Norwegian researchers had proven conclusively that firsts are the "smartest" of all birth orders. Behind this flurry of discussion lay the assumption that since laterborns have demonstrably lower IQs than firsts, they would not be as "successful" as the lucky firstborns.

The Norwegian researchers examined the military records of over two hundred and fifty thousand young men, analyzing birth order data, health status, and IQ scores (controlling for such factors as parents' education levels, income, maternal age at birth, birth weight, birth spacing, and family size). Their results were clear: They showed a decrease in intelligence test scores with increasing birth order. IQ scores dropped one to two points from firstborn to secondborn to thirdborn, and so on. When they examined almost sixty-four thousand pairs of adjacent brothers (comparing firsts and middles, or middles and lasts), they found the same pattern. Interestingly, larger birth spacing—the interval between one child and the next—*decreased* the difference in standardized scores.

But I think these results have been blown out of proportion. While I don't doubt that these variations in IQ scores by birth order do indeed exist, I also believe that one or two IQ points makes little to no difference in terms of an individual's likely success in life. So while firsts are technically "smarter" than middles, the long-term impact of this on quality of life remains unproven.

The most recent interpretations of intelligence—which were not addressed in the Norwegian study—argue that there are multiple factors at play. It's not just traditional IQ; social and emotional intelligence are essential as well. These have a huge impact on success in the workplace and in personal relationships with friends and family. Success is not just about knowledge and abstract thinking. It's also about personal relationships—an arena in which middles generally excel.

Middles do face some hurdles

No matter how much weight you might place on raw intelligence or ability, clearly environment plays a role in whether an individual is given the opportunity to reach his or her potential. A child with no access to reading materials, for example, will be hard-pressed to find ways to grow intellectually and improve upon his or her innate skills. And some fascinating studies reveal that middles, in particular, have *less* opportunity in terms of education and money to reach their full potential than do other birth orders. But if this is the case, what effect does this have? Not the one you might expect.

One study of education in East and West Germany (using data from 1945 to 1978) demonstrated that being a laterborn child significantly increased the probability of *not* having an educational degree or having only lower secondary education. A Canadian study, published in 2010, again using a large data set, reported that an increase in family size is significantly correlated with a *reduced* likelihood of post-secondary education.

My own research, conducted while I was a postdoctoral researcher, indicated that firstborn boys were given more money for college. These results were corroborated by a study of Missouri college students that showed that middleborns received substantially less assistance with college expenses than other children. Actually, in that study when the amount of money contributed for college expenses was considered across the three birth orders, 33 percent of middleborns received no financial support while only 13 percent of firstborns and 17 percent of lastborns weren't given money toward college. And most studies on birth order and university attendance in the United States, Canada, and Europe indicate that there are many more firstborns at college and in graduate school than other birth orders.

If middles are receiving less support from parents to develop their skill sets, why is it that my research, both anecdotal and scientific, shows middle children actually fare very well in later life? The reason is that education and intelligence are not the only factors implicated in success. In fact, they may not even be the most important contributors. Over the centuries that the debate over intelligence has raged, it has been virtually impossible to measure the effect that intelligence has on success outside the classroom; there are simply too many moving parts. Intelligence is complex, and success is complex.

To be a trailblazer one must be imaginative and driven. From all I know about middles, once they find their niche they are able to make up for the parental attention or resources they lacked as children. Whatever their natural intelligence and however well they manage to develop it academically or experientially, as children middleborns learn to rely on themselves and tend to push themselves. This helps them greatly when it comes to carving their own paths through life.

The key is using what you have

As a child, Theodore Roosevelt had many things working against him. One of two male middleborns in the family, he was bracketed by an older and a younger sister. Teddy was asthmatic and weak, and spent many quiet hours as a young boy holed up in his brownstone in Gramercy Park, New York, endlessly devouring books instead of attending school. He had little formal instruction before heading to college and no experience with vigorous athletic endeavors. But rather than give in to a sedentary life, he chose to challenge himself.

As is the case with so many middles, Roosevelt was not easily defeated by circumstance. Rather than succumbing to his ailments, he surmounted them by embracing an energetic lifestyle and opening his eyes to the wonder of the land and all that the people of America could do to either save or destroy it. In 1883, Roosevelt set foot on the dusty plains of North Dakota for the first time—a city boy looking to hunt buffalo in the Badlands. Just a week before his arrival, a herd of ten thousand bison had been slaughtered by commercial hunters. Soon there would be no bison left on the prairies at all. Throwing himself wholeheartedly into the roughrider lifestyle, he became entranced by the wide-open landscape and painfully aware of the forces of modernism that placed this beauty at great risk. On that trip to the Dakotas he was infused with a love of nature that would lead him to fight vigorously for radical changes in land management.

"Intelligence is what you use when you don't know what to do," said the late Swiss psychologist Jean Piaget. This statement reflects a perspective that helps us understand how middles operate. By dint of their position in the family, middles like Teddy Roosevelt learn to be opportunists. This, in turn, helps them put what intelligence they have to good use. While achievement is related to academic success, people with the same intelligence perform quite differently on achievement tests. In fact, the correlation between measured intelligence and achievement rarely exceeds 50 percent. This statistic once again makes clear the importance of additional factors that motivate achievement, such as personality, executive function, and emotional intelligence. Let's take a closer look at this.

Typically, executive function is thought of as the cognitive system responsible for planning and initiating appropriate actions, and inhibiting inappropriate ones. For instance, when you greet a superior at work, you're likely to shake hands, not slap him or her on the shoulder: It's your executive function that helps sort out which behavior is correct for any given situation. Executive functions are the processes that control and monitor behavior: the self-discipline of the intellect. They help us process what is relevant and ignore what is not. Individuals with attention deficit disorder (ADD) or attention deficit/hyperactivity disorder (ADHD), for instance, typically have poor executive function, finding it hard to concentrate and filter out extraneous input.

Emotional intelligence focuses on the ability to identify, control, assess, and manage one's own emotions and those of others. While important to success, it is often considered separately from the type of intelligence measured on typical IQ tests. Many people struggle with social cues and navigating group dynamics. Without the ability to interact well with others, opportunities for achieving change in the world are rather limited. My experience suggests that middles enjoy good executive function and excellent emotional intelligence, and this affects their social behavior in such a way that they often become trail-blazers, sometimes in spite of their personal circumstances. We'll be exploring emotional intelligence in greater detail in chapter 9, "Middle Children as Parents."

That Roosevelt should eventually become known and admired as the *Cowboy President*—a paragon of masculinity and strength—would not have been thought possible when he was a child. The Roosevelts had settled in New York City over a hundred years earlier and were about as removed from the rugged prairie lifestyle as city dwellers could be. Despite Roosevelt's lack of conventional education, and the fact that his background in no way prepared him for his new role as defender of the West, he used his planning skills, his self-control and drive (executive function), and his emotional intelligence to go against type and become a trailblazer of conservation.

THE EFFECT OF FAMILY DYNAMICS

Middles want to be different

When I first started graduate school, I was fascinated by family dynamics in general and the role of sex and birth order in influencing these dynamics in particular. Unlike many psychologists, I had always appreciated the importance of biology. As a young child I was fascinated by animal behavior and later was amazed by the similarities that seemed so glaringly obvious between many behaviors of animals and humans. Who, upon watching Jane Goodall's footage of chimpanzees at Gombe, is not struck by how much like a human mother Flo seems? Biology always seemed to me to be a unifying lens through which to view human and animal behavior.

Many people struggle with the question of how much of an individual's personality, inclinations, and aptitudes a person is born with, and how much emerges depending on environmental factors. Studies done on animals, such as when a nervous mother's baby is given to a calm mother to raise, clearly demonstrate that both nurture and nature have significant roles to play in development.

Undoubtedly, there are biological and environmental conditions over which children have little or no control that can have an immense impact on them: extreme poverty or wealth, neglect or overindulgence, disability or giftedness, school environment and culture. Children develop strategies to deal with their environmental circumstances; these strategies affect which aspects of their personalities are suppressed or brought to the fore.

In this way, middle children seek systems and behaviors that help them define their role among their families and the greater world around them. Since they're rarely in the pseudo-parental authority role of the firstborn, nor do they experience the responsibility-free role of the baby, middles are left to determine their own role. When they do so, it's typically in relation to their siblings: In order to make themselves as unique as possible, they define themselves as *what their siblings are not*. Also, middleborns seem more concerned than other birth orders with being successful in relation to their siblings. When you start out already a few steps behind your brother or sister, a more successful strategy is to take a completely different path.

Trying a little bit of everything

Lindie's older sister, Maxine, is three years her senior, and Diane is two years younger than Lindie. Their father had rowed in college, made it to the 1976 Olympics in Montreal, and encouraged his girls to be athletic. Maxine, with her long legs and incredible stamina, was a stellar runner. In middle school she won every long-distance track event. By the time she got to high school, she developed a problem with recurrent shin splints and turned her attention to swimming. At college she swam competitively and won multiple medals.

Maxine's athletic prowess was impressive, and middle child Lindie was intimidated. She tried a little bit of everything—like trying on pants for size. When she was younger, she liked running, but she quickly discovered her heart wasn't in it despite excellent running times in the 100-meter sprints. At fifteen she decided she wasn't cut out to be an athlete, and she gave up organized sports. Lindie later admitted that she probably just hated being compared to her older sister.

This situation is somewhat similar to Darwin's in that he, too, shied away from the paths modeled to him by his father and his older brother. Perhaps unconsciously he sought to define himself as unique; ultimately, he was comfortable with the decision to follow his instincts rather than follow the leader. Darwin actually benefited from being a middleborn. Had he been the *firstborn* son, his father might have insisted that he become a doctor after all, and Darwin would never have followed his passion and traveled to the Galápagos Islands, thereby changing our understanding of evolutionary biology.

The effects of parental pressure

In an early study from the 1980s, researchers broke down environmental differences into two categories: shared and non-shared. Socioeconomic status and culture are shared environments. Darwin, for example, and his brothers and sisters grew up in the same beautiful Georgian mansion, the Mount, and all benefited from his father's wealth and status. What was different for each sibling was the non-shared environment.

Sibling competition and parental attention are part of a non-shared environment—and for each child in a family, this experience is quite unique. As a middleborn, Charles Darwin felt less pressure than the firstborn to fall in line with his father's expectations. Not as celebrated as the first and not as coddled as the baby, he felt compelled to carve out his own path.

Even when parents are trying to be equitable, each child in a family is given different amounts of attention and investment from parents. In addition, each child experiences the competition from their siblings in a unique way. As two researchers recently noted in a review of research on shared/non-shared environment and parent-child relationships, a majority of siblings report experiencing substantial differences in parental favoritism. "In spite of strong social norms that parents should treat all of their children similarly," they conclude, "only a minority of the mothers report feeling similar intensity of affection for their different children, or say that they give similar attention, control, and discipline to their children."

Oh the places you'll go . . .

The reality is that parents' feelings about each of their children, and their expectations of them, vary dramatically, and this naturally influences their behavior. Sometimes, parents' expectations are shaped by their own views of birth order differences. If they expect their first to be dominant, they inadvertently reinforce any dominant traits that might already be evident. One study looked at 105 parents' perceptions of their children, giving them checklists of adjective pairs, such as *spoiled-unspoiled*. At one point the parents were asked to describe what they would expect an only, oldest, and youngest child to be like by rating them on the adjective scale. Then they were asked to describe their own children.

Parents' descriptions of their own children and the hypothetical children of the same birth order were positively correlated. Parents with more than one child were likely to describe their firstborn offspring more positively than their lastborn. Like many studies, this one didn't include middle children; however, studies that look at people's perceptions, or rather *preconceptions*, of middleborns suggest that there is no clear picture of where middles fall on most traits (other than the fact that they are never described as spoiled). Many people just place them in the middle of the dimension or have no opinion at all. This suggests that parents themselves, as well as others, may not have a very clear image of middles, leaving this birth order relatively free of parental pressure.

These results echo those of an earlier study in which adults gave more positive ratings and had higher expectations for firstborn children. If firstborn children take on a parental-like role of authority in the family, it shouldn't be surprising that parents view them as the responsible ones. As the firstborns tend to conform to parental authority and beliefs, parents often invest highly in them with correspondingly high expectations for their success in school, the workplace, and relationships. And in the pursuit of such success, parents provide the needed resources.

Also, parents with no previous experience to draw upon in terms of childhood achievement may set an unnaturally high standard for performance from their firstborn. This kind of parental pressure can be difficult to manage. In Lindie's family there was significant pressure on Maxine, the track star, to find another niche in which to excel after she became injured. Had she not pushed herself so hard, she may not have incurred the injuries in the first place. One could also argue that had her parents not encouraged (or pushed) her to continue competitive athletics, she would not have tried swimming. The significant difference to note here is that while Maxine felt pressure from her parents, Lindie, the middle child, made choices in relation to the pressure she put on herself.

Less pressure can be a *good* thing

Because everyone else in the family worked so hard to excel at their chosen sports, Lindie's parents were somewhat frustrated by their middle child's lack of motivation. It didn't occur to them that her attitude toward athletics was a direct result of her sibling's excellence. They also never considered that the positive attention they showered on the oldest daughter would have any impact on their middleborn's decision-making, yet Lindie felt it was simply too hard to define herself as an athlete in competition with her sister.

But this dynamic didn't hold her back for all that long. When she was a senior in high school, Lindie fell into a long conversation with Maxine's physical therapist, and they started talking about yoga. "It was as though a light went off in my head, and I thought, 'This is it,'" Lindie says. "'I found my thing!'" Throughout college and later in graduate school she became a serious yoga practitioner. It didn't matter to her that no one at that time recognized yoga as a legitimate athletic pursuit, because it gave her immense physical and psychological satisfaction. Eventually, Lindie moved away from home and opened the first yoga practice in a small town in the California desert. It became popular enough for her to open a franchise, and she now has seven yoga studios scattered throughout southern California.

Because of her middle child status, Lindie blazed her very own trail instead of taking her cue from her sisters or her parents. She tried something new, an activity she could claim as her own, that helped her define herself as separate from her siblings. It took her a while to figure out what her own special niche was supposed to be, yet once she discovered it, she was just as willing to dedicate time and effort to her chosen pursuit as her sisters had dedicated to theirs.

But less pressure can have its drawbacks

Johnny was born in Massachusetts in the spring of 1917, the second boy of a family of nine children. His older brother played football for his high school and was a star student. Joseph Sr. was grooming his oldest son to become a politician. Joe Jr. was handsome, intelligent, and serious-minded, and was sure to make his family proud.

Johnny, one of the middles in the family, was a skinny boy with a cheerful attitude, a Boy Scout who spent his summers with his family in Hyannisport, and his teen years at boarding school. He was often ill, suffering variously from appendicitis, colitis, and a bad back. Where his brother was studious, Johnny was the class clown—once blowing up a toilet seat with firecrackers. He eventually went to Harvard College (as did his older brother), earning a degree in international affairs. Afterward, the army rejected him due to his back ailments, and he joined the navy. He toyed with the idea of becoming a journalist, but he wasn't sure; he felt he had plenty of time to figure things out.

Both Johnny and his brother served in World War II. In 1944, Joe Jr. volunteered for Operation Aphrodite in which the crew of a plane packed with bombs was supposed to eject to safety before the plane blew up over its intended target. But disaster struck: The aircraft exploded prematurely, and Joe Jr. died instantly.

Everything changed for Johnny when his older brother was killed. Suddenly, there was a vacuum to fill. He had quite enjoyed his role as a more independent agent, sociable rather than serious, with no particular sense of urgency to his studies or his pursuit of a career. Now his father's attentions turned to him.

That's when John F. Kennedy decided to get into politics. Eventually, he would become the thirty-fifth president of the United States. One has to wonder what direction JFK's life might have taken had his older brother survived the war. It is highly unlikely, given his health issues and his reputation as a jokester, that he would have entered politics were it not for his brother's early demise.

This middle child did find his calling in life, but only after the long shadow of his brother's ambition stopped consigning him to the dark edges of the stage. Middles must be careful not to be so passive as to allow themselves to be overlooked or overshadowed. If they can learn to trust their instincts and embrace their independence rather than look for attention from parents, they could be destined for greatness.

THE IMPACT OF PERSONALITY

Out with the old, in with the new

Openness to innovation and to being different, as well as a distrust of existing power and authority, are behaviors learned by middles as part of the sibling competition for parental attention and investment. As we've discussed, middle children are more likely to try different strategies than the ones they see in use around them, banking on this risk paying off. This reaction to their non-shared environment helps them develop excellent intuition, flexibility, foresight, and willingness to evolve.

The third of four children, "Little Noni" didn't follow trends; she created them. Back in the 1980s this outgoing Catholic middle child tied shredded rags in her hair, wore lingerie as clothing, shocked the Pope by sexualizing religious imagery, and launched a global musical phenomenon that would soon become known by only one name: Madonna.

Raised by her design-engineer father and stepmother outside Detroit, Michigan, Madonna's childhood was dominated by rules and religion. Early in life she felt the need to distinguish herself by working hard and playing hard, and she didn't feel compelled to follow the pack. Every step she took toward success was characterized by pushing the envelope and flouting authority. Back when she wasn't yet a household name, she proclaimed to Dick Clark, "I have the same goal I've had ever since I was a girl. I want to rule the world."

In her first televised music video, she wore a mammoth white wedding dress and veil, and a chunky leather belt emblazoned with the words BOY TOY. It was an iconic performance that put fledging MTV on the map. A few years later she published a radical book called, simply, *Sex*, that led to an energetic public discourse on sexuality and feminism. Her videos were banned from MTV for being too racy. Not long after that, Madonna starred in *Evita*, for which she had to wear period costumes and sing classically. As the musician Sting pointed out, "She's outrageous, she's provocative . . . she's as feared as she's desired; she leads while others follow."

Madonna Louise Ciccone has been an enduring presence in popular culture for three decades, primarily because of her talent for reinvention and her inclination toward taking risks. As is the case with so many middle children, once they find their passion, they're fully dedicated to it. For many, they seek to influence the people around them with their outsize visions and sensibilities. Far from being shrinking violets, middle children often have a powerful drive, and a remarkable ability to shrug off other people's criticism.

Middles think outside the box

A study I conducted early in my career highlighted for me just how open middles are to new ideas compared to their siblings. In a survey that was sent to people with an interest in genealogy, participants were asked to rate how open they believed they were to new and radical ideas. Since most people like to think of themselves as open-minded, one might have expected very little variation in the results. Not so: *Under* 50 percent of firstborns claimed to be open to new and radical ideas, compared to *over* 85 percent of middle and lastborns.

It was interesting to me that middles were revealed as being more likely to believe in outlandish ideas (such as cold fusion) and to embrace change than other birth orders. In my own experience, my father (a middle child) was very open to new ideas, especially in science and technology, despite the fact that he was a strong believer in finding evidence to prove it. Many years before laws made car seats mandatory and child car seats were commercially available, my dad built me one of my own. It was a sight to behold: Resembling a small blue leather recliner, it was attached to the car seatbelt with ties that locked me in. Dad was a forward thinker who was not afraid to start his own trends.

We can see this tendency to embrace new ideas played out in consumer behavior as well: A 2005 study of innovation and conformity sought to examine the impact of birth order on consumption. Scales were designed to assess attitudes toward branded products, brand switching, comparison shopping, innovativeness in fashion and products, and susceptibility to interpersonal influence. These reflected an individual's openness and attitude toward risk taking.

The survey was given to undergraduates in the American South, and the results compared firsts and laterborns. They found that firsts were more likely to be swayed by friends and group norms, answering positively to such questions as: *I frequently gather information from friends and family about a product before I buy,* and *To make sure I buy the right product or brand, I often observe what others are buying and using.*

Laterborns proved themselves to be marginally more open to

product innovations, as seen in their responses to such statements as *I like to try new products to see what they're like*, and *I feel that the tried-and-true ways of doing things are the best at work and in my life*. Their answers reflected middleborns' and lastborns' willingness to try out that new and different concept even if the old one works.

Since being open to experience can be taken to extremes, middles do need to be careful not to be gullible. Accepting the possibility that new ideas are feasible may show laudable open-mindedness, but it also increases the potential of embracing an idea or action that's ill-conceived. In a study on sibling birth order effects, researcher and author Frank Sulloway discovered that laterborns were nine times more likely to support Gall's theory of phrenology—a now-discredited but once popular Victorian belief that bumps on the skull are illustrative of personality. So as long as middle children maintain a balance between embracing innovation and using judgment and common sense, they should be able to avoid being too credulous.

Carving their own path

The boy had tousled reddish hair, and sat at the very back of the empty room. The previous month, the Lakeview Mother's Club had held a rummage sale and bought a bunch of machines that looked like gargantuan ochre-colored typewriters. The eighth grader was leaning over the ASR-33 teletype, seemingly engrossed. On the desk next to him sat a GE computer whose black screen flickered with green digits.

When the teacher poked her head in, the boy didn't even turn around. "Bill," she said, "aren't you supposed to be in Math right now?"

Bill spun around. "I'm allowed to skip Math," he answered, reddening. "I'm working on some new language on BASIC. It's for a tic-tac-toe game."

Parents and teachers often find middle children somewhat perplexing. Although they're usually not vocal attention-seekers like firsts or lasts, middles quietly and steadily pursue their own interests, often in the face of adult skepticism. They don't mind bucking trends and taking calculated risks. Back in the nineteenth century, when Darwin was zealously collecting and categorizing insects, his father considered him an eccentric lazybones. In the 1970s, when the teenage Bill Gates first developed his interest in emerging technology, his elders were astonished at the hours he spent poring over computer code and dissecting machines. His desire to come to a deeper understanding of computing and his willingness to dedicate himself single-mindedly to this pursuit were at the core of the personal computer revolution that has changed our world in countless significant ways. Yet he broke some rules to get there.

Bill Gates had an older sister named Kristi, who became an accountant, and a younger one named Libby who is a stay-at-home mother. When he first got in trouble for exploiting bugs in the Computer Center Corporation's PDP-10—he was trying to find a way to wheedle free computer time—he was banned from using their equipment for a summer. Just a few years later he unwittingly transmitted what was probably the first ever computer virus, causing the national network of interconnected computers to crash. This time his punishment was more severe: no more computers for his entire junior year. Far from being lauded for his interest and dedication, Bill was considered a bright but somewhat difficult boy. He seemed to get himself into trouble with his insistent risk taking, even though his outward manner was neither foolhardy nor rash.

Risk taking can pay off for middles

Ultimately, Bill Gates's lack of concern with pushing boundaries paid off big time. He dropped out of Harvard in the mid-1970s and developed the Microsoft Disk Operating System, MS-DOS, for IBM in 1980. Ten years later over one hundred million copies of the operating system had been sold. This computer nerd blazed a trail through the world of technology and radically altered how business and communication is conducted in our modern era.

His phenomenal success in the business world is an excellent example of how conventional paths to success are not the only route. Without the ability to control impulses and direct attention, and to think outside the box, even the most brilliant child will find it challenging to navigate life successfully. In 2004, *Time* magazine called Gates "One of the 100 people who most influenced the 20th century," along with such other luminaries as Pope John Paul II and Nelson Mandela (both also middles). Gates's philanthropic foundation has donated $4 billion to charitable causes since its inception in 1994.

"There will be a day, not far distant, when you will be able to conduct business, study, explore the world and its cultures, call up any great entertainment, make friends, attend neighborhood markets, and show pictures to distant relatives—without leaving your desk or armchair," Gates wrote in his book, *The Road Ahead*. In 1995, before the advent of IM, YouTube, instant video downloads, iTunes, and virtual reality, this notion was almost impossible for most people to fathom. "It will be more than an object you carry or an appliance you purchase," he continued. "It will be your passport into a new, mediated way of life."

This gifted, unprepossessing, self-disciplined middle child who recognized and exploited his enthusiasm for modern technology was at the very forefront of developing this "new, mediated way of life" that so many of us are now utterly reliant on.

Using risk as a strategy

Researchers Frank Sulloway and Richard Zweigenhaft recently completed an intriguing study looking at major league baseball players, analyzing their base stealing strategies in relation to birth order, as well as taking a more general look at risk taking in sports. They conducted a metanalysis of twenty-four studies (with over eight thousand respondents) of birth order and participation in dangerous sports such as football, hockey, lacrosse, and wrestling. A sport was considered dangerous based on injury rates, expert or participant ratings of risk, and contact versus non-contact nature.

Laterborns were one and a half times more likely than firstborns to participate in dangerous sports. The researchers also conducted an analysis of older and younger brothers who both played baseball in the major leagues. The sample consisted of seven hundred men who had a brother who was also in the league. Younger brothers engaged more frequently in specific tactics that were more risky—in terms of danger or payoff—such as base stealing. In addition, they were actually more successful than their older brothers in those attempts.

Firsts did better in terms of tactics that require high levels of restraint, such as batting average and avoiding strikeouts. This highlights the fact that while both younger and older brothers are equally successful at the game, they simply specialize in different strategies for success. Middleborns, who are a significant segment of the laterborn or younger sibling category, are part of this risk-taking population. They often take measured risks when they believe those risks are most likely to pay off. As we'll see, this is applicable not only in baseball but in other aspects of their lives as well.

Middles push boundaries in spite of themselves

As General George S. Patton said after World War II, "Take calculated risks. That is quite different from being rash." Middles operate this way. While they aren't as risk averse as firstborns, neither are they reckless. As the baseball study suggests, middleborns take risks when they're likely to actually pay off. Their relatively high levels of conscientiousness (in comparison to more reckless lastborns) make them more careful evaluators of the costs and benefits of risk taking.

Darwin is once again a good example of the temperate middle. Courteous and rather humble, he was stealthy and consistent in his efforts. The prevailing religious and ideological convictions of the times were diametrically opposed to his science-based, painstakingly documented research. On top of this, his own wife was intensely religious; she was raised Unitarian and had a deep-seated belief in God. While he was brought up as an Anglican and had once entertained the idea of becoming a parish priest, he later became skeptical of religion and its doctrines. Charles Darwin did not seek out fame or notoriety, but his passions led him to become a national hero who, upon his death, was given a state funeral.

Bucking conventional wisdoms can create tremendous upheaval and stress, yet middles often thrust themselves right into the middle of the fray. They risk ridicule, opposition, and failure. Darwin himself was often violently ill, suffering from vomiting and palpitations that incapacitated him for months at a time throughout his entire life. He believed these symptoms worsened significantly at times of stress such as when he was due to present new research (a highly "risky" move, considering the prevailing beliefs about creationism). One important message for middles is not to let your dislike of conflict keep you from your goals. Do your best to make your point, produce your evidence, give the logical argument, and remember that it's not about you personally. Life is stressful, but you have lots of friends to lean on—after all, they lean on you all the time.

Who gets things done?

As we've seen, middleborns' openness leads them to think outside the box and to be more willing to take risks than firstborns. One element of their personalities that tempers this openness, softening the potential downside of being a risk taker, is their level of conscientiousness. This is one of the five factors that personality tests are designed to measure.

Conscientiousness is about self-discipline. For instance, someone who is efficient and organized tests higher on conscientiousness than someone who is easygoing or careless. When behavior is planned rather than spontaneous, this also shows conscientiousness. What's especially relevant to us is that middles share some positive characteristics of firsts and lasts, while avoiding the negative characteristics (such as dominance and neuroticism).

Typically, middles aren't as confrontational or aggressive as firstborns can be: Firstborns score high on measures of dominance and conscientiousness, which contributes to their sense of drive and purpose. But this dominance can also be off-putting and work against them. Lasts are more flighty than middles, scoring highly on sociability, openness, and agreeableness. This is helpful in forging relationships, but lasts' relative lack of conscientiousness makes them less dependable and trustworthy than middles.

Middles score high on sociability, exhibiting some of the most favorable elements of extroversion, openness, and agreeableness. So they are sociable individuals and also quite conscientious, and they achieve a better balance between these two elements than other birth orders. This is an advantage that can lead middles to be more effective in gaining trust, establishing efficient collaborations, and innovating and creating change than other birth orders.

Conscientiousness is critical to success. Without consistent effort, no success, whether in the arts or business, can be sustained over time. Although middles are not as conscientious as firsts, this can be interpreted as a positive: They aren't overly controlling or too detail-oriented. Madonna, for instance, may love to shock, but she is also a serious businesswoman with an attention to detail and an astonishing drive. At age nineteen she left Detroit for the first time and arrived in New York City with thirty-five dollars in her pocket. She had never before been on a plane or in a taxi cab. Less than ten years later she was a world-renowned artist. Guinness World Records lists her as the most successful female recording artist of all time.

In addition to being a singer, Madonna is constantly reinventing her style and her music, and is open to trying new ventures. In 2007 she signed a groundbreaking $120 million, ten-year deal with the concert promoters Live Nation. Having recognized that artists are not making money from CDs anymore, she understood it was time to embrace the shifting paradigms in the music industry. Her ability to comfortably take calculated risks combined with her conscientiousness make Madonna a true middle child.

MIDDLES AND THE FUTURE

As we have seen, since middleborns can't get what they want at home by being the biggest and strongest or littlest and cutest, they develop niche-picking skills early on. The middle child attempts to maximize opportunities for parental investment or seeks investment elsewhere—with peers, for example, as we'll explore in chapter 7, "Middles as Friends and Lovers". They're predisposed to experimentation and un-conventionality as a way to distinguish themselves.

Middle children are savvy enough to develop and exploit diplo-matic and cooperative strategies as responses to an environment de-fined by the hierarchical advantage of their older or younger siblings. As a consequence, they have an easier time finding themselves, figur-ing out how to exploit their own talents, and bringing out the best in the people around them. Therefore, even though they aren't known for their dominance or assertiveness, middleborns turn out to be maver-icks and entrepreneurs of the highest order.

Despite his lack of formal education and serious family tragedy, Teddy Roosevelt pushed himself hard, eagerly plunging into new and uncharted waters. His zeal, emotional intelligence, and determination drove him to become the youngest man to assume the presidency of the United States. But even that was not his greatest achievement. Roosevelt ended up overcoming his personal challenges and blazing the trail of land preservation in an era when the majority of the popu-lation saw nature as expendable. His motto, "Speak softly and carry a big stick," is typical of a middle child's brilliant negotiating skills and willingness to create an atmosphere in which significant change is achievable.

This middleborn's ability to see the big picture and his courage to resist the status quo led to the creation of national parks and monuments in eleven states. The groundbreaking Antiquities Act of 1906 allowed the government to designate landmarks of historic or scientific interest as national monuments. "Leave it as it is," he said of the Grand Canyon. "You cannot improve on it."

Unhampered by set parental expectations and willing to try new things, middle children are more likely to be innovators than firstborns. Because this tendency of middles to nonconformity goes hand in hand with a desire to distinguish themselves and a strong sense of determination, they are able to achieve more fundamental changes in science, business, and politics than other birth orders. Middles have radically changed our past, and they have the ability to change our future.

WHAT YOU SHOULD KNOW ABOUT TRAILBLAZING MIDDLE CHILDREN

1. **Middleborns have hidden smarts.**
   Although there is evidence that middles score lower on IQ tests than firsts, the difference is negligible. Middles have excellent executive function and emotional intelligence, which helps them excel with people. That's why they are so successful at effecting social change.

2. **Obstacles become opportunities.**
   Middleborns are driven to overcome their disadvantages and should trust in their innate strengths. They need not be discouraged by their parents' expectations or their lack of attention and focus on them.

3. **Middles carve their own path in life.**
   In order to stand out from their siblings, middle children often develop interests that are different from their brothers and sisters. Adults can be perplexed by middles who don't follow the crowd but should recognize the complex factors that go into making their choices, assess their real motives, and deemphasize sibling competition.

4. **Taking calculated risks is a smart move.**
   Middle children are more open to change and new ideas
   than firsts but are not addicted to risk like lastborns. Although middleborns have some potential to be gullible,
   being in risky situations tends to cause stress and this
   keeps most middles solidly in the middle ground.

CHAPTER FIVE

Middle Children
Are Justice Seekers

The barbershop in Rochester, New York, opened early for business. Men in black coats and top hats milled around, smoking cigarettes and pipes, and arguing about the upcoming presidential election. Registrars of the eighth ward sat inside the brightly lit store, behind huge ledgers and a variety of boxes and papers. It was 1872, and the people of Monroe County were registering to vote.

Or, rather, the men were.

Shouldering her way through the crowd, a middle-age woman in a long, dark gown with a lacy white collar marched into the shop. Accompanying her were her two sisters and about fifty townswomen. All was suddenly eerily quiet. What they were about to do was unheard of.

For her actions the woman would be indicted and put on trial. She would either face prison or be ordered to pay a fine. She would be the butt of countless political cartoons. But she was undaunted.

Susan Brownell Anthony, middle child in a large Quaker family, dedicated her life to fighting for women's right to vote. She became a well-respected and, ultimately, hugely influential civil rights leader. Although highly conscious of her plain looks and lack of oratory skills, she gave up to a hundred speeches a year about women's suffrage.

Nothing could hold her back—not when the United States marshal turned up at her house to arrest her after she illegally registered to vote. Not when she was offered bail but refused to pay it, wanting to stay in jail instead in order to make her point. Not when there was fighting within the National Women's Suffrage Association (which she had founded) or when she was publicly tried and found guilty of breaking the law. This middleborn had justice on her mind, and she fought for it until the very end of her life.

AN INSTINCT FOR ALTRUISM

A recent study examined the traits that people associate with specific birth orders. In a survey of 196 undergraduates at Stanford University, middleborns were ranked as the most envious and the least bold and/ or talkative of any birth order. Many people assume that because middle children don't get the attention they deserve as children, they become embittered and envious adults who don't often have other people's best interests at heart.

But what I've found is that this perception simply doesn't gel with reality. Middles actually grow up to be *more* finely attuned to the needs of others than their older or younger siblings. While middle children certainly have their faults, one highly admirable trait they share is the desire to help others; this leads them to make career and lifestyle choices that tend toward justice seeking. This instinct for altruism is deeply embedded in their psyches and reveals itself in myriad ways.

As we have seen, middles driven by their curiosity and conscientiousness have changed the worlds of science, business, politics, and the arts. But they have also distinguished themselves by standing up for what they believe in. More than any other birth order, middles have an altruistic streak that has led them to take on causes in the name of justice. Susan B. Anthony willingly put herself into enormous debt in order to disseminate feminist teachings in her weekly journal, *The Revolution*. Its motto was "The True Republic—men, their rights and nothing more; women, their rights, and nothing less." Though she died fourteen years before women were given the right to vote, she was influential in carving the path that led to women's emancipation.

We only need to look at a quick snapshot of history for innumerable other examples of justice-seeking middles. One of the founding fathers of the United States and its third president, Thomas Jefferson, was a middle child. In the 1700s his guiding vision for this new country was that it should become an "Empire of Liberty" and assume responsibility for spreading freedom around the world. Malcolm X, born into a blended family of ten, sought the liberation of African Americans from racism and died for the cause. Desmond Tutu—second of three children and a South African human rights activist and Nobel Peace Prize winner—has made raising awareness about AIDS, tuberculosis, homophobia, poverty, and racism his life's work. These middles and countless more have been moved by the injustices around them to fight for positive change.

Rising to the challenge

One middle child from Poland provides a particularly good example of how middleborns often overcome hurdles in order to be of service to others. In 1980, Lech Walesa—an uneducated, unemployed electrician—was milling around anxiously in protest under a huge sign that read STOCZNIA GDANSKA. The Lenin shipyards in Gdansk employed seventeen thousand men and women. After the Russians invaded Poland at the end of World War II, the shipyard began producing super trawlers, hydrographic units, and troop landing craft for the Soviet Union. But thirty-five years after the war, the Poles were suffering. They had just seen huge hikes in meat prices, making it unaffordable. They suffered constant power black outs. Everyone was tired of working so hard for so little. Yet today the protest was petering out.

Walesa was a charismatic, blunt-spoken character, the middle child in a family of seven. His father had died at the end of the war, and his mother married her husband's brother, merging their two families. He rebelled against his stepfather, preferring to spend time with friends rather than with family. As a child, he often got himself into scrapes and was a nuisance to adults.

On this warm August day, the thirty-seven-year-old was incensed by how the workers were being treated; he wanted the right to form a union so they could negotiate pay raises. Burning with the desire to make changes, he scaled the iron gates of the shipyard and jumped into the fray. He rallied the men and women, imploring them not to leave. He challenged them to stand up for themselves and believe they deserved fair treatment.

Eventually a thousand workers at the Gdansk shipyard launched a sit-in strike that had a massive domino effect all over the country. Less than ten years later the entire Communist bloc collapsed—not only in Poland but all over Eastern Europe.

Lech Walesa's defiance of authority, along with a penchant for taking risks, was critical to his development as a leader who helped free Poland from the restrictive clutches of Soviet rule. His stubborn determination, his optimism, and his courage led this middle child to seek justice for his people, eventually becoming a Nobel Prize winner and the president of his country.

Walesa's story of activism is an example of how middle children rise above the limitations of their own circumstances to make a difference for others in their communities or in the world at large. Although he was a simple man with no international, business, or political experience, he learned to speak effectively in front of thousands (ultimately representing his nation to the rest of the world); did not give up the fight even after being fired and imprisoned; and persuaded a famously intractable government to make radical changes. Against all odds this rather blunt, simple man became a game-changer who exhibited many of the characteristic middle child traits that are part of being a justice seeker. Middles:

- side with the underdog
- are peaceful warriors
- practice what they preach
- help themselves by helping others

Naturally, there are exceptions to every rule. Not all middle children end up dedicating their lives to positive social change. Most famously, Henry VIII is an example of a middle child who did not benefit society but turned the religious framework of his entire country upside down just so he could marry whom he pleased.

Nonetheless, many middles are driven to work for the good of others. By studying the reasons why middles fight for causes rather than for their own personal betterment, we'll develop insights into their personalities that are inspiring, whether we are middles ourselves. But we'll also learn what middle children need to watch out for, since they're notoriously trusting and can be taken for a ride.

What it means to be a justice seeker

We all know people who give more than they get, and middles tend to fall into this category. They are the most giving of the birth orders. A natural outgrowth of this tendency is that middles gravitate toward work and hobbies that focus on helping others.

Firstborns tend to be rather self-involved. They have usually been the only child for a number of years. Parents focus on them exclusively until siblings arrive, and even then the oldest child typically stays in the limelight. Since firsts feel the pressure and are driven to please their parents, they usually seek conventional success. This might mean following in their elders' footsteps when choosing a profession or perhaps prioritizing money and status over finding an occupation that is more personally satisfying.

Lasts are the most self-indulgent of the birth orders. Accustomed to getting their own way, they often don't have much patience with the foibles of others. Since they're the baby of the house and have older siblings to help them, they are cut more slack by siblings and parents alike. Often, because they are more self-centered and spoiled than middles, they don't end up becoming highly sympathetic adults.

Joe is a middle child who comes from a family of three boys, each eighteen months apart in age. Their father was a heart surgeon who commuted into New York City while their mother stayed at home. When Joe was a teen, he spent a lot of time in the skateboard park at the edge of the nearest town. His older brother, Henry, wasn't very athletic and instead pursued his studies with an intensity Joe never shared. The youngest, Chad, was the clown of the family. His parents were sure he'd be a comedian or an actor, and even though they themselves were conventional, they encouraged him in his pursuits.

Although Joe felt his parents disapproved of his skateboarding— their silence seemed to be an accusation of sorts—he kept it up even as an adult. His skating buddies were like a second family to him, and when he graduated from school, he moved west to live in southern California, where the skating culture was more accepted. To make money he worked as a prop master on film shoots.

All along, Joe nursed a passion for documentary filmmaking. As a teen he would borrow his father's super 8 camera and film the older kids in the parks. He made a short film in high school about the homeless people who lived under the bridge on the poor side of town. Once he moved to L.A., he started writing scripts and showing them to the producers of the films he worked on. By the time he was thirty, he was a documentary filmmaker who specialized in making short films about controversial topics. His last one was on transgender teens. "I was always driven to give voice to others," he explains, "and my work allows me to do that. I feel really lucky."

What makes Joe a justice seeker? The French philosopher Auguste Comte coined the term *altruisme* in his four-volume *Système de Politique Positive (1851–1854)*: It comes from the Italian word *altrui*, which means "belongs to others." He was likely also influenced by the French legal phrase *le bien d'autrui* or "the welfare of others." Comte defined the term as having the desire to do good without reward. In fact, there are some hidden rewards to behaving altruistically, and middles who follow this path do reap the benefits. Since altruistic individuals are seen positively by others, this can be a secret motivation. Equally, they get personal satisfaction and become part of a community through social activism. In Joe's case, the fact that he makes minimal money from his labor is of little consequence to him because of the pleasure he gets from pursuing this line of work. Many middle children react to the circumstances of their upbringing by developing skills and interests that lead to a dedication to causes over income.

History's martyrs are middle children

The mob cheered frenetically. Jan Hus was stripped of his white garments, and his hands were tied behind his back. A guard wearing full body armor chained Hus's neck to the stake and began piling wood and straw around him. This teacher and reformer from Prague was one of over a hundred thousand people to die in the sixteenth century— burned at the stake, beheaded, or tortured—for trying to reform the Catholic Church.

The Protestant Reformation involved a radical shift away from the traditions established after the Renaissance, toward greater accountability for those in power. Martin Luther, the oldest son in his family, was a German priest and professor of theology who defied the Catholic Church by calling into question the practice of selling indulgences. During the next few decades this protest became a direct assault on church authority, eventually culminating in a dramatic realignment of religious borders and affiliations throughout Europe.

Numerous studies have sought to determine why certain people accepted Reformist ideas when others so vehemently opposed them. The one I find most interesting compares birth order with an individual's likelihood to fight and die for new ideas or beliefs. After studying over seven hundred prominent players involved in the Reformation movement, birth order expert Frank Sulloway found the influence of birth order to be substantial (noting also that it is consistent throughout all social classes). Laterborns were far more likely to embrace reform than firsts. So although Luther, the original instigator of the religious upheaval, was a firstborn, it was actually laterborns who were willing to give their lives for the cause. Of those who participated in the Reformation and were *over* forty years old, laterborns were seventeen times more likely than firsts to support the new faith. This is highly significant because, typically, younger people are more likely to be reformers while older people can be set in their ways.

Since neither middles nor lastborns are ever the sole focus of their parents' attention, they naturally tend to feel less aligned with authority. Even in our modern society, the role of the firstborn child—in particular the firstborn son—is singular. They have more responsibility than the other siblings, and feel more closely aligned with their parents and their parents' philosophies. When firsts *do* go against parental authority, it's usually caused by unique frictions between two difficult personalities. More often than not, firstborn children have a vested interest in maintaining the status quo and end up becoming adults who are unlikely to embrace change or take risks.

Sulloway also conducted a detailed analysis of martyrs and their birth orders, which has particular relevance to our thesis. Of the individuals in his Reformation sample who were executed for their beliefs, 96 percent were laterborns. And, interestingly, most Catholic martyrs (who were trying to hang on to tradition) were firstborns since firsts are less interested in rocking the boat. "Laterborns were martyred for their religious fanaticism," explains Sulloway, "whereas firstborns were martyred for their continued adherence to the old faith."

JUSTICE SEEKERS SIDE WITH THE UNDERDOG

As a little boy, Alfred had a severe limp. He was skinny and insecure. In his eyes his father, a wealthy merchant, was a hero, and his mother was indifferent. One of the middle children in a family of seven, he felt intense competition with his older brother, Sigmund, who belittled him incessantly.

This sickly boy was Alfred Adler, an Austrian doctor in the early 1900s. Eventually he became a world-famous psychologist who was especially fascinated by the dynamics of personality. Adler broke away from Freud's approach to psychoanalysis, which he saw as looking too much at the past to explain the present. Instead, he embraced psychotherapy and personality theory, which saw the external—the social realm—as having huge impact on the development of the internal.

One of the best known early birth order theorists, Adler posited that the firstborn is "dethroned" by the next child, and the lastborn is indulged and therefore has little social empathy. Although middles may be squeezed and become somewhat rebellious, he argued that they become the most successful of all the children in any given family. He believed that middle children feel a strong need to prove themselves and achieve a sense of superiority, and this need translates itself into a healthy competitive attitude. Adler said the "middleborn is inclined to believe there is no power in the world that cannot be overcome."

We have explored middles' rebellious streaks and their tendency to question authority. In the home, since they enjoy minimal personal power, they bolster themselves by forming coalitions with friends and associates in order to feel a sense of control and belonging. They are good at cooperation and great at negotiation within their family. It helps them get what they want. They favor compromise and instinctively understand that their chances for success are greater when they're more flexible. The secondborn—especially if that secondborn is a middle—doesn't like subjugating him- or herself to authority. The sum of all this is an inclination for middles to side with the underdog and a belief that with the correct approach, they can right the wrongs they see around them.

Middles are protective

It makes sense that since middles sometimes feel they've been treated unfairly in the home, they are especially attuned to notice and abhor injustice toward others. They're caring and protective. It's a natural next step that middles would be driven to help others, and this is supported by copious counseling literature.

In the book *Why First Borns Rule the World and Last Borns Want to Change It*, Michael Grose asserts that because middles rebel against orthodox thinking, they tend to believe in and fight for causes. They're more likely to try to protect someone they perceive as a victim against political or social injustice than they are to embrace self-centered goals. While firsts need a purpose such as earning money or status in order to feel successful, Grose argues that secondborns get behind causes to give their lives meaning. "[Middles] have a highly developed sense of justice," Grose explains. "They genuinely want to right some of the wrongs of the world or help those that are on the wrong end of injustice."

When Joe the filmmaker was in sixth grade, he would sometimes come upon a gaggle of boys on the edge of the dusty soccer field behind the school. Chad, his younger brother, was often in the middle of the group, being teased by the older boys. Although Joe was scrawny for twelve, he couldn't just idly stand by. He would launch himself into the melee and drag Chad out by the sleeve of his jeans jacket. "I hated that he was being ganged up on. It was so unfair," he says. These instinctive protective actions, combined with a spirit of independence fostered by his position in the middle of the family, led him to his interest in the homeless as a teen and then later to his focus on depicting the voiceless in his documentaries.

Lech Walesa makes an interesting subject in this regard. As a middle not by birth but by circumstance (two families were joined when his mother married her brother-in-law), he felt relegated to the sidelines because of the conflicts that arose after merging the households. His relationship with his stepfather was tense, and this contributed to his antiauthority stance. Howard Gardner, a leadership scholar, makes the point that children who have a "contrasting relationship" with their parents—one favorable and the other not—often feel a sense of ambivalence toward family. "The impulse to wield power," he writes, "represents an attempt to resolve this anxiety-producing conflict."

I would take the argument further. Middles can have ambivalent relationships with their parents because their role in the family is not as clearly defined as their siblings'. They often don't quite know what is expected of them and are aware of not being the center of attention. While this doesn't necessarily make them angry or bitter, it does encourage in them a tendency to stand up for those who are maligned—to "wield power" but on the behalf of others. In Walesa's case, while not driven by the desire for power or moral authority in and of itself, he was certainly driven to fight for the rights of the underprivileged.

Birth order and the Supreme Court

Why do some members of the Supreme Court accept legal doctrines while others resist them? Does party affiliation and nomination of justices have any relationship to birth order? Kevin McGuire, a professor at the University of North Carolina at Chapel Hill, wanted to test whether there was a correlation between birth order and political ideology. Knowing that the process of socialization—which takes root in childhood—determines adult attitudes toward social norms, rules, and authority, he figured it would be enlightening to see how these childhood roles manifest in the later life decisions of the justices.

First, he discovered that since the beginning of the twentieth century, 60 percent of Republican appointees to the court have been firstborns or only children. Democratic presidents, in contrast, are five times as likely to nominate lastborns to the court. We can therefore deduce that since firsts identify with authority and endorse existing rules, they are seen by others as more likely to have ideologically conservative preferences. They're more leery of intellectual innovation, while being more supportive of the status quo than laterborns. Subsequent siblings, who are usually more creative and adaptable—and likely to be open to new ideas—revealed more liberal political preferences. As McGuire concludes, "Ideology travels with birth order and very closely indeed."

Whatever your politics, it's safe to say that those who vote Democratic or liberally rather than Republican usually place social justice causes higher on their list of priorities than economic considerations. One subtle but remarkable finding was that Republican lastborns often vote more liberally than Democratic firstborns, which helps explain the liberal voting record of a lastborn Republican such as Justice John Paul Stevens and the conservative record of a firstborn Democrat like Robert Jackson. Birth order is clearly a predictor of voting tendencies, with the likelihood of liberal voting increasing as birth order increases.

Middles and *stare decisis*

The youngest justice ever to be appointed to the Supreme Court was William Douglass. He was given the nickname "Wild Bill" for his independent and unpredictable positions on the court. The middle of three children of an itinerant family on the West Coast, Douglass had to deal with extreme poverty and constant illness in his youth. His father died when he was only six years old, yet he overcame these hurdles to become one of the longest serving justices ever, presiding on the bench for almost thirty-seven years. *Time* magazine called Wild Bill "the most doctrinaire and committed civil libertarian ever to sit on the court."

Douglass is relevant here because of his proven independence when it came to approaching decisions on the bench. *Stare decisis*,

Latin for "to stand by that which is decided," is the doctrine of precedent under which it is necessary for courts to follow earlier judicial decisions when the same issues arise again. How a justice approaches legal precedent tells us how willing that judge is to form a fresh, independent decision based on new information or specific circumstance, or how inclined he or she is to stick with the tried and true. "[A justice] comes to formulate his own views rejecting some earlier ones [decisions] as false and embracing others," this middle child declared on the United States Supreme Court. "He cannot do otherwise unless he lets men long dead and unaware of the problems of the age in which he lives do his thinking for him." As a middleborn, Douglass proved himself more willing than other judges to think outside the box, forming independent judgments on each case before him rather than relying on the legal reasoning that previous courts had made.

McGuire's study proved illuminating on this front, too, revealing that firstborn justices are more likely to be reluctant to challenge or overturn precedent than laterborns. Laterborn judges (such as Douglass) were proven to be more activist than earlier-borns and more likely to support challenges to existing democratic and legal processes. McGuire conducted an analysis to investigate how often each member of the court joined the majority coalition that invalidated a law or altered a precedent. Indeed, he found that firsts and onlies were reluctant to band together with colleagues in overturning existing federal and state laws. Lasts, on the other hand, revealed themselves to be very willing to question the decisions of elected officials.

And middles? They were more adaptable. Since they're willing to vote with the majority with nearly identical frequency whether the court was overturning precedent, middles are shown, once again, to be open to alternatives and comfortable with changing the existing rules.

Douglass fits into the middle child mold in other significant ways as well. He was an avid environmentalist, championing the idea of giving inanimate objects, such as trees and rivers, standing in court. He also launched the nation's first law review entirely dedicated to environmental issues. In addition to showing independence on the court, he was a true trailblazer like so many middleborns.

Crime and punishment

The man frantically waved a political banner above his head. Constable Jones marched up to him and ordered him to cease and desist. But J. Smith would have none of it. Ignoring the policeman's request, he hoisted the banner up again and began shouting. The police called in reinforcements, and soon Smith was surrounded.

But still he wouldn't stop. "I have rights!" he cried out. "I have a right to peaceful protest!"

Smith was dragged away and thrown into a van. Kicking at the van doors, he screamed and fought. It was New Zealand, 1999, and he was booked for resisting arrest and assaulting a police officer. The judge found him guilty of causing a public disturbance.

In a similar case, a young New Zealander named Lyle was blocking the entrance of a hotel to protest the Chinese government officials staying there. Guests could not come and go at will, and the staff became uneasy. Hotel security approached him and asked him to leave the property because he was impeding entrance to a place of business. Lyle, too, was arrested for being a public nuisance and found guilty of civil disobedience.

A Ph.D. student from New Zealand used these two cases, among others, as examples that highlight social issues in order to see whether birth order affects the severity of sentences handed down to convicted offenders. He believed that firsts would be harsher judges of individuals who defy the status quo and authority, and that secondborns (which in this study included middles and lastborns) would be more likely to sympathize with the underdogs. Why? Because he posited that when people perceived as underdogs break the law due to a cause they strongly believe in, other underdogs feel that lessens—or even justifies— their crime. Pairs of siblings were given the altered transcripts of various court cases, including those outlined above. Participants were asked to determine the length of the convicted offender's sentences or their fine, depending on how serious they felt the crime to be.

In both these cases, firstborn and secondborn participants agreed that fines, not jail time, were warranted—but in the case of banner-waving Smith who so vigorously resisted arrest, secondborns imposed a fine that was 50 percent lower than firsts. The hotel protestor was also found to be a more sympathetic character by secondborns, who levied a fine that was almost half that imposed by firsts. These results show clearly that laterborns are more likely to sympathize with individuals who appear to be acting out of moral righteousness.

MIDDLES ARE PEACEFUL WARRIORS

A precocious black child living in Georgia in the 1930s, Martin Luther King Jr. discovered he couldn't go to the same school as his best friend, a white boy. As a teenager, he traveled to Georgia to enter an oratory contest and proudly came away with the second prize. But on his return journey, he was forced to stand at the back of a segregated bus so the white students could sit. It was a bitter pill to swallow after his success.

Although his grandfather had been a sharecropper and many blacks of his generation had limited opportunities for social advancement, King was afforded an excellent education. The family lived in a middle-class African American neighborhood in Atlanta, Georgia. Like his older sister and younger brother, he was highly intelligent and driven. He skipped two grades, entered college at fifteen, and went on to get a Ph.D. in philosophy—but he still couldn't drink from the same water fountain as his white peers.

These commonplace inequities deeply offended King's sense of justice. From an early age on, he defended other people's honor and believed he had the right to equal treatment. Martin Luther King Jr. grew up to dedicate his life to ending racial segregation and discrimination. He was the youngest person ever to win the Nobel Peace Prize.

Despite living in polarizing times, King struck a chord with Americans, both black and white. He was extremely resilient and patient. "We've got some difficult days ahead," he said in his speech to sanitation workers in Memphis in 1968. "But it really doesn't matter with me now, because I've been to the mountaintop . . . and I don't mind." This ability to see a larger vision, to tamp down the impatience for change and accept a longer term view is both practical and effective in the long run. King was also an intensely righteous man, driven by a clear sense of right and wrong and moral duty: "The arc of the moral universe is long," he declared at the National Cathedral in Washington, D.C., "but it bends toward justice."

Patience is a common trait in middles since they seem to spend their childhood waiting for their parents to be done dealing with the cranky first child or managing the needy baby. Similarly, the search for parity and truth which King embodied is typical of middles who side with the underdog—and then make up their minds to actually do something about it.

How far will middles go?

If middles are driven to effect change on behalf of those less fortunate, one might think they're more militant than other birth orders in their quest for change. Sulloway looked at this question, testing his hypothesis that birth rank is related to tough-mindedness by figuring out which birth order is most aggressive or even violent in its pursuit of a cause or ideal.

First, Sulloway studied the birth order of prominent antislavery reformers. Abolitionists were divided into two camps: those who believed violence was justified and necessary, and those who believed no good could come of violence. After surveying sixty-four reform movements in American history, Sulloway concluded that abolition attracted the greatest number of laterborns—but also that the *militant* abolitionists were more likely to be firstborns. Even though firsts are more likely to support the status quo than other birth orders, when they *do* rebel, they tend to go all out.

The black power movement of the 1960s consumed American politics at that time (as did the Vietnam War). Riots and lynchings were not uncommon, and the struggle for social justice meant treading on dangerous fault lines. After traveling to India, Martin Luther King Jr. became a strong advocate of a nonviolent approach, whereas other middle children, such as Malcolm X, saw violence as not only viable but critical to success. Given Sulloway's theory, it's perhaps not surprising that the leader of the most radical group of all, the Black Panther Party—whose members were often seen carrying assault rifles and wearing military garb—was a firstborn boy.

King's position was one informed by a great deal of scholarship. He had been brought up to consider the moral inequities he faced from a philosophical perspective. Once he decided, at seventeen, to become a social activist, he read widely, searching for his platform and trying to figure out the core principles of his movement for equality. After reading Henry David Thoreau's *Civil Disobedience*, he came to believe in justice over law. During the Montgomery, Alabama, bus boycott he cemented his belief in nonviolence even though he was widely criticized by blacks and whites alike for working *with* whites rather than against them and compromising too readily. But he cannily assessed these methods as serving him best in his mission for justice.

As we explored in previous chapters, middles develop extraordinary negotiation skills and are instinctively more likely to embrace new ideas. These two tendencies make middles the perfect peaceful warrior, as contradictory as that may sound. Lech Walesa and King, as different as they are in terms of personality and approach, share this middle child trait. As Sulloway states, when middles rebel, "they do so largely out of frustration, or compassion for others, rather than from hatred or ideological fanaticism. Middle children make the most 'romantic' revolutionaries."

Moderates take the cake

A recent study took an in-depth look at how different birth orders see themselves and their siblings. It was split into two sections. The first examined the adjectives that would best describe participants' own behavior and beliefs and those of the siblings in their family. The second studied motives—what these individuals believe makes them and others behave a certain way.

The researcher collected data from over five hundred adults, all from families of three siblings. He presented them with items that fall into larger descriptive categories such as the following:

- earnest (conscientious, responsible, not lazy)
- antiestablishment (nonconforming, rebellious, unconventional)
- liked (charming, popular)

Firstborns scored highest on being earnest, and lowest on antiestablishment and liked—a combination unlikely to produce a justice seeker. Lastborns scored last on being earnest, tied with middles on being antiestablishment, and scored highest on being liked. This is a somewhat better combination for an individual who might be altruistic. I would propose that since middles scored higher than lasts in terms of conscientiousness (which was part of the earnest category), they would be more likely to carry through on their actions than lastborns would.

Middles ranked themselves and were ranked by their siblings as being moderately earnest, moderately antiestablishment, and moderately liked. In part two of the study, motives were analyzed by looking at three categories:

- power (controlling, dominant)
- achievement (through performance, independence)
- affiliation (cooperative, good-natured)

In this case, when making comparisons within birth order categories, middles scored higher on achievement than on power. I interpret this as indicating that they're likely to meet challenges successfully and care less about personal advancement. Middles' need for achievement is stronger than lasts', and they have the drive and emotional commitment to go against the grain.

What we see here is that middle children are persistent enough to challenge the world view and share a nice balance of conscientiousness and openness, which more often than not leads them to action. Middleborns see themselves as agents of change and believe in their power to effect good.

Middles are more successful with words than swords

Rolihlahla Mandela's father had four wives and thirteen children. The boy's given name meant "troublemaker." Despite spending almost three decades in prison, the enduring image the world has of this middle child is one of him smiling broadly and waving while working nonstop on advancing the causes of his beleaguered country.

Nelson Mandela, antiapartheid activist, Nobel laureate, elder statesman, and survivor of twenty-seven years of imprisonment, is arguably the most famous middle child justice seeker of all. He was born into a royal family of the Xhosa tribe in what was then South Africa's Cape Province. While the tiny village where he was born was bucolic, the country around him was ruled by apartheid. Mandela and other black Africans were denied their most basic rights. Driven to bring about change, he became a lawyer who could pack courtrooms as he butted heads with white prosecutors and judges.

So how does Mandela fit into our picture of middles as moderate militants—people gripped with the desire to change the world for the better but who prefer to do so through persuasion and persistence rather than violence?

Despite his words, and on occasion his actions, Mandela exemplifies the middle child approach to pushing through change in a recalcitrant society. His main goal was to seek justice and equality for black South Africans. After the Sharpville massacre of 1960, during which sixty-nine blacks were killed by white policemen, Mandela felt his insistence on nonviolence had been a mistake. A year later, when he became the leader of the armed wing of the African National Congress known as Spear of the Nation, he had come to believe violence was the only way to achieve radical change. Not long thereafter he was forced to go on the run, and after seventeen months he was arrested and taken to Johannesburg Fort. Convicted of sabotage (to which he pled guilty) and conspiracy to aid another country in invading South Africa (which he denied), he was given a life sentence.

Even from behind the walls of the Robben Island prison where he spent most of his incarceration, Mandela's influence continued to spread. As apartheid began to crumble, international pressure forced his release in February 1990. Facing the crowd who had come to greet him, he said, "We express the hope that a climate conducive to a negotiated settlement would be created soon, so that there may no longer be the need for armed struggle."

A canny middle child in action: With his excellent negotiating skills, Mandela proposed peace yet warned that the authorities had better take him seriously. He is a good example of a moderate militant and quintessential middle child who, in the end, achieved his goals through patience, negotiation, passion, discipline, and charm.

MIDDLES PRACTICE WHAT THEY PREACH

What people say they would do and what they actually do are often two different things. Measuring an attitude is not as persuasive as measuring behavior. One study of civil disobedience found an excellent scenario to test the hypothesis that laterborns are more likely to stick their necks out for the sake of others than firstborns. Although the sample size is relatively small, researchers analyzed data from arrest records in North Carolina that clearly showed a birth order pattern when it came to standing up to authority.

In the mid-1990s, Kmart had a problem on its hands. At their distribution center in Greensboro, North Carolina, workers complained about working conditions, leave time, and benefits. For two years these protests continued to mushroom until local ministers, community activists, college professors, and college students became embroiled in the conflict. An agreement couldn't be reached, and Kmart was boycotted. More than 150 people were arrested over the course of three months, including twenty Guilford College students.

Seventeen of these students were tracked down and questioned; they gave answers on behalf of seventeen close same-sex friends (thereby increasing the sample size). The same questionnaire was given to a control group of thirty-nine other students from the college who had not been arrested.

The results were stunning: 100 percent of those arrested twice were laterborns, and 50 percent of those students arrested only once were also laterborns.

This study reveals two important things. First, it supports the thesis that laterborns are more likely to take risks than firsts. Anyone standing on a picket line who has already been arrested once is exhibiting a rather daring willingness to accept the risk of being arrested *again*. Second, it emphasizes the tendency of laterborns to feel for others (to be empathetic). Although this particular study involved a small number of students, the fact that fully 100 percent of those rearrested were laterborns confirms that they often put the cause of others before their own self-interest. I would expect that a significant proportion of these activists were middleborns.

Disenfranchised but not daunted

Throughout history and in modern times millions of individuals have suffered and continue to suffer. Many become disenfranchised. Within these groups there are some who suffer in silence and accept fate, and there are those who act to change their situation or to help others. It's my belief that because of the specific role they've played within their own families, middle children are more likely to help those in need than other birth orders might.

Let's look at a human rights advocate such as Elie Wiesel. Born in the Carpathian Mountains of Romania at the very end of World War I, Wiesel, his parents, two older sisters, and his youngest sister were hauled off to Auschwitz. Both parents and his youngest sister were killed. Although Wiesel was a middle child and the tumultuous circumstances of his teen years created a family environment that was highly traumatizing (and doubtless affected his later actions), as a young boy nestled among his sisters in a village in which he initially felt secure and well loved, Wiesel was beginning to develop a sense of how to rise above the crowd and create a niche for himself. Later, as a survivor of appalling atrocities, he saw himself as a conduit for the stories of the millions who had suffered like him. He wrote more than forty books, including the best-selling *Night*, giving voice to the voiceless killed by the Nazis. Although disenfranchised, Wiesel was not daunted or paralyzed into inaction. As a middle child he was more inclined than his surviving older sisters, for instance, to take on the role of becoming a justice seeker.

A number of factors influence this. In social psychology there is a phenomenon known as "the bystander effect" in which people who witness an emergency or a crime do not act to help the victim. Researchers create a situation in which someone has a serious problem in public— say, an epileptic fit or a fall—and then test how long it takes a bystander to step in and help. The more people witnessing the event, the fewer people act to help. This can be the result of two basic impulses:

1. **Social influence: bystanders monitor the reactions of others to decide whether they should interfere or not;**
2. **Diffusion of responsibility: bystanders convince themselves that *someone else will deal with it*.**

It is my contention that middle children such as Wiesel are unique in their reactions to the travails of others. As we've already established, since middle children identify with the underdog, they feel the empathy necessary to try to improve the lives of people in that position. And since middles are independent, they don't much care what others around them are doing. As with skateboarder Joe, over time these middleborns come to see that they have the power to make changes—even if those changes are slow and methodical rather than dramatic. It's the sense of self-determination and the belief in the merit of questioning the status quo that make middle children act. As we have seen, their increased conscientiousness also incites action rather than falling back on the idea that someone else will do what's right.

You could argue, of course, that lastborns share many of the same characteristics as middles. Joe's younger brother, Chad, for example, also identified more with outsiders than did his oldest brother (who eventually became a surgeon like their father). Yet lastborns can be impulsive, self-centered, and inconsistent. Though they may perceive themselves as an underdog compared to the firstborn child, they're more accustomed to getting what they want through histrionics than stealth and perseverance. Consequently, lastborns are somewhat less likely to act to help others who are disenfranchised.

Middles find their voices

The air raid siren went off, and yet the young girl stayed in her seat while her classmates all raced out. It was the 1960s in California, the height of the Cold War, and everyone was terrified by the threat of a nuclear holocaust. But the girl wasn't going to be swayed by what she thought of as government propaganda and fear-mongering.

That child was Joan Baez. Not long after this incident, she heard Martin Luther King Jr. speak and was profoundly moved by his words. Because of her father's work in health care and with UNESCO (the United Nations Educational, Scientific and Cultural Organization), her family had lived in many different towns across the United States as well as throughout Europe and the Middle East. Baez was the middle girl in a three-child family and felt from early on that social justice is "the true core of life."

Like so many middles, Baez felt moved to action and used her singing talent—and phenomenal popular appeal—to spread her message of nonviolence, honoring civil and human rights, and protecting the environment. When asked in an interview about her inspiration, she explained, "It's not because I think about it and figure it out; it's because I get very quiet and somehow or other there's a directive that comes to me." She feels compelled to do good, to stick up for her beliefs, and to try to influence others. Although Baez was arrested twice and thrown in jail once for civil disobedience, it was her distinctive music that was the most effective conduit for her message of peace and justice. She found the most effective way to be heard by millions.

Growing up, middle children are given more freedom; this means they are freer to develop and follow their passions than firstborns are. Because middles are more conscientious than lastborns, they're more likely to *act* on those passions than the baby of the family. In a position of relative weakness in terms of family hierarchy, middleborns empathize with those who are less fortunate and, as adults, often direct their passion and energy toward helping underdogs. As a consequence, many middles choose a life of service to others. They put their money where their mouth is.

THE PITFALLS FOR ALTRUISTIC MIDDLES

The most famous case of a middle child being taken in by an unworthy cause is Patty Hearst. Most people are familiar with the picture of the kidnapped newspaper heiress standing, straddle-legged, in front of a massive snakelike symbol representing the Symbionese Liberation Army, a guerrilla group. She's wearing a jaunty beret and full camouflage, and she is carrying a machine gun.

Patty Hearst was born into wealth and privilege, the third of five daughters, granddaughter to the publishing magnate William Randolph Hearst. As a child she had been apolitical, enjoying her comfortable family life. Yet at age nineteen she was kidnapped from her apartment in San Francisco. During months in captivity she came to adopt the left-wing guerrilla group's mission as her own. This culminated in her participation in a bank robbery in the Sunset District, near where she had grown up. She was caught, arrested, put on trial, and sentenced to prison.

This particular phenomenon is highly unusual. It is known as Stockholm syndrome and describes situations in which hostages become irrationally sympathetic toward their captors. Nonetheless, one might ask whether Hearst's older siblings or younger sister would have been as susceptible to the rhetoric of this political faction as she was, being the middle child. Clearly, it was not her natural instinct to be so radical. After she was pardoned, Hearst rapidly reentered the mainstream, married, became a mother, and led a life away from the spotlight.

Patty Hearst may be an extreme example, but she's a cautionary tale nonetheless. Middles are so quick to empathize that they can sometimes put their efforts behind causes or people that turn out to be unworthy. Making well-considered decisions about which causes to support is critical lest middles get taken for a ride.

Middleborns don't think much about self-preservation. Anyone who feels sufficiently moved by the plight of others tends to put those interests ahead of their own and thus risks getting themselves in trouble. Lech Walesa, a staunch Catholic with a growing family, was fired as an electrician for his political activities and spent many years out of work. After the Gdansk shipyard strike, he was imprisoned for eleven months. His dedication to social justice caused his family serious hardship, but it was in the name of a greater cause. Martin Luther King Jr. was arrested, beaten, threatened, and eventually assassinated for his beliefs. Nelson Mandela spent much of his life in prison. While these are all extreme examples, middles often do invite danger into their lives by embracing risk and change.

For some middle children their hearts might win out over their minds: When donating time or money to a cause, they could stretch themselves too thin. Frequently, middle children make career choices based on the moral value of their work rather than the salary. If you're married to a middle or have a middle child, it's important to consider bracing for a future in which money may not be a priority.

MIDDLES HELP THEMSELVES BY HELPING OTHERS

The Dalai Lama, leader of Tibetan Buddhists—and, incidentally, a middle child—has expounded at length on the personal satisfaction one derives from dedicating one's life to being kind and compassionate. Although Tibetan Buddhists are denied the freedom to practice their religion in Tibet, they insist on the pursuit of justice with no sense of rancor or hatred. "The greatest degree of inner tranquility comes from the development of love and compassion. The more we care for the happiness of others, the greater is our own sense of well-being," the Dalai Lama explains. "Cultivating a close, warm-hearted feeling for others automatically puts the mind at ease. It is the ultimate source of success in life."

It's quite natural for middle children to gravitate toward helping others because it gives them a sense of satisfaction and happiness. This comes from feeling a close bond with others. Middles are, at core, social beings who like to feel part of a community or self-formed family. In this sense, by focusing on social justice, middle children set themselves up for a life that they find personally fulfilling, perhaps without even intending to do so. In this modern era of extreme flux, where traditional conduits to success are constantly being reassessed and redefined, this is crucial. Middles actually end up helping themselves by helping others.

In his book *A Whole New Mind*, author Daniel Pink argues that qualities such as empathy, joyfulness, and meaning, dismissed as frivolous in the past century, will be the very qualities that predict success in modern life, especially now that technology has become paramount. According to Pink, the era of "left brain" dominance will give way to a new world in which "right brain" qualities become all-important. "The future belongs to a very different kind of person," Pink states, ". . . creators and empathizers, pattern recognizers and meaning makers." As we've seen in part one of this book, middle children excel in many of these right brain arenas. They think outside the box, are imaginative and flexible, and are often selfless. They can see the big picture, act on their passions while remaining grounded, and are moved to action by causes other than making money.

Middles develop lives underpinned by purpose and meaning. Since middle children tend to veer toward social justice, seeking personal fulfillment through helping others, I would suggest that their traits will serve them well in the world of the future. In the next part of the book I will delve into the specifics of everyday life—work, love, and family relationships—to reveal practical ways that middles can tap into their remarkable and underappreciated abilities.

WHY MIDDLE CHILDREN ARE MOTIVATED TO DO GOOD

1. **Justice provides the purpose.**
   Since middle children occupy a position of relative weakness in the family hierarchy, middles often feel like underdogs and empathize with the disadvantaged. Activism and fighting for justice on behalf of others gives middles a sense of purpose.

2. **Middles won't sit on the sidelines.**
   Even if circumstances are difficult, middles believe in the power of action. Since they are more empathetic than firsts and more conscientious than lasts, they are more likely than other birth orders to act on behalf of those who are needier than they are.

3. **They are not afraid to push the envelope.**

   In the eyes of a middleborn, authority figures are not in-fallible and the status quo isn't set in stone. They don't believe there is any power in the world that can't be over-come. This confidence and drive leads them to embrace new ideas—and fight for changing outdated or unjust ones.

4. **But they don't make a scene.**

   Middles tend toward moderation rather than extremism. Wily in finding ways to approach problems and create necessary change, middles have patience and persistence that make them formidable foes.

5. **Middles can give too much.**

   While their generosity is laudable, middle children need to make sure they protect themselves from unscrupulous people and unworthy causes. Many middles have sacri-ficed for the causes of justice, and they can take their self-lessness to extremes.

PART TWO

UNLEASHING the SECRET POWER of the MIDDLE CHILD

CHAPTER SIX

Middle Children
in the Workplace

Who would have thought you could make a computer to order? Just as one customer at a burger joint might want his hamburger with pickles, hold the ketchup, while another prefers it with lettuce but no pickles, technology consumers don't always want the same features in their computers. Not everyone likes or needs to have 30GB of memory, and some buyers really want video capability but don't like paying for a DVD burner. Fifteen years ago, giving the consumer the power to custom design their own computer (and have it be affordable) was a truly radical idea that redefined the global supply chain of the twenty-first century.

It took someone with the ability to think outside the box—as well as use powers of persuasion and negotiation to change people's perceptions and work as a successful team leader—to fundamentally change how computers were being bought and sold in the 1980s. One teenager from Houston, Texas, was that person. Although he'd been working odd jobs since he was twelve years old, the idea of a vocation, occupation, or career was not first and foremost in his mind—but following his passions was.

As a freshman, his dorm room at the University of Texas was a sight to behold. Computer components were strewn across the floor, carcasses of disassembled units littered his desk, and tools of all kinds were everywhere. According to his parents, he was "wasting" his time tinkering with this "computer stuff." They had wanted him to become a doctor.

A frantic last-minute purge would begin whenever he got wind that his father, an orthodontist, and his money-manager mom were about to drop by his dorm room for a visit. He would sweep up the stray components, deposit them in his roommate's bathtub, and yank the shower curtain closed. Away would go the tools and the half-dismantled computers.

The boy would later admit: "My parents telling me to stop doing it is probably what caused the company to get created."

VOCATION, CAREER, OR DAY JOB?

In many ways workplace dynamics reflect those at play within families, thereby creating a kind of birth order ripple effect. When recognized, this can be beneficial rather than detrimental. Middles can capitalize on the strengths they develop throughout their childhood and avoid some of the negatives, helping them find rewarding day-to-day work.

Michael Dell was the second child in a family of three boys. His parents had high expectations for their sons and encouraged them to work from an early age so they would develop a sense of the value of money and their own potential to make it. In Dell's case, he was a singular kid from the very start. After taking a high school entrance exam at age eight (he didn't get in), he made good money as a bus boy in a Chinese restaurant at age twelve. He started investing in the stock market when he was fourteen and then brought in thousands of dollars selling newspapers at sixteen.

This middleborn was more guided by his interests than by a grand scheme to revolutionize the technology supply chain. "You have to sort of have an instinctual feeling or an idea about something. And you've got to be passionate about it," Dell explained. Experts agree, saying interest and passion are keys to finding happiness, equilibrium, and success in the workplace. "Find what you really love to do and then go after it relentlessly. And don't fret about the money," said Steve Hannah, CEO of the satirical website the Onion, "because what you love to do is quite likely what you're good at. And what you're good at will likely bring you financial reward eventually."

Sometimes we don't choose a career; it chooses us. Sometimes we land a day job, and it ends up being a career. Occasionally we're dedicated to a hobby, and it turns into a vocation. Vocation comes from the Latin word *vocare*, which means to call. A vocation is thus a calling; it is more about finding and pursuing a purpose—something middles are inclined to do (as we saw in chapter 5)—than merely punching a time clock. "The deepest vocational question is not 'What ought I do with my life?'" says author and educator Dr. Parker Palmer. "It is more elemental and demanding. 'Who am I? What is my nature?'" Michael Dell, who created Dell Computers from his dorm room at age nineteen and went on to become the youngest man ever on the list of the Forbes 500, allows that the motivation for creating his monolithic company came from within. "It was kind of like a big, big game for me," Dell says.

In contrast, the word *career* comes from the Latin word for *cart* and the French word for *racetrack*, suggesting that pursuing a career is like racing around in circles. When you take pleasure in climbing the hierarchy—achieving satisfaction from raises and promotions rather than pursuing work for work's sake—you're building a career. Most of us are happy enough to fall into this category: Building a satisfying career can be highly rewarding even when it isn't the core purpose of your life.

And, finally, holding a job is about getting a paycheck, generally so you can focus more on your life outside work or perhaps because you've got limited choices. While this is the kind of work that is typical for many, it isn't ideal. During our professional years we spend about 30 percent of our time working, so it's vastly preferable to have labor that is satisfying in and of itself.

OUR MODERN WORKFORCE

According to sociologists, the number of hours Americans and Europeans work today has actually declined by almost 50 percent since the Industrial Revolution. Back then, work was highly labor intensive, and factory floors were crowded with men, women, and children who put in as many as twelve to sixteen hours a day, six to seven days a week. Production has since been massively streamlined, and much of the developed world's work takes place behind a desk and in front of a computer. Yet despite the nominal decrease in working hours, our modern workforce is married to technology—making it seem that our work is never done but carries on unabated even once we technically stop working.

In addition, we change jobs much more frequently than in the past. Late baby boomers held eleven different jobs between the ages of eighteen and forty-two, according to the Bureau of Labor Statistics. This suggests that to be happy at work, people must determine their personal and professional priorities; fully understand their strengths and weaknesses; and make informed decisions (in a global sense and also on an everyday basis) that help them succeed. Taking into consideration the specific strengths and weaknesses that we develop as a result of our birth order is a useful and enlightening approach to making these kinds of work-related decisions.

This begs the question: What exactly does it take to be happy and successful in our place of work? In 2002 a Department of Labor report produced a list of the top personal qualities employers are looking for in their employees. Here's how middles shape up in terms of what employers want from their workforce.

Table 1. HOW WELL DO MIDDLES FIT WORKPLACE CRITERIA?

Qualities Employers Desire	Desired Qualities Middles Embody	Desired Qualities Middles Need to Work On
Responsibility	• Effort and perseverance toward a goal • Vitality and enthusiasm	• High standards and attention to detail • Concentration even when doing an unpleasant task
Self-esteem	• Knowledge of skills and ability • Aware of impact on others	• Belief in self-worth • Knows emotional capacity and needs; knows how to address them
Social	• Has understanding, empathy, and adaptability • Takes an interest in what others say and do	• Asserts self
Self-management	• Assesses own skills accurately • Has well-defined and realistic goals • Monitors progress toward goal attainment; self-starter • Exhibits self-control • Is not defensive when receiving feedback	
Integrity/Honesty	• Can be trusted • Chooses ethical course of action	

These areas, highlighted as being of primary importance to workplace success, represent aspects of our daily lives that we must all manage to one extent or another. If we have a good handle on our abilities, we'll be able to gauge where to invest our time and effort. If we give up at the first sign of failure, we can't hope to achieve personal success or success for our organization. When we're adaptable, we can better overcome obstacles. Being able to work without someone always looking over our shoulder is crucial. And, naturally, being dependable and empathetic helps us gain people's confidence, so that we can attain increasingly more responsibility and influence.

In studying what middle children bring to the workplace, I've uncovered five key ingredients they can exploit to find success and happiness in their careers. Typically, middles do the following:

1. **Find *internal* motivation**
2. **Roll with the punches**
3. **Have perseverance and perspective**
4. **Put themselves in others' shoes**
5. **Self-manage**

This chapter will help middles better understand which career paths suit them, whether they're just starting out or are already mid-career. Determining where their talents lie and what holds their interests—or, better yet, fuels their enthusiasm—are important starting points. Insight into personality traits will help them take the right first steps or correct themselves when they veer off course.

What are the specific traits middle children develop at home, and how do these play out—positively and negatively—in work situations? For all their considerable strengths, middle children have some tendencies that can cause trouble in the office. Although they self-report as being happier than their siblings in their day-to-day work lives, they do face some challenges as a result of their learned behaviors. What are the major pitfalls, and what can they do to overcome them? What kinds of jobs are good matches for middle children, and which should they avoid?

KEY INGREDIENT #1:
MIDDLES FIND INTERNAL MOTIVATION

Sarah hated being a lawyer, but she couldn't let on to anyone, least of all her father. Since she was a little girl, he would sit her on his lap and tell her stories about the courtroom. He'd smoke his pipe and close his eyes, and she could see how exhausted but passionate he was. As a teenager, Sarah would often listen in on his closing arguments, absorbing the drama and seriousness of purpose that pervaded the wood-paneled room in the old courthouse downtown. After finishing college, it was a no-brainer that she would work in his law offices for a few years and then apply to law school.

As the firstborn in her family of three boys and two girls, she always felt she occupied a special place in the family. When things got noisy in the kitchen or her younger siblings were fighting, she'd knock on her father's study door, and he'd let her enter his quiet inner sanctum filled with the sweet smell of his pipe tobacco. Law school was fairly interesting, though by the end of her first year she already suspected that she'd be no good as a prosecutor. That is what she'd always imagined herself doing, though, and she hoped that once she got inside the courtroom, she'd see things differently. She would learn to be good at putting bad guys in prison. Her dad loved his work, and she would, too.

But now she dreaded going to work every day. Every time she was assigned a new case, she had to overcome a sense of doom. The very last person on earth she wanted to admit this to was her father, yet when she went home for Christmas, she found herself in his study early one morning, telling him that she'd made a terrible mistake and that she needed to figure out what she really wanted to do in life.

Although he had never pressured her to become a lawyer, it remained an unspoken assumption that Sarah and her father shared personality traits and interests, and ultimately this put her under unintentional pressure. Her younger sister, Julie, became a stellar athlete and went on to participate in triathlons. Her two brothers had very divergent careers: a banker and a session musician. When she looked at them and assessed their lives, her siblings seemed pretty content with their choices. Sarah couldn't figure out how she'd gone so wrong.

The pressure to fulfill expectations—even unspoken ones—is much greater for firstborns than for other siblings in larger families. Of course, trying to live up to expectations by no means automatically leads to disappointment or failure. Research shows that firsts are over-represented among National Merit scholarship participants, SAT high scorers, doctoral candidates, engineers, and scientists. According to a 1990 *Baylor Business Review* article, twenty-one out of the original twenty-three astronauts were firstborns. Firsts can be driven and successful—but they can also blindly follow the path in front of them. When Sarah considered what led her to pursue a career that ended up being so unsuited to her personality, she realized it was simple: She just hadn't thought enough about what her inner motivations were.

Matching internal motivation to career moves

A 2001 study on birth order and careers revealed that firsts and onlies gravitate toward such prestigious careers as lawyer and doctor. "As they have more children, parents tend to become more open and relaxed," one of the researchers explained, "and that may allow for younger children to be more risk taking." In their view, this then gives laterborns more flexibility when choosing careers; this explains why they found middles and lasts to be more artistic and oriented to the outdoors (jobs thought of as less secure). Middle children might enjoy such occupations as being a drama coach, park ranger, museum curator, or firefighter.

As we can see from Sarah's family, parents place different demands and expectations on their children depending on their ordinal positions in the family. The two middle siblings in her family—the athlete and the banker—took quite a bit longer than Sarah to figure out what they wanted to do with their lives in terms of work. Julie, the middle girl, was largely driven by her athletic talents and avidly participated in races throughout college. Afterward, she taught at a summer camp and then became an assistant swimming coach at her former high school. She didn't worry much about bringing in a big paycheck: Her priorities were having enough time to continue with her sports and working with kids. At around thirty years old, she settled into a career as a physical therapist at the nearby state college. Although she had to go back to school to specialize in her field, by that time she knew exactly what she wanted from her work life.

Kyle, meanwhile, was the first boy in the family and the third child (the second middle child). While growing up he sometimes resented the attention his father showered on Sarah, but eventually he came to realize that he benefited from a certain freedom that his oldest sister didn't seem to enjoy. While he hated studying (especially history, which he failed in tenth grade), he excelled at math. He was very personable and enjoyed pursuits that were exciting.

Julie and Kyle, the two middle children, perceived themselves as more independent than Sarah. They spent more time and effort considering how well their personal inclinations fit with their particular skills, consequently choosing professions that were more suitable for them in the long run. After assessing their motivations, they were able to choose career moves that made better use of their particular skill sets.

One large study looked at what makes people choose one job over another. Five hundred adult students (all from three-child families) were questioned in order to determine the motivation behind job selection for firsts, middles, and lasts. The three motives tested in the study were achievement, affiliation, and power.

- *Achievement*: Do respondents set attainable but challenging goals? Do they need or want a lot of feedback on performance?
- *Affiliation*: How important is it for them to establish and maintain friendly relationships with others in the workplace?
- *Power*: How strong is their desire to influence the activities and thoughts of others?

Although the author expected middles to score higher than other birth orders on the need for achievement, his research actually demonstrated otherwise. He believed middle children's history of attention seeking within the family would drive them to put greater emphasis on attaining goals and getting constant (preferably positive) feedback. In fact, their history seems to have led to the need for achievement being just one motive in a string of other equally important motives.

Lasts scored highest on the need for affiliation, which measures the importance of sociability and friendliness. Not surprising, middles were a close second. In the need for achievement, firsts ranked at the top with middles squarely in the middle. And in terms of power, firsts once again came first, with middles revealing the most moderate approach to power by ranking it as of medium importance.

This provides an insight that can easily be overlooked but is highly valuable: Middles tend to value process over results. In workplace situations this can be a source of great strength. It suggests middles put more time and effort into assuring that their everyday work experience will be enjoyable and successful, rather than focusing too intently on specific goals for the future. As we saw with Michael Dell, his focus was more on doing what seemed fun and natural than making money. The interest came first, and the money followed later. "The true search is for what you believe in," says Po Bronson, author of *What Should I Do With My Life?* "Let your brain be your heart's soldier."

Drawbacks to following inner motivation

As great as it is to be motivated by causes and to feel a genuine personal connection to your chosen field of work, laying aside practical considerations can have its drawbacks. Multiple studies have found that laterborns are less motivated by money than other considerations when choosing their professions. While this isn't negative in and of itself, it can lead to uncertainty when it comes to bringing in a steady income. Creative endeavors, as well as many careers that rely on interpersonal relations such as social worker or community activist, are notoriously low paying.

Middles are drawn to ideas over data and concepts over the concrete. Careerbuilder.com conducted a survey of almost nine thousand people and discovered that middle children are more likely to earn $35,000 or less a year than firsts or lasts. Some of the middles I profile in this chapter have brought in the big bucks, but we don't normally associate middle children characteristics with those of a CEO. We tend to think of CEOs as dominant, tough-minded, competitive, conventional, and lacking in empathy—traits required to rise to the top. But laterborn leaders have a different management style and rise to the top of their chosen fields partially because their personable style of interaction with employees is motivating. Also, their willingness to take risks with both strategies and products can lead to enormous success. So middle children can actually have the best of both worlds if that's where their passions lie.

There are naturally plenty of middles who strive just as hard at work but with less financial reward. A mantra we have all heard over and over again is that money doesn't buy happiness. Middles seem to know this instinctively, and as long as they are aware of the consequences of their career decisions—in all arenas, not just financial—the likelihood is high that they'll find satisfaction in the workplace eventually, regardless of income.

Middleborns can chafe under authority

Let's go back to Sarah, the firstborn who became an unhappy prosecutor, and her younger sister, Julie (the middle), who ended up a physical therapist after years of trying to figure out what she wanted to do. As a kid back in Wisconsin, Julie found herself resenting her sister's know-it-all attitude and the fact that their father always deferred to her when asking the kids what they wanted to do on weekends or their family vacations. One of the reasons Julie so enjoyed athletics was that Sarah could barely hit a ball or run a sprint. She liked the attention and encouragement her coaches gave her, and felt powerful and autonomous whenever she participated in an athletic competition—even if she didn't win.

But after college, at her first job in the summer camp, she just couldn't get used to the camp director and his bevy of supervisors. Over and over again she would get irritated at being told what to do and be reminded that she wasn't in a position to make rules or decisions. Finally, as a physical therapist working individually with college athletes, she found work in which she could really be her own boss.

Family dynamics can replicate themselves in the workplace. While it's all well and good for middles to allow their inner motivation to guide them, there are times when they must learn from those in positions of authority and take orders—both in the workplace and at home. Work that relies on a rigid hierarchical structure is probably best avoided, such as some government, clerical, and law jobs, medical specialties, and financial analysis.

It's important for middle children to separate their home experiences with older siblings or parents and find a level of comfort with authority figures in the workplace, or they may find themselves unable to successfully navigate the hierarchy at work.

KEY INGREDIENT #2:
MIDDLES ROLL WITH THE PUNCHES

Cara Carleton Sneed was the middle child in a family of intense strivers. Born in Austin, Texas, she was a hard worker who set extremely high standards for herself. The mediator in her family, she constantly sought to appease and manipulate. "I became the family diplomat," she explains in her autobiography, "always intervening in every family argument, listening to every side, empathizing with everyone, and trying to find a way to bridge the gaps." She would later find these skills invaluable in her quest to be a "change warrior" for business.

But as a college graduate, the young woman wasn't clear what her next steps should be. After just one semester in law school, she quit; it wasn't for her. She taught English in Italy and took on temporary secretarial jobs, trying to figure out what to do with her life. After a few years she was accepted at the University of Maryland Business School and then ended up taking a position in AT&T. Less than twenty years later, Carly Sneed Fiorina was the first woman to head a Fortune 20 company, credited by many with breaking the proverbial business "glass ceiling" for women.

Fear of change—or fear of the unfamiliar—can be crippling in the workplace and usually inhibits advancement. "It's not the strongest nor the smartest of the species who survive," Fiorina said, "but those who are the most adaptable to change." In business and politics, a crucial ingredient of success is the ability to make decisions based on what the particular situation calls for rather than out of fear or desire to keep things the same. This applies to the jobs we pursue as well as the choices we make once we're in a particular career. "What separates the winners from the losers is how a person reacts to each new twist of fate," middle child Donald Trump has famously said.

Embracing change is a form of risk taking, and as we've seen, middles are much more open to taking risks than firsts but less likely than lasts to enjoy risk for its own sake. Consequently, middles would make good ER nurses, for instance, because they're faced with rapidly changing situations that call for quick thinking many times each day. Equally, being an entrepreneur or a firefighter would fit this personality profile, too.

Fiorina worked her way through the ranks to become vice president of AT&T, where she masterminded the spinoff and initial public offering of Lucent Technologies. After being ranked the most powerful woman in business by *Fortune* magazine in 1978, she migrated to Hewlett-Packard and became CEO for the next six years. During her tenure there, Fiorina broke off the technological equipment division and formed the wildly successful Agilent Technologies. Despite vigorous pushback from board members (including Walter Packard, the son of the company's founder), she initiated and completed a massive merger with Compaq. Known for her bold moves and her ability to roll with the punches, this middle child used the skills and strategies she learned growing up and became famous for embracing and implementing daring changes in the business world.

The dangers of being too fast and furious

Fiorina's role as a change warrior was not without its failures and controversy. In a humiliatingly public coup, she was ousted as CEO of HP and then listed by Condé Nast *Portfolio* as one of "The 20 Worst American CEOs of All Time." Making audacious moves and pushing through change can be immensely valuable, but it can also be dangerous and destructive. It's crucial to know when to retrench and reconsider.

An infamous middle child who seized opportunities a little too indiscriminately was Jeffrey Skilling, the former CEO of the energy trading company Enron. He wasn't able to put on the brakes when things got out of hand, and he's now serving time in federal prison for fraud. At Enron he created a culture of risk that was taken to extremes: During sales weekends, he and his sales force would embark on wild off-road trips in Baja, encouraging the philosophy that *nothing can touch us*. The second child of four, Skilling didn't especially stand out from the crowd either as a child or as an adult. He had to fight for recognition—and he fought hard, eventually achieving a reputation as a brash player. Along with the growth of his power and bank account, he began to change his image in order to get more attention and feel more comfortable in his fast-moving world. His need for self-improvement and risk taking masked a deeper problem: a fundamental lack of self-esteem.

The result was disastrous. In 2001, Enron was the largest company ever to file for bankruptcy. In one fell swoop, twenty thousand people lost their jobs.

Skilling is not a typical middle child in that his need for success and excitement became all consuming; it clouded his judgment to the extent that he lost sight of right and wrong. Usually middles' open-mindedness leads to a responsiveness that helps them be productive in the workplace, rather than leading to a recklessness that ends in ruin.

KEY INGREDIENT #3:
MIDDLES HAVE PERSEVERANCE AND PERSPECTIVE

Being the middle child in a gang of seven boys, in a family with sporadic income, couldn't have been easy. In the early 1900s at age two, Leslie Hope was accompanying his mother on her jobs as a cleaning lady in London, England, while his father drank too much liquor and found occasional work as a stonemason. Later, they left England and passed through Ellis Island on their way to Ohio. But once they arrived in their new home, Hope faced further hurdles. American kids teased him, turning his name backward and calling him "Hopelessly." Allowed a huge amount of freedom, the teen often caused trouble and got into fistfights. To help the family survive, he had one job after another—selling newspapers or outdated shoes and running errands for his uncle's butcher shop. Constantly fired, he always found new work. His ultimate mission? To become a great comedian.

Leslie Hope failed his first screen test for Pathé in 1930. He was fired from his first production company for cracking a joke about the movie he'd just shot. It wasn't until the 1940s that Hope (who had changed his name to the "chummier" Bob) made a name for himself. He stuck it out through the tough years, doggedly pursuing his passion for show business. Despite his setbacks, he had great confidence in his ability to make it as a comedian. His conscientiousness and consistency certainly paid off: For the next few decades Bob Hope became one of America's most prominent and popular superstars, dominating radio, film, and television.

But that wasn't all. In the end, Hope was perhaps best known as a supporter of U.S. troops, headlining sixty tours for the United Service

Organization (USO) during World War II, Korea, Vietnam, and the Persian Gulf wars. As a war reporter, John Steinbeck wrote of him: "It is impossible to see how he can do so much, can cover so much ground, can work so hard and can be so effective." Not only did Bob Hope show perseverance, but he also dedicated a good portion of his time to helping those he saw as needy. His perspective on the world and his desire to give back were rooted in his childhood experiences as the middle child in a rough and tumble family.

Becoming a performer is a surefire way of assuring that you won't be lost in the crowd. Firsts are sometimes too tightly wound and studious to make it as actors or comedians, and lasts often want to be entertained by others rather than do the work of entertaining. Middle children such as Richard Burton, Sarah Jessica Parker, and Jennifer Lopez all found a way to use their people skills—their ability to be whoever you might want or need them to be—to find great satisfaction and success on stage and behind the camera. And here's a surprising fact: Johnny Carson, David Letterman, Jay Leno, Conan O'Brien, and Tim Allen are all middle children. The assumption might have been that lasts would be the clowns of the family, seeking attention and playing to their audience. But in show business, where perseverance is arguably even more important than talent, middles reveal themselves to be particularly driven.

They're in it for the long haul

Without perseverance and perspective, people give up too early and too easily. Having staying power in a work situation is critical to success, yet knowing when to quit or change plans is also critical. "Although perseverance and tenacity are valuable entrepreneurial traits, they must be complemented with flexibility and a willingness to learn," states a 1999 *Harvard Business Review*. This is where perspective comes in. Because middle children tend to see the big picture, valuing concepts and abstract ideas more highly than other birth orders, they're more likely to know when to keep going and when to call it quits.

Donald Trump is a middle child who manages to keep his work goals and his everyday life in perspective. "I'm a busy guy," he explains, "but I set aside quiet time every morning and every evening to keep my equilibrium centered on my own path." He explains that this helps him stay independent and block out the noise from other people with different agendas. As a middleborn, Trump understood early on that he not only had to work hard but that he also needed to maintain a sense of autonomy and perspective. Such professions as advertising executive and secretary also play to these strengths.

According to the Careerbuilder.com survey, middle children report that they are the most satisfied with their current positions than all the birth orders. To me this suggests they have the wherewithal to ride out the lean times, waiting for their opportunity to shine, and are able to find joy and meaning in the journey toward success, not simply because of the success itself.

But middle children can lose sight of details

The tendency of the middle child to see the big picture rather than the details sometimes means the nitty-gritty realities of the present day— balancing checkbooks, catching small errors, being practical about immediate necessities—can take a backseat. Employers, however, tend to place a premium on workers who are able to see beyond today and grasp more abstract and longer-term goals.

Middles aren't the most detail-oriented people. They're better at big picture projects, strategic thinking, and developing abstract ideas or concepts than they are at being precise and focused. Their sociability can lead them to interact too much with their coworkers, decreasing their efficiency.

Elissa, a middle child of three (two boys and a girl), is a first grade teacher in Florida. What she loves most about teaching is figuring out how to communicate with the children. It's a riddle she has to unlock, and when she's successful, it's the most satisfying feeling in the world. But as a kid she had always hated details—she was constantly in trouble with her mom for not vacuuming her room thoroughly enough, not hanging her clothes, not tidying her desk. She just couldn't really see the point. As an adult she was often late handing in the report cards for her class, and she rarely filled in her job satisfaction questionnaires in time. It drove the principal nuts. He could see that most of the time Elissa was great at her job—figuring out how to reach kids even when they posed a serious challenge—but her lack of attention to the routine of her work was a headache.

These problems are relatively easy to overcome. Recognizing organization or attention to detail as areas of weakness is the first step. Middle children then need to avail themselves of checklists and calendars, which will help them with planning and focus. Learning to delegate to coworkers who have a greater affinity for detail work is also a good strategy and plays toward middles' strengths: working in teams.

KEY INGREDIENT #4:
MIDDLES PUT THEMSELVES IN OTHERS' SHOES

Current workplace managers complain that young people often are incapable of seeing themselves as part of a larger force. This leads to difficulty communicating, which hurts them as well as others. As child psychologist Mel Levine explains in *Ready or Not, Here Life Comes*, solid interpersonal skills are the key to successfully negotiating relationships in later life—for example, when navigating office politics or maintaining a romantic relationship.

Our ability to convey thoughts accurately, convince others, cement relationships, and behave politically all develop as a result of the interactions we have as children with peers (friends and relatives) and adults (parents, teachers, mentors). Because of the jockeying for power that takes place in their families, middles are predisposed to see themselves as part of the larger world. They don't usually have the privilege of operating in a bubble, and this actually helps them develop interpersonal skills and put them to use in the workplace.

Middle children become accustomed to playing the communicator role, and so they grow up seeing themselves as warm and sociable. Because they're able to put themselves in other people's shoes, they genuinely like and excel at being the middleman. Careers that require very little social interaction, such as computer programmers, sound mixers, and accountants, might prove challenging to a middle child who highly values company.

A pharmaceutical study from the mid-1990s shows how middles perceive themselves and the role this perception plays in their choice of work. It focused on one hundred pharmaceutical students, asking them eleven questions about their listening/empathy skills and eleven questions about their assertive/aggressive tendencies. The purpose was to figure out who wants to become a pharmacist and why, and to use this information to find individuals better suited to this particular position.

With good cause, pharmacists are considered detail-oriented, controlling, and insular. In the past they haven't been required to interface much with customers. Recently their role has been shifting, however, from a hands-off profession centered on dispensing drugs, to a more patient-oriented approach. Counseling and education have become ever more critical. Older research suggested that those who entered pharmacy school were low in warmth and had introverted personalities—and were largely motivated by the high salaries.

The results of the new study were broken down by birth order. There were far fewer middle children in the student ranks than firstborns. Since laterborns in general, and middles in particular, are more empathetic and interactive than firsts, they veered away from pharmaceutical study in which their interpersonal communication and flexibility skills would not be put to good use.

What do diplomats, mediators, secretaries, waiters, and other service occupations have in common? These jobs require significant people skills. A secret power that middle children possess but sometimes don't recognize fully is their ability to build bridges over rough terrain that would intimidate others. They are oriented toward others; it's natural for them to listen, consider, build consensus, and then move forward.

A good secretary must constantly interpret what is wanted and what is actually needed. Waitstaff must have patience and endurance, and be able to communicate cheerfully in spite of physical exhaustion. Similarly, business leaders cannot grow their companies without listening to what consumers want, interpreting what they actually need and can use, and then working persistently to provide it to them in an efficient manner.

Not yet twenty years old, Michael Dell had only a thousand dollars in the bank—but when he saw his opportunity, he grabbed it with both hands. Rather than telling consumers what was available from a menu of rigid options, he listened to what they actually wanted and then gave it to them, cutting out the middlemen. "This theme of listening has been really important for us," he has said.

This may not sound radical now, but back then it was. Dell's fledgling company grew 80 percent per year for eight years, and 60 percent per year for six years after that. The phenomenal growth is a direct result of predicting what people want, listening to their feedback, and then being willing to adapt quickly to provide them with exactly that.

The perils of being *too* empathetic

Mary Jane was a great ER nurse. No matter how late it was, she always had energy for new patients. All the other nurses relied on her good humor and her patience. As the intermediary between the sick, scared patients and the businesslike doctors, she knew she was an important piece of the puzzle that kept the ER working smoothly. She enjoyed great rapport with her coworkers when things were quiet and was wonderfully efficient when things got busy.

Her supervisor was an older woman named Hannah. After Mary

Jane had been at the hospital for almost five years, Hannah retired and Mary Jane became the head nurse, overseeing dozens of nurses and hundreds of patients a day. At home, she celebrated with her partner and her kids. She was thrilled with the promotion and looked forward to taking on extra responsibilities. She felt she'd earned it.

But after a year she realized things at work weren't going so smoothly anymore. Lately, on the night shift, the atmosphere would get downright crazy. She had always felt in control before, but now everything was going haywire. One nurse in particular, Jamie, never did his share of the work, and the others all complained. Mary Jane knew it was a serious problem, but she couldn't bring herself to fire him. She talked to him over and over again, and even tried to make up for his mistakes. Finally she understood that she was endangering patients. After she called him into her office and told him that he'd had too many warnings and it just wasn't working out, she went home feeling defeated. The stress was really getting to her. For the next few months, until she agreed to see a therapist, she lost all enjoyment of work. As top nurse she was a total flop.

At first it was hard for Mary Jane to see why the therapist insisted on talking about her childhood so much. Work was the problem, not her childhood! She had been a happy kid, the middle child in a family of two girls and two boys. Her parents divorced when she was ten, but they had a friendly relationship and saw each other all the time. Her dad lived just a few minutes away. But then she cracked it: She was too kindhearted and considerate, and this led her to be a reluctant disciplinarian. When she was in a top-management position, it made her uncomfortable to wield her power over others, as her older brother had over his three younger siblings. The therapist encouraged her to see her role as an enabling one, explaining that when she had to exert authority over others, she could (a) use her social and empathetic nature to be kind but direct, (b) remember that she was actually *helping* other people overcome weaknesses, and (c) give them a chance to find a better match at work.

When middles assume leadership positions, they can be overwhelmed by the stress of trying to take care of their subordinates. While they're great at brokering consensus among people with different opinions, they can be rendered indecisive if they're the decision makers and get stuck worrying too much about what others want. Continually, and perhaps blindly, putting others' needs ahead of their own can cause them serious problems. In addition, they themselves suffer when their needs are not met and risk becoming frustrated or angry if they perceive themselves as giving too much and not getting enough in return.

This can be mitigated if middles accept that in the long run the better approach is to find a happy medium— first by being decisive and self-oriented when their own concerns are important to the health of the job or business, and, second, by recognizing that their coworkers and bosses are autonomous. Middles alone should not carry the responsibility of other people's disappointments or needs. Sometimes, to create a happy work environment, everybody has to fend for themselves.

KEY INGREDIENT #5:
MIDDLES SELF-MANAGE

Let's go back to Elissa, the rather disorganized teacher from Florida. There was one little boy in her first grade class who was driving her crazy. Every morning he would arrive sluggish and grumpy, but by the afternoon he would be so pumped full of adrenaline and energy that she could barely get him to sit still and participate in class. One spring afternoon she arrived home sweaty and spent. She admitted to her husband that this little boy was her nemesis. Elissa loved kids and loved being a teacher, but it was just so exhausting trying to figure out how to get him to calm down and help him learn. It was affecting her attitude at work, and other teachers began commenting that she seemed "down."

Elissa grew up in a three-child family in Florida. Her oldest sister had cerebral palsy and needed a lot of attention. Her younger brother was a rabble-rouser whose red hair and freckles automatically made him everyone's favorite. Sometimes Elissa felt that she was the only one in the family with the patience and stamina to deal with them both. Her parents worked very hard to make ends meet and often took on extra jobs that meant working at night. As a teenager, Elissa frequently took care of family dinners and got her siblings to bed.

It's not that she minded—in fact, she quite liked being in charge. She devised a system of star charts that rewarded her siblings for good behavior. Whenever she became impatient with her duties or felt she needed time alone, she would remind herself that what she was doing was really useful. She had to learn to control her emotions, and she decided that she was great at being a caretaker. Becoming a teacher was the fulfillment of her dreams, but now this little boy was seriously testing her limits.

It goes without saying that unless you have the ability to exercise self-control, daily life in the workplace will be a challenge. Without the talent for self-management, and organization, each work task becomes a mountain to scale. "Why does affect [emotion] matter in organizations?" the authors of an article in the Academy of Management Perspectives newsletter asked. "Affect matters because employees are not isolated 'emotional islands.' Rather, they bring all of themselves to work, including their traits, moods, and emotions, and their affective experiences and expressions influence others."

In Elissa's case, she knew she needed to work on the extent to which this boy was impacting her emotions, and she needed to control how she presented her frustrations in the classroom. The fact that she took the time to recognize his effect on her and determined to address it was already a big step toward improving her approach and her outlook. She was able to develop a routine for herself in which she celebrated her small successes with her husband, Jon, rather than complaining about her challenges. She also began making a point of seeking help from the principal, who had many years of experience in special education. This middle child benefited from having been trained, so to speak, by her family situation to be an effective self-manager.

Middle children step up to the plate

Personality traits are generally split into the "Big Five" factors, one of which is conscientiousness. This is about showing discipline, being dutiful, and planning well. Impulse control is a key element of conscientiousness. If a person responds positively to such statements as *I'm exacting in my work* or *I get chores done right away*, the person has high conscientiousness. Equally, if the response to a statement like *I make a mess of things* or *I shirk my duties* is positive, then the person's relative conscientiousness is low.

It's perhaps not a big shock, considering what we have learned about middle children so far, that they fall in the middle as far as being conscientious is concerned. They are not overly fastidious and organized like firsts can be, nor do they fly by the seat of their pants, as lasts often do. Much of being successful in the workplace relies on avoiding extremes. If you don't have tantrums when a coworker invades your turf; if you can manage a subordinate's (or, in Elissa's case, a student's) foibles without losing your cool; if you can approach big projects without drowning in the minutiae, you have a leg up on others.

Middles are sandwiched between siblings at home, and therefore when it comes to dealing with issues of dominance and control in the workplace, they're typically not overbearing. It's unlikely they'll be highly emotive, lose their tempers easily, or become defensive at the slightest criticism. This makes middleborns easy to work with and for. They excel in jobs that require them to show patience and to act as a go-between such as a family counselor, personnel manager, or hairdresser.

Yet middleborns have trouble saying *no!*

Calvin, who lived in New York City and wanted to be an opera singer, had a startling soprano voice. In order to afford the apartment he shared with three roommates, he worked as a catering waiter at large events. It was a job he had held already for almost ten years, and he loved it. It paid well and was predictable, and he got to meet lots of interesting people.

The biggest work problem Calvin faced was all the extra shifts he took on. He really wanted some time off so he could be with his girl-friend; she complained constantly that he was too busy. But whenever one of the other waiters or waitresses called in sick and the manager asked if he'd fill in, Calvin always said yes. He just didn't want to leave anyone in the lurch. Growing up as the second boy in a family of four, he had become accustomed to always helping out. But now it was get-ting to be too much.

Middles are people pleasers. It's hard for them to say no. Some-times it takes being pushed by someone in the inner circle—a family member or a partner—for them to be able to say no to a colleague or superior in the workplace. They're accustomed to being under some-one else in the hierarchy, and they often take pride in their reputation as uncomplaining doers.

At a university meeting I once attended, Frank Sulloway asked how many of the professors in the room were firstborns. Almost every hand shot up. How many were middles? I saw a hand or two. And lasts? A few more hands were raised. In faculty meetings dominated by firsts, things can get very loud. Everyone has an opinion, and everyone wants to voice it. Firstborns are more likely to make radical pronounce-ments and to reveal their emotions quickly. They're not afraid to fight for their turf. Lasts are accustomed to attention and aren't afraid to speak up.

These kinds of meetings can get contentious rather fast and often end in stalemates. With middles in the room, however, everything is toned down a bit. They bring balance to the discussion, and often resolu-tion. However, since they are reluctant to rock the boat, middle children must be sure to protect themselves from being bulldozed in such situa-tions. Keeping silent in the face of overbearing firsts or indulgent lasts does not make use of middles' abilities to bring people to resolution.

Middles need to learn to face conflict

Although the Department of Labor guidelines don't specify conflict resolution as a vital component of workers' employability, being able to communicate effectively in high stress or contentious situations is a skill most people must put to use daily. Because middle children have great negotiation skills and high self-awareness, they typically manage conflict with finesse. Sometimes, however, they seek to manage it by simply avoiding it.

To evade all conflict is impossible. What's crucial to success is *how* conflict is resolved. A 1981 paper on communication strategies highlights three basic strategies used by people experiencing conflict. People can do one of the following:

- shift topic or deny the problem (avoidance)
- fault or blame others (competition)
- act with the goal of seeking a mutually beneficial outcome (cooperation)

Middle children are naturally inclined to want to deny problems (avoidance) because they like getting along with others. It's part of how they define themselves. They're rather unlikely to fault or blame others since they tend to be quite self-aware. And yet they're also adept at seeking mutually beneficial outcomes (cooperation) because of their agreeableness.

Consequently, middles need to step up, take a deep breath, and face their workplace issues with the same diplomacy and tact they used at home when they were children. Part of being a good self-manager is knowing when to face the music, when to launch into an argument, when to stay quiet, and even when it's time to dig in your heels regardless of what your friend, coworker, or boss might think.

Table 2. HOW MIDDLES' PERSONALITY TRAITS PLAY OUT AT WORK

Middle Child Personality Traits	Positives	Negatives
Agreeableness	• Good team players • Get along well with others • Achieve consensus	• Can't say no • Avoid conflict
Sociability	• Enjoy working with others • Good at working in groups	• Not always efficient • Can feel isolated depending on work environment
Empathy	• Care about what others think • Contribute to comfortable work environment	• Can't say no • Top management is stressful (firing, etc.)
Moderate Conscientiousness	• Responsible, not anal • Get things done • Don't lose sight of the big picture	• Not always sticklers at work
Openness	• Willing to listen	• Impractical at times
Low Dominance	• Creative • Able to learn and grow • Seen as part of team (even if boss)	• Don't always choose the right direction • Not great at enforcing hierarchy

Table 3. DEALING WITH MIDDLES' WORKPLACE CHALLENGES

Problem	Solution
Avoid conflict	• Remember you're a good negotiator and can help others resolve conflict
Can't say no	• Before agreeing to something, consider the costs and benefits
Resent hierarchy	• Be aware: your boss is not your older sibling • Talk things out • Adopt lastborn strategy: go to superior
Too empathetic (hard to fire or correct people)	• Think of this as an opportunity for them to learn something important about themselves
Not detail-oriented or efficient enough	• Think of the big picture • Learn to delegate—portion out time • Work with headphones or door closed • Connect and partner with detail-oriented coworkers

LOOKING TO THE FUTURE

As we explored in the first section of the book, middles tend to be anti-authority and think outside the box. They're willing to take risks (within reason); show genuine flexibility when faced with problems; are usually quite accessible and even humble; and are good at building consensus between people. Because they are in the unique position of following the older kid's example and yet also leading the younger siblings, they thrive on personal relationships and develop great people skills.

So what does this mean specifically in terms of their fit for particular jobs?

Table 4. GOOD JOBS FOR MIDDLE CHILDREN

Middle Child Inclinations	Best Job Fit
Scientific/mathematical: *Investigative work*	• Family physician • Private investigator • Teacher • Medical technologist
Language/arts/music/drama: *Artistic work*	• Drama coach • Editor • Photographer • Actor/Comedian • Advertising
Human/interpersonal relations: *Socially oriented work*	• Social worker • Nurse • Law enforcement • Service person • Sales • Community activist • Human resources/Personnel managers • Diplomat • Assistant/Secretary • Entrepreneur • Hairdresser • Mediator
Risk taking/trailblazing: *Athletic and outdoor work*	• Competitive athlete • Park ranger • Museum curator • Firefighter • Pilot

As you consider a move toward a satisfying career, or if you're try-ing to help your middle child find his or her place in the work world, it's important to keep in mind how quickly our world is changing. YouTube and Twitter have been around only for a few years. Imagine what new jobs, lifestyles, and challenges we'll all face in the coming decades. Take nanotechnology, for instance. Between 1997 and 2005, investment in nanotechnology research and development by govern-ments around the world grew one-hundred-fold to over $4 billion. Ac-cording to the Nature Publishing Group, by 2015 about 8 million people will work in a field related to nanotechnology. While it has in-fluenced every corner of our lives, from medicine to transportation to agriculture, just over a decade ago most of us couldn't even have imag-ined the opportunities this new arena would present to the world's workforce.

Since our society is faced with the constant need to adapt to re-cent discoveries and the unknown, middle children enjoy a distinct advantage over other birth orders who are tied more tightly to the tried and tested. Overwhelmingly, middles have qualities that sup-port their prospects of finding a vocation, achieving career goals, or enjoying a daily job that fulfills their needs and fits their personali-ties. "Imagination is more important than knowledge. Knowledge is limited," Albert Einstein said. "Imagination encircles the world." And middleborns, with their learned strategies, have the imagina-tion, energy, and flexibility to turn a variety of workplace environ-ments into fertile ground for their personal development and satisfaction.

PUTTING MIDDLES TO WORK

1. **Birth order affects the office, too.**
   Dynamics at work often reflect those of the family and produce a kind of birth order ripple effect. It's important for middles not to allow the negative dynamics at play in their childhood to affect them at work.

2. **Middleborns tend to do what they want.**
   Middles are under less pressure than firsts to fulfill certain career expectations and so have greater freedom to match their personalities and desires with their choice of work.

3. **But middles like to be part of a group.**
   Middle children are hardwired to see themselves as part of a larger world and like jobs where they can intermingle with others.

4. **It's okay to be selfish . . .**
   Middles need to think of their self-interests more often. They should put their needs ahead of others' on occasion. When middles draw the line between self-sacrifice and generosity, and learn the importance of taking care of their own needs, they'll find it much easier to say no every now and then.

5. **. . . but it's not okay to be disrespectful of authority.**
   If middle children can shake off the habit of finding authority irritating, they'll stand a greater chance of being able to navigate office politics successfully.

6. **Organization will help middles succeed.**
   Recognizing that, in the workplace, attention to detail can be critical, middleborns should use organizational tools (calendars, to-do lists, short-term goals) to help them focus more effectively on the immediate needs of their business or their coworkers.

CHAPTER SEVEN

Middle Children
as Friends and Lovers

In private they called each other Nattie and Googie, and in public they were famous for their comedic timing and on-set chemistry. They spent decades cracking jokes about domestic life, sparring light-heartedly on camera and over the radio waves. He was born Nathan Birnbaum, son of Orthodox Jews from Brooklyn by way of Eastern Europe, and she was Grace Allen, an Irish Catholic girl who grew up in San Francisco. They were married for thirty-eight years. Some three decades after Googie's death in 1964, her husband wrote a book titled *Gracie: A Love Story*.

And theirs was a long-lasting one by any measure. Even late into his nineties, comedian George Burns would talk aloud to his beloved wife at Hollywood's Forest Lawn Cemetery, pacing up and down her marble mausoleum, smoking his ubiquitous cigar and asking for her advice.

Burns was one of twelve children. His father died of the flu when Burns was six years old. As one of many middles in such a huge family, he was accustomed to taking care of himself and using his imagination and energy to make money from a very early age. When he fell in love with Allen, she was engaged to be married to someone else—but Burns was smitten and wouldn't take no for an answer.

Over the many years of their marriage, they worked side by side in a successful business partnership, and they also kept their marriage strong. "I'm the brains, and Gracie is everything else, especially to me," Burns once said. After his wife's death, he reportedly couldn't fall asleep until he slept on the bed she had spent her last months in. Notwithstanding his faults (and he certainly had some), George Burns was dedicated and generous. In a June 1978 interview, Arthur Cooper wrote of him, "In truth, Burns is one of the gentlest and kindest of men. Even when prodded, he cannot find a mean word to say about anyone. If he ever had any enemies, he has managed to outlive them."

These traits helped him keep a love story going longer than most. "In the long run, nobody is living a valentine," writes Martin Gottfried, Burns's biographer. "But in real life, I don't think you can get a better marriage than George and Gracie's."

Middles: sticky yet supple

It's no easy feat to maintain a cadre of close-knit friends or to stay happily married, yet middleborns tend to do both remarkably well. What makes them such great friends and lovers? My research points to three essential characteristics of their personalities:

1. **dedication to chosen family**
2. **agreeableness**
3. **openness to experience**

Ever heard of rubber glue? It's a great adhesive, yet you can also unstick something if you've made a mistake and move it around. In many ways, middles are like rubber glue when it comes to relationships: They have the loyalty and dedication to their partners and friends, and so they stay close, but they also have the flexibility to shift when circumstances demand.

As children, squeezed between siblings at home, middleborns have to develop the ability to get what they want by being clever—rather than loud like the firstborn or cute like the last. They learn how to hold on to their friends by becoming good listeners, and being flexible and tolerant. George Burns was famously loyal: to his brand of cigars, to his friends, and to his wife. Yes, he made fun of Allen and of himself, but he was relentlessly dedicated to her and gave her credit at every turn. "For forty years my act consisted of one joke," he was fond of saying. "Then she died."

On becoming independent adults, middleborns benefit from those very skills they developed as youngsters, which help them navigate both platonic and intimate relationships with greater ease than other birth orders. While it is common for middle children to be thought of as unassuming, when it comes to their interpersonal relationships, they have strong feelings and expectations. Guided by a deeply embedded value system, they set high standards for themselves as friends and lovers.

Naturally, for every positive there are negatives. In some cases middleborns fail to maintain close relationships with their parents. They can fall into bad habits, such as being too self-effacing or laid-back. It's often easy to take advantage of them, and they can be more vulnerable than others to peer pressure. Here we will look carefully at the traits that make middleborns so successful at friendship and love, and the potential traps they should avoid. And if you're not a middle yourself but are in love with one, you'll gain a deeper appreciation of what they need from you as a partner.

MIDDLES ARE DEDICATED

It wasn't love at first sight. For years Susie and Ned were neighborhood friends, walking to the school bus stop together in the early mornings. In their last year of high school they broke up with their respective mates and suddenly saw each other with different eyes. They began dating. Even though Susie went to college in California and Ned stayed in Maryland, they were married just a few years after graduating. Susie is a middle child, and Ned is the firstborn of two sons.

Petite and brunette, Susie was not the liveliest conversationalist as a young woman, but she radiated a sense of calm and control that tended to put people at ease. She never lacked a friend to turn to and was an avid member of various social groups in school and college. After dating for seven years, she and Ned were confident that they'd found their life partners, and neither of them wavered in their decision to tie the knot at such a young age.

Married for almost ten years now, both admit that Ned likes to make the rules and gets his nose bent out of shape whenever something unexpected comes up. Susie tends to be more agreeable, supporting her husband's way of doing things while not always caving in to every demand. What makes them feel like a real team in running their family, though, is the diplomatic way Susie handles the inevitable hurdles. "I can freak out sometimes, and she never makes me feel stupid for reacting that way," Ned explained. "Because of her sensitivity, I feel closer to her each time we overcome some obstacle."

Shortly before the birth of their second daughter, Ned lost his job as an account manager with an advertising firm. After a few months he became so demoralized about his prospects that he stopped looking for new work and started being unhelpful and irritating around the house. Once her maternity leave was over, Susie would get home each day from her job as a law clerk only to find him stretched out on the sofa watching TV. Ned was also miserable and constantly complaining. Despite wanting to stay together for their two little girls, he and his wife teetered on the brink of divorce. What got them over the hump, Ned maintains, is how much Susie valued their relationship even during the rough patch. "She's so dedicated to making things work and so tolerant, even when I was being totally unbearable," he said. "That's what saved us. And she was like that from the start, when we were just kids. That's why I married her."

As we can see in Susie and Ned's situation, being dedicated and loyal is vital to creating and sustaining a sense of intimacy. Showing consideration, even when in disagreement, is part of what keeps middleborns and their friends and lovers feeling connected. Despite the trauma of job loss and depression, and the ensuing emotional upheaval, Susie showed a willingness to ride the ups and downs of an intimate relationship, which allowed her to survive the tough times with her husband. It took almost one year and a cross-country move from Maryland to Washington State for them to find their feet again, but they were ultimately able to rebuild their relationship. Susie explained, "I felt strongly that we were a *team*, and I made a point to remind him of that whenever things were tough." Once they settled in Seattle and Ned started his new job with a small online advertising agency, they actually felt closer as a couple and more capable of managing any future problems that might crop up. Had Susie not been as dedicated a partner, this middle child may have been more easily swayed by her feelings of anger and disappointment instead of allowing her husband the time and space he needed to get back on track.

Middles gravitate toward chosen family

Middle children are highly social beings. They have better interpersonal skills than firstborns. Firstborns try to bully their friends into doing things their way, just as at home they lord their advantage in terms of age and size over their younger siblings. And lastborns, like only children, tend to be more spoiled and stubborn.

Middles gravitate toward chosen family—their friends and lovers—because they're not competing with them for attention based on the accepted familial hierarchy. Instead, they feel they can open up and be relaxed without concern for either protecting their position or having to fight for it. As a result, they value these relationships so highly that they're fiercely dedicated to them. For friends that means calling often, seeing each other frequently, and being available both physically and emotionally. For lovers that means fostering a sense of safety by showing commitment through even-keeled and consistent dealings. Middleborns are adept at this: Their devotion to their chosen family reveals itself through the constancy of their attentiveness.

In a recent study I did on birth order and relationships, middleborns scored highest on questions related to being able to talk about important things to one another, doing special favors for friends, and lending items to friends. They rated such statements as *My friends and I can count on one another to keep promises* and *I make up quickly after an argument* much higher than did firsts or lastborns. Another study showed that middleborns are no slouches when it comes to giving of time, attention, or tokens of affection. Norwegian researchers asked participants about the cash value of gifts given and received over the Christmas holidays, revealing that middleborns are more likely to give valuable presents to friends than either first or lastborns would. This shows their willingness to openly express just how much they value that relationship. They are unfailingly giving and dedicated, at least where friends are concerned.

The fallout of favoring chosen family over birth family

But the dedication that middleborns show toward their chosen friends and family doesn't always extend to their birth family.

Interestingly, Susie rarely called her mother during the year she struggled with Ned. "I've just never felt close to my parents in that way, whereas I rely a lot on my friends," she explained. This is common among middleborns. Although they don't hold on to bitterness toward their parents for neglecting them as children, they also don't tend to feel particularly close to them once they become adults. Middleborns feel they didn't get much attention from their parents, so they tend not to give their parents much attention in return.

While you could argue that middle children's strong ties to their peer group are actually a sign of their resourcefulness—rather than an indication of dissatisfaction with their childhoods—there is no doubt that their birth families get short shrift in terms of middleborns' time and attention. In a 2003 study I asked participants to rate such statements as the following: *A person should be willing to sacrifice anything for one's family*; *A relative in need can be a nuisance*; and *We should not allow ourselves to be distressed by the misfortune of others*. The answers revealed that middleborns have distinctly less positive attitudes toward family than either first or lastborns, and they show greater faithfulness to commitments and obligations to their friends than to their birth families.

So we see that their birth family can be regarded by middles as more of an obligation than a resource, at least among college-age individuals. This can have a serious chill effect.

Susie's husband was the one who noticed the effect their marital discord was having on her relationship with her parents. Weekend calls and visits became less frequent, and by the time they packed up the house and moved, they hadn't seen her parents for almost four months. "She was expending so much time and effort on me that she had none left over for her parents," he said. "And they were sad about it, too; I could tell."

When it comes to family and friends, it doesn't have to be either/or

Often, middleborns aren't consciously expressing negative feelings toward their birth family by not staying close. Rather, their disinclination to maintain intimacy with those in positions of authority within the family (i.e., parents) is an unintended oversight. Once adult middleborns become aware that they are ignoring or minimizing interaction with family, misunderstandings or hurt feelings can easily be avoided. A few calls, a thank-you letter, or an effort at inclusion from a middle child toward his or her parents can go a long way to avoid unnecessary misunderstandings.

One weekend morning Ned brought Susie a cup of coffee and mentioned that she hadn't called her mother in a long time. At first Susie was defensive, insisting that she had just been too busy with the move to think much of her parents. Also, she had started a new job. What could anyone expect? Since the little ones were still fast asleep, Susie and Ned sat in the kitchen for almost an hour and talked it through; she realized that he was, in fact, right. It had been over a month since she had last spoken with her mom, and she had totally forgotten her sixtieth birthday was coming up. After that, Susie initiated a weekly Sunday afternoon call home and made plans to have her parents fly west and stay with them over Easter break. Instead of leaving communication with her parents to chance, she now makes the effort to reach out more often, and with greater consistency.

The good news is that as middleborns age and have their own families, they develop a different perception of their childhood family interactions and become more inclined toward closeness with family members. In fact, many middles, as adults, say that they don't regret their birth position growing up because it gave them more freedom to figure out who they really were. Their older siblings faced more parental responsibilities and expectations, and the baby of the family was coddled too much. Grown up, middleborns often recognize that their birth position helped turn them into strong independent adults. "I never felt that important at home; that's why I'm so independent now," Susie acknowledged. "In a way it's the reason I have such great friends who give me support when I need it."

In an intriguing twist, many middle children actually feel quite close to their siblings and value those peer relationships. While Susie, for instance, grew ever more distant from her mother and father as she was navigating her relationship troubles, she did often call her younger sister Jill, an attorney in New York City, for moral support. When they were teens, they hadn't spent much time together, but their bond became much closer after they both had their own children.

As middle children mature, they will increasingly seek the wisdom and perspective of elders outside their peer group and will benefit from a more thoughtfully maintained relationship with their own parents. Parents of middleborns need to remember that their middle child's independence—and perhaps emotional distance—does not necessarily correlate to a lack of affection for them. If parents can avoid being overly sensitive to perceived slights, they are likely to enjoy a less stress-filled relationship with their adult children whether or not they always remain in close touch.

MIDDLES ARE AGREEABLE

Back in the early 1970s, researchers went into classrooms in Riverside, California, and took aside seventeen hundred grade school children individually to pose questions such as this one: *Suppose you were picking teams to play ball during recess. Who in your class would you most like to have on the team*? Although the researchers were actually studying peer popularity from the perspective of race, the results showed that laterborn children were far more popular with their peers than firstborns were.

While studies show that lastborns and middleborns are equally social, the baby of the family usually wants and expects to have things his or her own way, while middles tend to be better at the give-and-take of friendship. This is one reason that they score high on peer acceptance, which measures how well individuals do socially by relating the *quality* of a child or adolescent's peer relationships to the *quantity*. This also explains why some studies show that middleborns are not only more popular in the classroom but also have more friends across their lifespan than other birth orders. It is clear that middles' personalities make them highly attractive as friends and partners.

A primary reason that middles are popular is that they respect others' opinions and desires, and this manifests itself in their agreeable natures. Middle children prefer being pleasant over being combative, listening over talking, and compromising over imposing their will. This agreeableness comes from the sensitivity they developed as children caught in the middle at home. Middleborns are perceptive observers: With less responsibility than firstborns and less attention than lastborns, they become adept at assessing and validating others' points of view.

We need only look at a random sample of famous middles to see that they are often known for their ability to make others feel that they're really being heard. Abraham Lincoln was famous for his willingness to listen interminably to regular townsfolk who visited him at the White House. Julia Roberts is a middle child with a reputation for showing kindness to coworkers. Bob Hope was not only married to the same woman for sixty-nine years but was said to be loyal and kind at every turn. Although earnest, Robert Kennedy (another middle child in the large Kennedy family) was also personable and energetic—one of the reasons he captured the imagination of the American public after his brother was assassinated, inspiring a battered nation to feel that anything was possible even in such difficult times.

One young woman, Christine, is a great example of middle's agreeableness and the impact it has on sociability. The third of four children, Christine has two older sisters and a younger brother. A tall, willowy woman with short-cropped black hair, she plays a mean game of tennis and loves board games. She grew up in a small town in central Florida where everyone knew one another. At a young age she had often taken a caretaking role babysitting neighbors' children, working as a nanny, and, as an adult, becoming a preschool teacher. Although she's a little on the shy side, she makes friends quite easily and will always go out of her way to be helpful to them even if it's inconvenient for her.

She often finds herself in the position of mediator—whether between her parents, who argued a lot when she was a child (they eventually divorced once the kids were out of the house), or between friends and coworkers. After college, Christine moved to a bigger city on the coast and started working as a fifth grade teacher. Some weekends she would spend hours with a friend consoling her about some spat with another buddy and giving advice on how to patch things up. While she rarely gets into arguments herself, she finds herself constantly helping other people deal with their problems. She likes to think of herself as a problem solver and a good listener; in fact, it defines her self-image. She gets huge personal satisfaction from giving to others.

Like most middleborns, Christine has a tendency to be compassionate and cooperative with others, as opposed to suspicious or antagonistic. In surveys—which are mostly measured by self-report or peer-report—middles consistently reveal themselves to be highly empathetic. This agreeableness on the part of middle children plays a significant role in making them attractive as both friends and lovers, since we naturally tend to gravitate toward those who make us "feel good."

Susie, married to Ned (the unemployed ad executive), became skilled at navigating relationships early on in life: At home she was caught between a burly, outgoing older brother—the star quarterback of the football team—and an adorable baby sister. As an adult, having learned to be adaptable and agreeable, she was able to roll with the punches when it came to a particularly tricky period in her marriage. Ned gravitated toward her because she balanced out his nature: She was social and optimistic while he was more private and circumspect.

Christine, the teacher, says that her friends come to her when they don't feel happy, and "they usually go away feeling better. Somehow I make them feel okay again." When someone is negative, critical, or intransigent, this dampens our desire to spend time with them, to share intimacies, and to make ourselves vulnerable. Middleborns, in contrast, are adept at accommodating their chosen family, making them feel valued.

But Christine admitted that she does sometimes ask herself: Am I getting as much as I give?

The difference between being agreeable and being a pushover

When you have an overly agreeable nature, it's tempting to seek peace at all costs, and, as a result, middleborns tend to shy away from conflict. Since middle children have excellent negotiating skills, they usually avoid drama and instead employ tact and diplomacy when involved in disagreements, especially when mediating between others. But when it comes to their personal lives, they often prefer to avoid disagreements altogether, sometimes burying their own concerns and desires. Moreover, they find it harder than most to say no to their friends.

Once again Christine is a case in point. While she feels well loved, she does sometimes get the feeling that there's an imbalance in her relationships that she is inadvertently encouraging through her own behavior. At least once a week she organizes an outing with friends (bowling, movies, a game of doubles, or dinner at a restaurant near the water), but every now and then she'd like to have someone else take the reins. She puts others' needs ahead of her own, and this certainly makes her a great friend—from her friends' point of view. Christine admitted that she hesitates before calling her best friend to talk about something that's worrying her because she doesn't "want to be a burden." The problem is that her more self-centered friends sometimes take advantage of her: They end up asking for endless favors without giving much in return. Christine finds it hard to cut those ties.

She has also fallen into the pattern of having serial monogamous relationships that end after a few years. Since she was little, she dreamed of being married and having five or six children, but even though she's very accommodating, her relationships don't ever get serious enough to lead to a permanent commitment. She gives her boyfriends plenty of freedom, so that's not the problem, and she never expects them to change their lives for her. But while she puts her heart and soul into relationships, she expects little in return. For many lovers that imbalance undermines what could otherwise be a strong and more equal partnership.

An important study of high school boys back in 1982 revealed that middleborns have lower self-esteem than first or lastborns, which makes them less likely to demand support from their friends and lovers when *they* need it. Middles don't like to muddy the waters in their relationships. They're often unwilling to be demanding because—unaware of how much they are valued by their partners—they fear risking their relationships. As we'll see in the next chapter on parenting a middle, peer pressure can be a concern for middles because they can be overly influenced by the opinions and actions of the people close to them.

Sensitive partners are the key to middles' happiness

Christine is in her midthirties now. As she's gotten older and has accomplished more in terms of her career, she's started to gain confidence and recognize that some of her relationships are in fact damaging to her. During her twenties she worked as a fifth grade teacher, before realizing that her passion was teaching high school. After four years as head of the English department in an urban public high school, she became the assistant principal of a smaller private school. Figuring out what was important to her in her career and combining that with her inherent skill set and passions helped Christine get a better perspective on her personal life—the relationships she fostered, and those she tolerated. "I'm not such a pushover with people anymore," she said. "And I think it's really making my relationships healthier. I guess I'm learning to say no." Over time, as she continues to become more comfortable articulating her own desires and standing her ground when something is important to her, she will also enjoy greater reciprocity from both her friends and her partners.

Since middleborns actually tend to be highly regarded as lovers and as friends, their inclination to be overly self-effacing is a hurdle that's relatively easy to overcome. A recent study of both boy and girl middles from an urban middle school found lower self-esteem among middle children who had same sex siblings, and higher self-esteem among middle children who were the only boy or girl in the family. Being the only child of your gender would naturally make you feel more unique. It follows that in order to have a good self-image, middles need to feel cherished as individuals and may require—though not demand—more attention in relationships than other birth orders. Middleborns appreciate getting a lot of love and support from their partners, and when they don't they can begin to harbor unnecessary doubts.

Let's take the case of Amy and John. They have been married for eighteen years, are in their midforties, and have two children: a son leaving for college in the fall and a daughter who is a junior in high school. John is a high school counselor, while Amy owns a small chain of hair styling salons. Both are successful at what they do, although Amy makes a bigger financial contribution to the family bank account.

For her work, Amy, a firstborn, often travels to industry expos and small business seminars. Sometimes John, the middle of three boys, frets about her being away so much. Her thick blond hair with its golden highlights attract a lot of positive comments. She's such a beautiful, outgoing, vibrant woman that he's sure she catches the attention of other men. When they first met, she was determined to make a success of herself, and now that her business is flourishing and the kids are almost grown, John occasionally thinks she doesn't need him as much anymore. He knows he has gained a few extra pounds and worries that his job isn't as exciting as his wife's. Sometimes he asks himself whether she'll stay interested in him.

Amy doesn't usually notice this malaise, but when she does, she makes a point of reminding her husband how much she loves and appreciates him. "I tell him I love him all the time," she says. "I know he likes to hear it, and I mean it. He and the kids are the most important things in the world to me." John's insecurity puzzles her, because he's a great husband and father, and she finds him as attractive today as when they fell in love—and she doesn't mind the extra pounds!

John suffers from self-esteem issues typical of middle children.

But because his wife is sensitive to his needs, she gives him the regular reassurance he craves. Seeking to avoid conflict, John neglects to ask for emotional support, yet he's fortunate to have a partner who needs little prompting. Also, because Amy knows how dedicated he is to her and to their kids—and because he shows so much sensitivity to *her* needs—she is, in turn, dedicated to making him happy. They manage to stay close by understanding each other's strengths and weaknesses.

In Christine's case (the young woman from Florida with all the friends), she's better off being somewhat more selective about who she spends time with. It's crucial for middleborns to surround themselves with friends who value and reciprocate their dedicated, easygoing natures. When middles open themselves up indiscriminately, there's a chance they'll be spending their time with friends or lovers who focus too much on themselves. As middle children grow into confident individuals and find suitably reciprocal partners, they'll develop a level of comfort communicating their own needs honestly and promptly.

MIDDLES ARE OPEN TO EXPERIENCE

Finally, the third fundamental relationship trait that middleborns manifest is their openness to experience. As we discussed in Part One, since they don't identify strongly with their parents and are used to being dominated by older siblings, it makes sense that middle children have a propensity to break the mold. To find their own niche in the world they have to be more open-minded and willing to try new things. Middleborns gravitate toward being unconventional, adventurous, and rebellious—and they've used this to their advantage throughout history.

Middle children spread their friendship happily among varying groups of people and are less constrained by society's expectations or class strictures. That partially explains why about half of America's presidents have been middle children: They identify strongly with all sorts of people and feel a sense of responsibility toward them. Middle children sometimes find their way into prime positions in the media—such as Johnny Carson, Jay Leno, and Conan O'Brien. Growing up in an environment where they are expected to carve their own paths, they seek to connect with others, often through comedy or journalism. Part of their appeal as interviewers and performers is the fact that they relate well to a wide spectrum of people.

Take Henry, a sandy-haired bachelor in his forties who is soon to be married to Lana, a lastborn. As a child Henry wasn't particularly extroverted, but he enjoyed being with his peers. He was always out on the streets, kicking around a soccer ball or shooting hoops. He would often referee the street hockey matches in the summertime. The third of five children, he got along with his siblings reasonably well, although he and his only brother were hardly the best of friends.

Growing up in a working class neighborhood, most of Henry's childhood friends came from the same background. A straight A student, he was the first in his family to go to college, getting a degree in architecture. Although he has now moved to a small house in a different part of town, he keeps in close touch with his old friends. On weekends he likes to kick back with his buddies, and whenever he gets the chance, he invites his work friends over as well. Childhood buddies in steel-toed boots and baseball caps hang out with professional guys in chinos and golf shirts. While Henry doesn't notice it himself, sometimes his new friends think his old buddies are "kind of rough around the edges."

Henry is a great example of how middle children have the flexibility to form friendships with most if not all types of people. Because they're open, middleborns benefit from a wide variety of friendships and can frequently accommodate very different—or even *difficult*—personalities in both their casual friendships and their romantic liaisons.

This dynamic is at play in Henry's relationship with his fiancée, too. Lana is the last in a family of four; she's ten years older than Henry and twice divorced. She grew up in Hong Kong to British parents and feels kind of rootless. Initially, she balked at the idea of another marriage, convinced of her own bad luck and sure that Henry would be unwilling to deal with her "difficult" personality. But after dating for two years, Henry wore her down with his good-natured spirit and his willingness to entertain almost any off-the-wall ideas. "And, you know, I love his friends," she said. "They're all so totally different." Lana credits Henry's accommodating personality with helping her feel comfortable in her own skin after her previous failed marriages.

What about openness in the bedroom?

As a researcher I wondered what kind of connection there was between being open to experience and intimacy. Could I link middleborns' openness with a willingness to experiment in the bedroom? And, if so, what would this indicate about middle children's attitudes toward monogamy—given that a tendency toward sexual experimentation might lead to the desire for multiple partners, which in turn could be detrimental to long-term, intimate relationships?

Many studies suggest that children who grow up in homes with inconsistent or rejecting child-rearing practices suffer in their intimate relationships as a consequence. They tend to reach puberty earlier, engage in intercourse earlier, and have more sexual partners than those who grow up in more stable homes. Attachment theorists also claim that different kinds of early childhood experiences are likely to influence whether you prefer long-term, committed or short-term, uncommitted romantic relationships. Since middleborns often feel neglected at home, it follows that this experience could have an effect on whether they're able to maintain healthy and long-lasting sexual relationships as adults.

Consequently, researchers have long assumed that laterborns—and, by implication, middleborns—are likely to be less faithful than firstborns. In his book *Born to Rebel*, for example, Frank Sulloway proposed that laterborns would be more likely than their older siblings to engage in high-risk strategies such as mate poaching and infidelity.

Since Sulloway had no specific data at hand, this suggestion was based on the results of his study of revolutions in science, for which he grouped middles with laterborns.

But what I've found is that middle children have complex personalities that defy such categorization. In a recent study I conducted on birth order and relationships, middles reported cheating on a partner in a monogamous relationship significantly less than did firstborns or lastborns. Over 80 percent of middleborns said they never strayed while in a monogamous relationship, whereas approximately 65 percent of firstborns and 53 percent of lastborns had never cheated. Interestingly, once someone did cheat, there were no birth order differences in the number of times they cheated. Marriage counselors corroborate this picture of middleborns' steadiness and reliability in intimate relationships, reporting consistently that they're less likely to be seen in couples counseling than firstborns, lastborns, or onlies.

I also discovered in my study of birth order and sexual behavior that there's a difference between what middles think and say, and how they actually *behave*. In terms of sexual behavior, I found that lastborns were the least restricted and firstborns the most restricted—and middleborns were in the middle. This means that firsts and lasts have stronger promiscuous tendencies than middles. But when I looked at questions related to *attitudes* toward sex, middle children scored highest, firstborns lowest, and lastborns in the middle. In other words, middleborn attitudes toward sex are quite open and nonjudgmental, but their actual behavior is not as freewheeling as this would suggest.

Also, when I measured behavior and attitudes toward sex and then related them to birth order and gender, the results in this study diverged from previously held assumptions. Men didn't exhibit any birth order effect when it comes to their sexual behavior (which falls in line with other studies showing that they typically have more unrestricted sexuality than females across the board). When we look at sociosexuality, however—which measures differences in the willingness to engage in sexual relations without closeness, commitment, and other indicators of emotional bonding—female middles showed reserve. Their sociosexuality scores were actually the lowest, suggesting that middleborn females are *less* promiscuous than other birth orders.

Because middle children treat their mates more like their friends—as valued resources to be actively cultivated and indulged—they're more comfortable working on these relationships and committing to exclusivity. These lovers, husbands, and wives are part of the family that middleborns have created for themselves outside their birth family, and they value them greatly. So when you combine middles' dedicated and agreeable natures with an inclination to be open-minded risk takers, you get a lover who is both steady *and* willing to experiment sexually. And in building healthy intimate relationships, middle children's' three core relationship traits make for a highly successful combination.

LOVE MATCHES FOR MIDDLEBORNS

Judging by these three traits that middleborns both value and exhibit in their relationships, it seems obvious that anyone would be lucky to have a middle child as a partner. Research corroborates this fact. According to an Israeli study that asked such questions as *Do you confide in your mate?* and *How often do you and your mate get on each other's nerves?*, the happiest couples of all are middleborns with any other birth order and firstborns married to lastborns.

Although middle children tend to push aside problems and can be somewhat *too* tolerant at times, they typically make well-balanced and fun-loving mates who don't apply blanket judgments on others and are willing to stay the course. Luckily for Ned, the out-of-work husband, his wife Susie—a middle—was willing to be flexible and forgiving, and they made a success of their marriage. "I know that when we're not close, when we're not being intimate, we grow apart fast," Susie explained. "So we always try to give each other time to really connect." Had Ned married a hypercritical first or a fiery last, he may have paid a steep price for his months of antisocial behavior.

The bottom line is that good communication is an essential element of any relationship, and middleborns are uncommonly adept at communicating. They simply need to give voice to their own needs as forcefully as they do for others. Successful relationships involving sustained intimacy demand a degree of emotional and personal vulnerability that is unique to sexual relationships, and also an aptitude for facing and resolving conflict on one's own behalf.

We have already seen with Christine from Florida that friendships can become strained if one party—the accommodating middle child—is too much of a pushover. On the positive side, while middleborns tend to avoid personal conflict, family communication research actually remains divided over whether conflict avoidance is necessarily a bad strategy. It can be seen as a cooperative mode in which the goal of both parties is to find resolution without resorting to fireworks. This means that middleborns can work through difficult patches in their relationships more easily than other birth orders. In fact, middles are more likely than other birth orders to see disagreements as "no big deal," which helps keep arguments in perspective. If both members of a couple share a similar strategy in dealing with conflict, they'll simply "let it go," and no resentment seems to develop.

So it becomes evident that the consistently gentle, thoughtful, and caring communication style of middleborns makes them great matches for firstborns, who can be prickly and self-important, and also lastborns, who can be dramatic and capricious. Some problems arise, however, when an agreeable and conflict-avoiding middle marries another agreeable and conflict-avoiding middle.

From avoiding waves to smooth sailing

Barbara and Doug are both middle children. They've been married for five years, and their friends think they're the perfect couple. Not only do they look as if they just stepped out of the pages of a fashion magazine, but they're always cheerful and energetic. Cindy, their little girl, just turned two years old and started at a little preschool around the corner. Now that the baby's a bit older, Barbara is thinking of going back to work as an editor, at least part time.

But all is not perfect in their household, as one of Barbara's best friends, Leah, knows. On girls' nights when they manage to spend some time together, Barbara confides in Leah that she worries Doug isn't happy about her returning to work—though he doesn't actually say so. In fact, he avoids the discussion as much as possible, and when she tries to approach the topic, he insists, "I'm fine with it!"

Barbara doesn't know how to handle this. In addition, since she brought up the subject, she feels that Doug is taking more overtime at the fire station. Maybe he thinks she wants to go back to work because they need the money, or maybe he's just trying to avoid her so he doesn't have to tell her he wished she'd stay at home. Meanwhile, Leah finds it hard to believe her friend doesn't just sit her husband down and hash it all out.

Since they're in limbo, Barbara hasn't done anything about approaching her old contacts for work. She's frustrated with the situation but unwilling to confront Doug over any of it.

In failing to openly address their individual concerns, Barbara and Doug are doing themselves a disservice: Each has to resort to guessing what the other's real motives and priorities are, and there's little clarity about how to proceed in making important life decisions. The danger is that they will fail to make decisions at all or make them for the wrong reasons because of the lack of transparency in their communications. Facing up to potential disagreement would be much easier than being forced to deal with resentments later, once hopes have been dashed or needs misunderstood.

They suffer from middleborn avoidance syndrome: shunning conflict at the expense of real intimacy.

The solution? Enlist some help

But Barbara and Doug got a lucky break: Their friend, Leah, helped solved their stalemate. She invited them over for dinner and after a few

glasses of cabernet sauvignon, she and her husband broached the subject of kids and work. The look of relief on Barbara's face was immediate, and among friends, Doug had no problem opening up about his
concerns. "I wasn't sure she'd have enough time for me and for Cindy,"
he admitted later. "And I didn't want her to think she *had* to go back
to work for the money." On the other hand, Barbara realized she had
never told Doug how much she loved her job as an editor. "Once he
realized how much that kind of work energizes me, he pretty much
changed his tune. We worked it out, but we definitely needed the ice
breaker." Afterward, they laughed about how many months of silence
had passed between them before they had had the courage to speak
openly to each other. They agreed that from then on they would just
say what they thought. Each trusted that the other was sensitive
enough not to blurt out some knee-jerk reaction.

Since then, Barbara found a part-time position as an editor at a
small weekly paper. Although she doesn't bring in much money once
child-care expenses have been paid, she knows that working outside
the home makes her more efficient and happier when she's with her
family. Now that they try to deal with questions head-on, both say
there's a lot less guesswork between them, and they're clearer about
their boundaries. Barbara wants to have some independence, and
Doug wants to make sure family comes first. Since both understand
the other's motives, it's easier for them to find acceptable compro-
mises.

Although there can be some avoidance of conflict, middleborns do
quite well married to other middleborns—as evidenced by the Israeli
marriage happiness study. On the other hand, if you're a first or a last,
you're most certainly less likely to be happily partnered with someone
of your same birth order. A first plus a first tends to result in two leaders spending a lot of time tussling it out. Lastborns also don't do best
paired with another last because they're both used to getting their own
way, and yet neither wants to take the lead. Onlies, who now represent
a growing proportion of our children, don't do particularly well with
other onlies because both have trouble sharing the spotlight. In addi-

tion, studies of personality indicate onlies are often perfectionists, which makes them very hard on their spouses.

Regardless of which birth order you partner up with, if you're a middle child, you should not be afraid to speak up about *your* concerns or needs. Go ahead and use your agreeable nature to your advantage when it comes to discussing problems with either friends or partners, but don't forget to advocate for yourself.

And if you're married to a middle, make sure to check in often with your spouse to discuss his or her inner thoughts. Your spouse may be keeping quiet about important things. By reciprocating the support and dedication that middleborns so willingly give, you can allow them the leeway to rock that boat when they need to.

BEING A MIDDLE PAYS OFF IN FRIENDSHIP AND LOVE

Middleborns are adaptive personalities, and I believe this is what enables them to establish such healthy reciprocal relationships with nonfamily—making them, in a sense, friendship specialists. "The middleborn child seems to be like type O blood: suitable to all," the authors of the Israeli study concluded. Not only do stable, adaptable middleborns seem to have the best chances of making a marriage work, but they also make dependable, lifelong friends.

On top of this, there are innumerable tangible benefits to enjoying close interpersonal relationships. As you age, you are less likely to suffer cognitive decline when surrounded by friends. One study showed that people actually live longer and happier lives—and are more likely to recover from illness or disability—when they maintain strong social connections. George Burns lived to be a hundred years old and credited his vigor to the energy he got from work and friends. Although Gracie died decades before him, George maintained a connection to her: visiting her graveside, talking about her at every occasion, and never choosing to remarry. At his death he said he looked forward to being joined with her again in heaven.

Middles hold the key to maintaining good relationships, and as long as they understand the most effective way to use it, it's a very valuable key. If they can find a healthy balance between dedication and mindless loyalty, between being agreeable and being a pushover, and between open-mindedness and recklessness, they're good to go. When middleborns recognize the many advantages they enjoy because of their natures, while also being aware of—and thereby avoiding—the potential pitfalls, they open the door to experiencing a multitude of satisfying and long-lasting relationships.

HOW MIDDLE CHILDREN LOVE

1. **Middles choose their own families . . .**
   Middleborns are highly social. Adult middles gain freedom from their entrenched family hierarchy by choosing their own "families." They're dedicated and loyal to their friends and lovers—sometimes to the detriment of their birth families and to themselves.

2. **. . . but need to work on maintaining actual family bonds.**
   Once grown and independent, middles can avoid misunderstandings with family members by staying in closer touch.

3. **In romance, middleborns give but don't always receive.**
   In love relationships, middles are both solid and flexible, making their partners feel safe. But they, too, need love and attention from their partners or they can begin to harbor unnecessary doubts.

4. **Middles need to fight for what's right.**
   Middle children can have trouble drawing the line in the sand with friends and lovers. They should be prepared to stand their ground when an issue is important to them.

5. **Middle children need to negotiate on their own behalf.**
   Although they're great listeners and are very generous, middles will be better off if they recognize when they're being imposed upon and then learn to say no. Using their negotiating skills *on their own behalf* helps them avoid being pushovers.

6. **Partners need to make sure middles talk.**
   Avoiding small conflicts and being flexible has its benefits, but avoiding bigger conflicts can backfire for middleborns. Seeking peace at all costs is dangerous. If you're married to a middle, make sure to check in with your spouse often to discuss his or her concerns. Your spouse may be keeping quiet about important things.

7. **It's okay to ask for what you deserve.**
   Because they are open, middles benefit from a wide variety of friendships, and can frequently accommodate very different—or even difficult—personalities in their romantic liaisons. But being too open-minded in a romantic relationship can lead them to being undervalued. People have the right to ask for reciprocity.

8. **Love meets in the middle.**
   Middleborns are great love matches for firsts and lasts, but when two middles are together, they can have avoidance issues. Learning to speak up about needs and concerns is key to keeping communication smooth.

CHAPTER EIGHT

Parenting a Middle

June Bug Johnson was extremely tall for his age. By seventh grade he had already hit the six-foot mark, and just a couple of years later he was six-foot-five. Early in the mornings and late at night after homework and chores, he could invariably be found on a basketball court in his hometown of Lansing, Michigan. Luckily for him, the "June Bug" nickname didn't stick beyond his childhood. As a fifteen-year-old, Earvin Johnson's skills on the court were so astonishing that he was given the nickname "Magic."

The middle child in a family with eight other children, Johnson didn't get any special treatment just because of his special talents. There were lots of mouths to feed and lots of work to be done. Often, he'd get home at night after practice, and all the food his mother had prepared was already eaten up. His father worked on the assembly line at the local General Motors plant and took on extra jobs at night. His mom was a school custodian. "My parents believed in work—not only for themselves but for their children, too," Johnson wrote in his autobiography. "I washed dishes, took out the trash, vacuumed, cooked, and took care of the twins—although I was only two years older than they were."

Johnson developed an obsession with basketball that his parents and mentors encouraged, but it was always kept within reason. He was expected to follow strict rules: No playing with balls in the house, for instance (instead, he'd throw balled-up socks at a mark on the wall), and school came first. In addition, he was always held accountable: If his father came home at three in the morning to discover his son hadn't shoveled the driveway as he had been told, he'd wake him up and make him do it right then. Although Johnson spent almost every waking moment courtside, his mother insisted he come into the bedroom early in the morning or late at night to tell her exactly where he was going.

Even though his father worked two jobs, he made time to play basketball with his middle child, and he gave his son a good run for his money, never letting him slack off. "Physically, I'm not the most gifted basketball player in the world. I've never been the fastest runner or the highest jumper," Johnson has said. "But thanks to my father, nobody will ever outsmart me on the court."

He was one of many children, but he never felt invisible.

Life gets hectic in families with multiple children, especially when resources are scarce. Numerous studies have documented that the availability of parental resources decreases with the number of children in the home—no surprise, I'm sure, to those with big families.

As I previously pointed out, parental resources are finite: Even when parents of large families have unlimited finances, they rarely have unlimited time for all their offspring. There is often not enough money or time to give each child what the parent thinks the child needs or what the child wants (which can be quite different, naturally). But we see from Magic Johnson's story that there are certain basic principles parents can live by, whether their families are larger or smaller, that help each child develop with good character and useful life skills.

A PARENTAL PICKLE

Parents of middleborns face a bit of a conundrum. In a family where the oldest is walking unfamiliar paths and needs constant guidance, and the youngest demands so much time, how can they give their middleborns enough attention? Every parent frets over whether they're doing a good enough job, and parents of middle children deal with additional guilt: In the chaos of everyday life, it's all too easy to overlook their middleborns.

Katherine, mother of four, says she worries about her secondborn because she's noticed he spends a lot of time alone in his room. "I realized that I praise the older one for his guitar playing all the time, but I never really comment on what Johnny likes. It's almost as if I only *tolerate* his interests." James, a dad of three, put it this way: "I rarely think of my middle child except when I'm feeling guilty for never thinking of her."

But much of that guilt is actually unnecessary.

In this chapter I'll show parents why. I'll help them figure out what they are already doing right and what they might be doing wrong with their middleborns. What are the signs to watch out for, and what are the valuable skills they're instilling in their child without even knowing it? I will answer such questions as these: *What should I do about the fact that my oldest and my youngest are happy to spend vacations with us, but my middle would rather go away with her best friend? Is eight-year-old Sarah too quiet and withdrawn, or just happily independent? Does my fifteen-year-old feel burdened because she has to babysit her little sister all the time, while her older brother gets to pursue his hobbies?*

We have spent much of the book analyzing the positive skills that middle children develop. Now it is time to focus on some of the concerns that parents have while raising these middles. I'll highlight some child-rearing habits that parents of middles should watch out for. For instance, middles tend to spend a lot of time hanging out with friends, and sometimes parents don't feel comfortable insisting on family time. While turning to their peers for the attention they are not getting at home can be a strategy that leads to good skills development, it can also make middle children more vulnerable to peer pressure than other birth orders.

There's no blueprint for raising a middle child, but there are certain red flags to watch out for. In addition, there are areas of concern that are actually *not* as acute as modern parents might think. Our understanding of what constitutes successful parenting is constantly changing, depending on current cultural attitudes and our own values. But, independent of parenting fads, middle children have specific needs that are quite different from the needs of their siblings. We'll be exploring these, too.

With this study of the unique experience of parenting middles, I hope to show parents that they're not doing so wrong by them, as long as they follow certain core parenting principles which I'll highlight. There is no reason that middles shouldn't grow up secure in the knowledge that they are developing skills that will stand them in good stead. And parents can stop worrying so much, while also being aware of the special needs that their middleborns have for such things as encouragement and respect.

WHAT IT'S LIKE RAISING MIDDLE CHILDREN

What parents of middles say

Hugo is the older middle son of four and has been spending all summer in sleepaway camp since he was eight years old. Since his brothers and sister refuse to go away to camp, Hugo's parents sometimes worry about whether he really feels part of their family. Charlotte is a seventeen-year-old middle child who spends every waking minute texting her friends, and she complains bitterly when she's dragged along to family events with her parents. They make strict rules about how often she has to commit to "family time" because they worry they don't know what's really going on in her life. She seems secretive and distant to them. Daniel, a tall and athletic fifteen-year-old middle, refuses to play any competitive sports. "I can't figure out what's going on," complains his father. "It's as though he's doing it just to spite us."

Is there something wrong with these kids or with their families?

Just as with any birth order, middles come in all types. Your experience raising one or more middles might be smooth and joyful, whereas for another parent it's harrowing and fraught with guilt. These differences in experience have multiple roots. Keep the following in mind:

- Middles are born with certain inherent personality traits that affect their relationships with their parents. For instance, home life for a middle with a *glass-half-empty* approach to life will be radically different from home life with a *glass-half-full* middle.
- Children define themselves in contrast to their older siblings. So while one middleborn may be an outgoing and lighthearted athlete, the next middle might be introverted and bookish.
- Adults have different parenting styles and aptitudes. In one family the middle may receive sufficient time and resources to grow up feeling appreciated and secure, whereas in another family the middle children may be virtually ignored and end up feeling less worthy than other siblings.
- Circumstances independent of birth order—such as family trauma or financial stability—can have signifi-

cant impact on the strategies that children develop in childhood. Thus, for example, a middle from a family of divorce might pose different challenges for parents than a middle with an intact family.

What middles say

With my perspective on the many great skills middleborns develop, it's sometimes surprising to me just how frustrated and overlooked many of them feel. Search any number of blogs, and you'll read about how angry middle children are that they're neglected. A common theme is that the firstborn is bossy and spoiled, and the baby is treated with kid gloves. "My parents claim they love me just as much, but I doubt it," writes one middle. "I act like nothing bothers me, but I really hate being a middle." Another girl wrote, "It's horrible. I feel like I have no talents, nothing." At the end of a long discussion about the miseries of being a middle, one boy admitted, "It's hard sometimes, but I think I take things worse than I actually should because I'm so sensitive."

In my everyday experiences with my friends and students, the feelings that grown middle children express about their role in the family vary substantially. While some, like my friend Sally, say unequivocally that they felt unseen and unappreciated, others like Jake, a graduate student, say they liked the freedom of not being scrutinized every second. And in the professional world, adult middle children express a far greater comfort level with their degree of independence than do the younger middles venting on blogs.

So what should parents make of this? Without a doubt, the home environment is crucial to a child's development: Family is the first social group we encounter, and, as such, it's how we learn to perceive ourselves and others. Birth order impacts development in an immediate and powerful way because the more children a family has in close succession, the less time parents commit to each individual child. This in turn leads children to develop niche-picking strategies in order to attract more attention. It's these strategies that can work in their favor if recognized and appreciated.

It is my belief that when middles understand how their family dynamics help them develop excellent life strategies, they'll feel less put upon in the home. Talk to your middle about the experience of being a middle child. Make sure they feel heard. Don't assume that because the middle is quiet that shows either happiness or unhappiness. Ask your middle child how he or she feels. A little acknowledgment goes a long way.

Dynamics in larger families

Few studies break out middle children from laterborns, and even fewer take into consideration age spacing. A seminal 1981 study took both these factors into account. Psychologist Jeannie Kidwell compiled data on 1,700 adolescent boys, positing quite reasonably that the more children in each family, the greater the potential for parental frustration. Kidwell wanted to know how teens in larger families perceived their parents. Did they feel their parents punished them more often or less often depending on the family size? Were they reasonable in explaining rules? Were parents supportive? Kidwell looked at the answers from the perspective of both birth order and spacing between children. From a punitive perspective, having larger families has a twofold impact on children:

- In trying to control their children's behavior, parents become more punitive the more children they have.
- Parents with bigger families have less time, energy, and patience, and therefore are less likely to explain their actions and engage in positive one-on-one interaction with the children.

As one might expect, as the size of a family *increases*, the level of perceived reasonableness and support *decreases*. Relevant to us is the finding that middle children consistently reported more negative perceptions than either the firstborn or the lastborn. "The middleborn child has no uniqueness associated with his position in the sibling structure," Kidwell explained. "The lack of felt supportiveness by his parents apparently reflects this deficit status."

As I discussed earlier, although parents from Western cultures usually share the goal of treating all offspring equally, the reality when seen from the viewpoint of the middle is often quite different. The middle child feels "pushed around" and is convinced the oldest and youngest in the family get special treatment. In addition, Kidwell determined that sibling spacing makes an enormous difference in the level of frustration experienced by middles. The greater the spacing between siblings, the greater the quality of the relationship. The closer the siblings are in age, the more inferior the quality of the parent-adolescent relationship becomes.

Am I advocating that parents have fewer children and increase the length of time between births? Not at all. I believe that families with multiple children can and should recognize the reality of the constraints on their time and patience, and establish various patterns of behavior toward their children—in particular their middles—that will increase their sense of understanding and support, and decrease the sense of frustration and neglect. The bigger the family, the more the middle children are squeezed. This exacerbates the challenges and frustrations they experience. When parents are aware of this dynamic, they can take steps toward diminishing it.

Think back to the environment in which Magic Johnson was raised: a secure and loving home, a sense of responsibility and accountability, and parents who encouraged passions and had fun with their kids. And as we'll see, for middle children the key component to a happy family is not really parental time and investment in and of itself but the particular nature of this investment.

ATTENTION ISN'T ALL IT'S CRACKED UP TO BE

In an effort to produce happy and successful children, today's generation of striving parents often overlook some basic truths:

- We cannot prevent our children from ever experiencing
  failure or danger.
- Failure itself can be instructive.
- "Success" is relative.
- Parental pressure to do well in school does not guaran-
  tee "success" and can, in fact, backfire.
- Passion and authenticity are often better predictors of
  success than grades.
- Having good people skills does not mean never
  disagreeing.

One of the most enduring and destructive parental myths is that
the more attention children receive, the safer, happier, and more successful they will become as adults. Parental instinct is to protect children at all costs—from failure, loneliness, disappointment, fear—and
yet, ultimately, it's a futile endeavor. Let's look at the effects of different
kinds of attention on various birth orders in general and middles in
particular.

"Mom, Dad, you've got to hold my hand!"

Charlotte sat in my office at the University of Redlands with a look
of utter confusion on her face. A first-year student, she was twisting
her cell phone in her fingers and looked as though she hadn't slept a
wink.

"You just have to figure out the first few chemistry classes," I said.
"You can always change the focus later if you realize it's not the right
thing for you." I had already been going back and forth with her for
over half an hour.

"But my mom said I did so bad in Chem 131 last semester that she thinks I should take more bio classes instead."

"What do *you* think, Charlotte?" I asked, a tinge of impatience creeping into my voice. My next advisee was due any moment now, and this year I had a record number to take care of: forty-four.

"I just don't know. I mean, I think I'd really like to take more English classes, but my parents want me to do premed. My mom called my high school chemistry teacher to ask her about it, but she couldn't get through. Can I just have a few more days?"

"You're registering *tomorrow*," I said, sighing. "You can wait, but you'll have a better chance of getting the courses you want if you register as soon as you can."

I was all too familiar with this problem. The year before, one of my students' parents had actually attended an advisory session *with* his child. A couple of years earlier a bright young man had been unable to complete a single conversation with me in my office without checking in with his mother first. Children are so attached to their parents, they come to college and find themselves unable to make decisions without their parents' approval. As young adults entering the "real" world for the first time, they are uncertain and overly dependent. It usually takes them their entire freshman year to wean themselves from the constant support and attention they're accustomed to from home.

Less attention leads to greater independence

Without a doubt all children need nurturing and guidance to become their best selves. Parents must provide an environment in which the child feels safe and loved, and is encouraged to reach his or her potential. But children also need to develop a strong sense of independence. Unless they feel confident that they've developed the skills necessary to make their own good decisions, they'll be haunted by insecurity.

One indicator of middle children's independent spirit is their relative financial independence as young adults. Who do middles turn to if they're in financial trouble? A study of seventeen- to thirty-five-year-olds shows that 87 percent of firstborns and 81 percent of lastborns would turn to their parents first for financial help, compared to only 63 percent of middles. Another study that focused on college students reveals that a higher percentage of middleborns say they receive no parental assistance with their college expenses at all—indicating a high level of self-sufficiency.

In his book *Ready or Not, Here Life Comes*, psychologist Mel Levine says that raising children who'll be successful adults is all about mixing and balancing elemental behaviors such as discipline and freedom, parental intervention and self-help, and free play and programming. So what happens when your parents are too busy or distracted to shower you with attention, such as is often the case with middle children? You learn greater self-sufficiency. You use your imagination. You come to understand that life is not always fair. In many ways you become better prepared to navigate the adult world. "The more we pour ourselves, our talents, concerns, and aspirations into our children, the less room they have to develop their own talents, concerns, and aspirations," says Madeline Levine, author of *The Price of Privilege*. "Overinvolved parents are clipping their children's wings."

Middles don't get much, don't expect much, and end up being asked to give a lot. They're asked to wait, to help with the baby, and to pick up the slack when the younger one is too inept or the older one is too busy with more important tasks such as homework. Many middles feel their parents demand less of them than others in the family, and although in some senses this is a slight, it also means they are ultimately freer to follow their own paths as they mature into adulthood.

Many of today's parents are admirably dedicated to the act of parenting, but here are just a few examples of the behaviors some overzealous parents exhibit that seem to be doing their children more harm than good:

Table 5. FALLOUT FROM OVERPARENTING

Action	Result
American college administrators say baby boomer parents are so intent on removing obstacles from their child's path, that they've nicknamed them "lawnmower parents."	Young adults don't learn resilience, negotiation, or creative thinking. They fail to develop important social skills.
High school teachers report being afraid to give poor grades for poor performance for fear of angry recriminations from parents.	Kids don't have to face the consequences of their action or their inaction, and don't learn from their mistakes.
Coaches report that the parents' level of intensity of involvement in their children's sports has increased phenomenally in the past two decades.	Athletic teens sometimes rebel and quit their sport altogether. They experience burnout and report feeling "trapped."

Books such as *Positive Pushing* by James Taylor suggest that when parents are too protective, it inhibits emotional maturity. This psychological vulnerability makes them less well equipped to deal with the obstacles and setbacks they'll inevitably have to face in adult life.

As we have already seen, middles get less time, attention, and resources from their parents, and they often suffer from this. But this suffering seems to be short-lived. As is abundantly clear, this lack of attention can lead to the development of some extremely useful skills, as attested by the earlier chapters on negotiation, trailblazing, and justice-seeking. Coupled with an understanding that an excess of attention can actually be harmful to children, parents of middles can rest assured that no child profits from a free-for-all, but any child can profit from a little benign neglect.

But is there negative fallout for middles?

When *The Psychology of Self-Esteem* was published in 1969, it changed the way parents approached their children's accomplishments for decades to come. Its author, Nathaniel Brandon, asserted that self-esteem was the single most crucial element of an individual's being. It was accepted back then that self-esteem, praise, and performance all rose and fell together, and so parents and educators entered the age where everything a child produced—be it artwork, a science paper, or simply their handwriting—was greeted with excessive praise: "Great job, kiddo!"

A number of studies have looked at the relationship between birth order and self-esteem; the most informative for us is, again, the work of Jeannie Kidwell. She found that school-age middleborns did indeed have lower self-esteem than firstborns or lastborns. She attributed (correctly, I believe) middleborns' low self-esteem to their self-perceived lack of uniqueness in the family: *There's the responsible firstborn, and there's the pampered baby . . . so who am I supposed to be?* This, in combination with the fact that middles generally receive less time and attention from parents, seems to lead to a decreased sense of worth.

Obviously, it's preferable to have healthy self-esteem than low self-esteem. Oftentimes, firsts and lasts (but especially lasts) get the extra praise that pumps up self-esteem even when they haven't done that much to earn it. Middles usually have to work hard for the praise they get. Contrary to what many parents believe, however—and what motivates them to hover over their children, showering them with unearned praise—high self-esteem does not actually correlate with success, as the book *NurtureShock* reveals. Authors Po Bronson and Ashley Merryman analyzed multiple recent studies and discovered that when a child has high self-esteem, it doesn't go hand in hand with improved grades or career achievement, nor does it reduce alcohol usage or violence. They also conclude that "excessive praise distorts motivation" and leads to an inability to deal with failure and develop persistence.

Just as all praise is not equal, all attention is not equal, either. If parents can give their middle children enough attention at the right time and in the right way, those middles will develop into individuals with a strong sense of self, good motivation and persistence, and "good enough" self-esteem. And what does good enough really mean? It's when an individual has a strong enough sense of self-assurance that he or she can weather failures and endure unrelenting hard work without feeling gypped or deflated.

THE MOST COMMON CONCERNS FOR PARENTS OF MIDDLES

Since we have spent considerable time focusing on what's right with middle children, let's turn our attention to the specific concerns that middles raise for their parents. In my own experience and through my research, I've narrowed down these concerns to five basic areas. I believe these can each be successfully addressed so that middles feel better understood and loved at home, and can enjoy their adolescence as well as benefit from it, as Magic Johnson so famously did.

1. "My middle child *never* wants to be without her friends. What's wrong?"

It was Friday night, and the Smiths planned on having a family dinner. It had been a hectic fall, and they wanted to spend some quiet time talking about the school year with their three kids: John, seventeen; Meg, sixteen; and Kyle, thirteen. As usual, Meg was nowhere to be found. She seemed to disappear constantly; either she was in her room talking to friends on her cell phone, or she was over at a friend's house doing homework, whipping up some cooking project, or checking on Facebook.

Despite the age gap, the two boys were good buddies and spent a lot more time with their parents than Meg. Her mom, Amanda, had started to worry that Meg was depressed because she acted as though she was avoiding her parents or hiding something from them. Amanda tried to remember when all of them had last spent a weekend night together, but she couldn't. In fact, the last time Meg had really given her family any attention was during their summer vacation when they were up at the lake for a week.

The experience of the Smiths is typical for many families with three or more children. Middles are social beings. At home they may seem quiet or disinterested, but with their friends they feel free to be themselves, and so they often prefer to be with their friends. In one of my first studies on middles back in 1998, I found out just how much they value their friends. I was analyzing the effect of political rhetoric on different birth orders by seeing what kind of terminology most influenced them. Politicians use what they hope are evocative terms to gain loyalty and trust, and I wanted to see where susceptibilities lie for the different birth orders. When making judgments, whose authority and messaging are they most influenced by?

Two hypotheses were being examined. First, I believed kin terms would be more effective than more distant relationship terms (such as "friend") in evoking a positive response, and, second, I thought middleborns would be less likely to respond to such kin term usage than first or lastborns. I presented three political speeches to my subjects. One used kin terms such as "brother can you spare a dime"; one used terms such as "my friends"; and the other used terms of citizenship, such as "my fellow citizens."

The middleborn response to the family terminology speech was very low (just like the response of firsts and lasts to the citizen speech). This means that familial authority doesn't sit well with middles. They are less likely to be influenced by appeals from authority figures and more likely to listen to their peers, whom they see as sharing their interests or agendas.

But is this reliance on friends good in the long run, or does it create potential problems where peer pressure is concerned? And should parents like Amanda insist on family time, one-on-one time, or allow their middles to withdraw, slowly but surely, from family life if that's their inclination?

How worrisome is peer pressure, really?

Anyone who has seen the 2003 film *Thirteen* is familiar with the abject horror that a parent feels when their impressionable, sweet-natured child makes a friend or joins a clique that leads the child down the perilous path of teenage rebellion. Countless movies, books, and real-life stories bemoan the lack of influence that parents have on their children. "The idea that we can make our children turn out the way we want is an illusion," says author Judith Rich Harris. "Give it up."

Harris's 1998 book, *The Nurture Assumption*, directly challenged the long-held belief that parental influence outweighs that of peers. Sigmund Freud made famous the notion that for adults to achieve happiness and clarity, they must first overcome the long-lasting and often crushing influence of their parents. Psychoanalytical theory embraced this viewpoint for decades. Harris contends, however, that researchers have in actuality not been able to find any causal links between specific social conditions in a child's environment, as created by the parents, and the kind of adult that a child becomes.

This is a radical and deeply unsettling idea for parents. If Harris's conclusion means that in the grand scheme of things parenting practices have negligible impact on children, then outside influences such as peers are even *more* influential than previously thought. So does this mean that how children turn out depends more on who they hang out with than who their parents are? According to Harris, children "are not yours to perfect or to ruin: they belong to tomorrow."

Clearly, when the parental relationship is not highly valued but friends are, the risk of being led astray is far greater than when authority figures are prime influences. A 2006 study in the *Journal of Economic Inquiry* using a huge pool of data to look at risk taking in adolescence sought to determine what the main causes were for youngsters engaging in such behavior as smoking, drinking, using marijuana, sexual activity, and crime. Was it the desire to be different? To be at the center of attention? Or was it peer pressure?

Looking at the results from the perspective of birth order revealed that middles and lasts were more likely than firsts to push boundaries by engaging in risky behavior. What's particularly pertinent here is that laterborn children had more sex and smoked more cigarettes than firsts. These two activities are associated with social behavior, and so perhaps it's not surprising that middles would be open to indulging in them. (Alcohol and pot come next on the list, but those are illegal and harder to get hold of.) The effect was also stronger in lastborns than middles, though it was significant for both.

We have already talked about the fact that middles are more willing to take risks than firsts, and in this case we can see that social activities which are risky but have a potential social upside for the participant are more attractive to those birth orders who highly value peer acceptance.

The researchers believed this tendency to break rules was largely due to the fact that laterborns are exposed to this kind of behavior through their older sibling(s), but that doesn't ring quite true to me. This assumption wasn't proven, as there was no data presented on whether or not the older siblings modeled this kind of risky behavior. In fact, typically in studies firstborns score lower on risk-taking behavior inventories as well as sensation seeking. Laterborns, on the other hand, are more predisposed to try new activities and take risks, so they score higher. Since we know they are more influenced by peers than firsts are, when these kinds of activities are suggested by friends, it is the laterborns who are more likely to be swayed than firstborns.

But there's another important consideration to keep in mind: It's highly valuable for children to be accepted by their own age group, and in and of itself, it's not bad to have lots of friends or even to prefer friends to family. Children who are left out, have few friends, or are bullied suffer deep emotional scars that carry over into adulthood. A 1968 study on peer acceptance and rejection found that children with low peer acceptance were nearly twice as likely to commit delinquent offenses than those who are more popular, while a 1987 study on peer relations and personal adjustment concluded that children with poor peer adjustment (especially those who also have aggression issues) are at risk for dropping out and engaging in criminal behavior.

This is a problem most middles are unlikely to encounter. Middle-borns tend to score exceptionally high in peer acceptance. A 1992 review of birth order research reported on several studies that indicated that among younger children, middles were represented in leadership positions more frequently and scored higher in popularity among their schoolmates than firstborns.

What parents can do about peer pressure

In the argument about peer vs. parental influence, I come out somewhere in the middle. There's a great deal of recent research suggesting that the way children view the world is strongly influenced by the environment they grow up in. Since individual tastes and personalities are formed when children are quite young—before the age of five—the influence of parents is vital. Child-parent relationships will influence the number and quality of social ties outside the home and the importance of peers to a child's sense of self.

In addition to a child's choice of social group, other elements are critical to development. Some of these are as follows:

- *Genes*: Certain skills, gifts, and challenges (such as dyslexia or ADD) are intrinsic to an individual.
- *Parenting style*: Abundant research and literature confirm the importance of certain parenting principles such as warmth, consistency, and accountability.
- *Number of children*: A child in a family of one will have a radically different experience of childhood than a child in a larger family.
- *Gender*: The expectations for girls and boys are often different, as are their behaviors and styles of communication.

Children don't pick their families but do pick their friends and social group. For middle children who tend to be greater risk takers than firsts, they might well gravitate to a crowd that enjoys pushing the envelope. Since they value friendship more highly than other birth orders (including lasts), this could mean that they engage in risky behavior simply because they don't want to disappoint their friends by saying no. They're more likely to get themselves in trouble—shoplifting or experimenting with drugs or alcohol, for instance—as a result of having friends that encourage such behavior.

But accepting that your middle is a social animal does not mean that you must accept lack of control over those they spend time with. Paying attention to their friends, allowing them to bring their friends home, and becoming acquainted with the parents of their friends will all help bring back some measure of control. From an early age onward, encouraging them to recognize their own feelings and opinions as valid and to act on their instincts (rather than what they think *others* want) will help them say no when it's important—whether it's when friends ask too much of them or when they are presented with an activity they would rather not participate in.

Table 6. STRATEGIES FOR PARENTS

Examples of Typical Middle Child Behavior	Parental Strategies
"John is never home—he's always at his friend's house."	• Create an environment at home where your middle and his/her friends like to hang out. • Offer opportunities to meet their friends (pizza nights, movies, skating party). • Recognize that hanging with friends has its benefits (and that being a loner isn't necessarily better).
"Jane is on Facebook *all the time*!"	• Create and enforce limits; be consistent. • Recognize the positives: In modern life there is not as much of a natural social community. Social media can create a valuable sense of belonging.

Examples of Typical Middle Child Behavior	Parental Strategies
"Susie never wants to go on vacation with us."	• Allow them to skip one vacation (maybe they could go away to camp or stay with a friend instead). • Tell them they can invite a friend along with you on vacation. • Listen, sympathize, and yet stay *firm*.

2. "I feel as if I don't even know my own kid!"

Martha was tired of hearing all about her son from his best friend's mother. "We'd be on the phone to arrange a pickup time after band practice," she explained, "and I'd get a comment like '*That's so cute about Jay's girlfriend! How long have they been together?*' And I'd think, 'What on earth are you talking about?!'" This kind of thing happened so often that Martha started paying closer attention to how much her kids shared with her. "I realized that Jay never tells me *anything*. And I don't know what to do about it." And yet with his friend's mother Jay was far from secretive or withdrawn; he was downright loquacious.

Along with their strong desire to be part of a peer group, middles also often exhibit a tendency to be chameleons. It's in their nature to be open to experience and flexible, and they like everyone they're with to be comfortable and get along. As a result, it's often easier for them to change at a superficial level in order to make others (and, by extension, themselves) more comfortable. They also have a strong desire to be part of the group; this chameleon behavior helps them fit in and understand others better by walking in their shoes.

Middles often reveal different personalities to their friends and teachers than to their parents at home. One mother, Sue, was at a school conference with her five-year-old middle daughter's kindergarten teachers and made a throwaway comment like, "Oh, well, you know what Gretchen's like! She's a lot to handle!" The teachers returned a blank look. "I paused for a moment and then started to explain," Sue said. "The Gretchen that I knew was nothing like the Gretchen they knew. At home she was always getting into scrapes, insisting on having things her way, and being loud and impulsive. But in school, she was compliant and sweet."

Table 7. STRATEGIES FOR PARENTS

Examples of Typical Middle Child Behavior	Parental Strategies
"She seems like such a different person to me than to others."	• Understand that this is a result of their flexibility and social awareness, not a negative commentary on their relationship with you. • Talk to teachers and friends to be sure you get insights into your middle's varying modes of being.
"I can't get Sasha to talk to me."	• Don't force the issue but be persistently encouraging and open. • Find ways to spend more time one-on-one. • Share your own personal stories without expecting anything in return. • Be willing to draw them out by being open about what you think they're feeling. • Try not to compare your middle to older or younger siblings or friends. If they're not feeling compartmentalized, they may be more willing to share.

Middles are often thought of as secretive, but what they're really doing is assuring themselves access to various people by changing their behavior to fit in well with whatever group they are associating with. Since middles do change their behavior depending on who they're with, researchers can have a hard time pinning them down, which is one of the reasons there's been so little research on middles as a distinct birth order group.

Having said that, parents do often complain that middles appear mysterious to them, and parents find this disconcerting. Here are some examples of what middles may be thinking but not sharing with you, and what you can do about it:

Table 8. STRATEGIES FOR PARENTS

What Middles May Be Thinking	What Parents Can Do About It
"I'm always bossed around by my parents and older brother/sister."	• Give them a chance to make decisions. • Ask their opinion often. • When with the entire family, allow middles to take the lead sometimes.
"The baby gets away with *everything!*"	• Make sure to hold your youngest accountable. • Acknowledge how you treat the baby of the family. Honesty helps avoid misunderstandings.
"Do I really measure up? Am I good at anything?"	• Make sure you take pictures of your middles for albums and to hang around the house. • Praise them for something specific they have worked hard on or achieved. • Make an effort not to give more praise to the older or younger siblings.
"I definitely don't want to try that. I might fail."	• Teach all children that failure can be a helpful learning process. • Reward effort, not just results. • Share stories about risks you took—both risks that panned out and those that didn't.

What Middles May Be Thinking	What Parents Can Do About It
"I can't ever say how I *really* feel, so sometimes I want to explode."	• Create a home environment in which it's okay to talk about feelings. • Ask open-ended questions such as "Anything on your mind?" • If your middle does explode, wait until it's over and then take time to calmly discuss how it happened.
"I feel discouraged so often."	• Help them see projects through by being encouraging and interested. • Praise the value of persistence frequently. • Model how hard work can lead to success. • Make a point of praising a finished *effort* no matter how "good" the final product is.

3. "My middleborn's focus keeps changing! It's driving me crazy."

While middles often end up feeling passionate about the work or hobbies they choose to participate in, it can take them a while to commit to one area of focus. This happens for a number of reasons.

First, middle children are choosing what they want to do compared to what their older sibling has already chosen for him or herself. In a sense they have less choice—or at least their choices are more complicated—because the firstborn has already carved out a niche and the secondborn has to react to that. Middles consequently have to strategize more, and this can mean making mistakes or taking circuitous routes in order to end up in the right place.

Second, since middles are inclined to try new things, it's easy for them to feel drawn to an activity or pursuit that seems interesting only to discover it's not really suitable for them after all. They're then willing to move on and try something new. Danielle, mother of three, explained that her middle son, Joe, had run through every spring sport (lacrosse, rowing, baseball) until finally, in high school, he decided on tennis. "We thought he was flaky," she said, "until we understood he was just testing things out until he figured out what really suited him best."

To parents it can seem that their child is not committed (or, even worse, unreliable and erratic) when in fact, their middle is simply trying on different hats. In many ways this tendency is actually beneficial to middles in the long run. When the desire for achievement comes from inner rather than outer sources of motivation, people are much more successful. For middles, realizing that they can figure out their own path increases their sense of self-worth, and it's more likely they'll be truly invested in what they do finally settle on.

Researchers on teaching practices in schools note that the link between motivation and achievement is all-important when determining what makes a student thrive. When learning is valued as an end in and of itself, it leads to feelings of efficiency, achievement, and curiosity. Since middles seem to be more motivated by the desire to master a lesson or class than to curry favor, they stand to benefit from the desire to learn and achieve for its own sake.

Parents can encourage their middles to try things and give them the support they need to become invested in the activities of their choice.

Table 9. STRATEGIES FOR PARENTS

Examples of Typical Middle Child Behavior	Parental Strategies
"Lily can't commit herself to anything."	• Recognize that for middles it can take time to figure themselves out. • Give them enough breathing space so they can determine their area of expertise. • Let them try different things. Failure can be a constructive learning experience. • Know that they'll find their passion eventually.

4. "My middle lets her friends walk all over her. She hates all conflict."

This is a concern I addressed in a previous chapter, but it's worth looking at again since parents are rightfully worried about bullying and are aware of the damage that can be done if their children's friendships are imbalanced.

Middle children are dedicated to their friends, loyal, and generous. Studies on gift-giving have shown this. While these are all positive qualities, this also means that they can allow themselves to be taken advantage of. Because middles dislike conflict and often avoid it, they would rather agree to something that makes them uncomfortable than make a fuss about it. It's not uncommon for middle children to go to extreme lengths to accommodate friends or neglect to stand up for themselves in situations such as disagreements with teachers or friends. Middles themselves often don't see this dynamic at play, whereas parents do.

The real question here is how much parents can or should interfere. Figuring out for oneself the skills necessary to navigate relationships—whether socially or at work—is critical to the development of a mature and confident attitude. But there are times when adults do need to step in and help their children understand what's really going on and give them tips on what steps to take. Since middles value their friendships so highly, they worry about losing friends and may need a gentle push from parents to fully understand the negative consequences of passive behavior. The key is not to attack the friends (which will make middles defensive) and not to attack the middle's approach (which will *also* make them defensive!). The best way to impact your child's behavior in these situations is usually tangentially: by telling stories of your own experiences or enlisting a close friend or relative to open up the topic with your child.

There's one critical factor that parents must take note of: When middles do cry out for help, they're not crying wolf. A study conducted at the Virginia Institute of Psychiatric and Behavioral Genetics looked at suicidal behavior in adolescents. Researchers asked questions relating to conflict with mothers, suicide attempts, thoughts of suicide, and depression. Almost two thousand teens with at least two or more siblings participated. Results showed that while middle children are only one quarter as likely to make a suicide attempt than firsts or lasts, this attempt was eight and a half times as likely to need medical intervention. We see from this that even though middles are less likely to take drastic measures to capture their parents' attention, when they do, they're really serious about it.

We can learn two lessons from this data: When middles are dissatisfied, they're not very likely to engage in dramatic attention-seeking behavior. Parents therefore need to watch out for small signs that could be red flags. Their middles are not going to pipe up every time they're feeling oppressed. And when middleborns are struggling with serious issues, they're apt to make a more forceful cry for help than their older or younger siblings would. When they decide they need help, they really go for it. Try not to ignore the red flag when the middle child is waving it in your face.

Table 10. STRATEGIES FOR PARENTS

Examples of Typical Middle Child Behavior	Parental Strategies
"Davis is always doing favors for others."	• Give your children various "scripts" to help them vocalize their own priorities/needs. • Remind them to first consider what *they* want or need. • Praise their patience and selflessness.
"Jana lets her friends decide everything."	• Offer your child ideas on how to engage friends on his/ her own terms. • Don't criticize friends directly; this will turn middles off. Rather, tell related stories that middles can interpret for themselves.

Examples of Typical Middle Child Behavior	Parental Strategies
"Sam won't go to the teacher/his friend to deal with a thorny issue."	• Remind them that people are generally forgiving. • Give examples of when conflict resolution is really helpful. • Praise them for their people skills. • Step in and model conflict skills when necessary.

5. "My middle child is so hard on himself; he just thinks he's useless."

Magic Johnson pushed himself hard, never feeling he was quite good enough, and for him this led to great achievements. But some middles are so critical of themselves that it inhibits rather than encourages their personal growth. It's easy to become discouraged when you're constantly comparing yourself unfavorably to others.

Middles have a strong desire to be successful. A Swedish survey published in 2010 asked firsts, middles, and lasts how much they cared about being "successful" at work compared to their parents, their friends, and their siblings. Middle children cared the least of all birth orders about being more successful than their own parents. (This is not very surprising because they're not as dependent on their parents as their other siblings are.) When it came to middles, however, they:

- cared *most* of all birth orders about being more successful at work than their siblings;
- cared *most* about earning "no less money" than their friends and their siblings;
- cared *a lot less* than firsts (but marginally more than lasts) about being more successful at work than their friends.

Researchers concluded that the more parents compare their children to one another, the more competitive siblings will be in respect to one another. "This might in turn affect educational and work-related choices," the authors explained, "as well as how people as adults deal with comparisons to others."

Middles want to match up to others, and this can put additional pressure on them. Just as the first wants to please parents and adults, middles are driven to prove themselves in comparison to their peers (friends and siblings). This is not inherently a negative, but parents should be aware of their middles' tendency to be hard on themselves and offer a lot of encouragement in response. Also, overtly making comparisons between children in front of them is likely to have a deleterious effect on your middle's psychological well-being.

Table 11. STRATEGIES FOR PARENTS

Examples of Typical Middle Child Behavior	Parental Strategies
"Lily is always comparing herself harshly to her siblings and friends."	• Never compare middle children to their siblings. • Take the time to point out their strengths. • Praise effort over talent. • Make them feel they're at the center of attention. (For example, don't always insist on hand-me-downs!)

GET TO KNOW YOUR MIDDLE CHILD

As a young athlete who needed a lot of physical and psychological nourishment, Magic Johnson by no means got all the attention he could have used to help him on his path to stardom. His parents had little money and even less time. But as one middle child in a pack of many, Johnson made do with what he was given—and that turned out to be plenty. Why? Because his parents managed to make him feel cherished. Despite the lack of time and money, they created a secure and supportive environment, insisted on responsibility and work, held their kids accountable, encouraged individual interests, and also had fun together.

Johnson learned the importance of persistence and practice, spending early mornings and late nights courtside, honing his skills. His parents taught him to be accountable and to show respect—so he understood that hard work and desire, not talent alone, lead to success. Johnson's mother and father passed down their own values to this middle child, embedding in him a sense of responsibility for his community as well as frugality. (He bought his $7 million home in Beverly Hills with cash.) Johnson had a stellar career in professional basketball but also later invested in downtrodden inner-city areas, operating his business in ninety-one cities and twenty-four states. He employed thirty thousand minorities and amassed a fortune of over $500 million. As one child of many, he did not feel relegated to the sidelines but, rather, saw himself as a useful and appreciated member of the family.

Parents have inordinate responsibilities, and the burden can be heavy at times. But keeping in mind the big picture—the desire to instill values and teach children to embrace challenges with poise and flexibility—helps parents operate with greater confidence. With any child, one of the key lessons one learns early on is to pick your battles. Since we know middle children's areas of weakness lie in their self-judgment, their perceived lack of warmth from parents, and their sometimes too-close ties to their peer group, parents need to be especially sensitive to building a distinctive relationship with their middles. Rather than focusing on being perfect or carving out unlimited time for the forgotten middleborn, parents can reap great benefits by acknowledging their middle's unique needs. Instead of fighting against their natures, parents can embrace them for who they are. They are likely to end up as positive and engaged members of society.

BEING A MOM OR DAD OF A MIDDLE

1. **Attention isn't everything.**

   Parental attention is not always the linchpin on which a kid's success turns. Independence is a critical skill, and dependence can be debilitating. So while middles have a valid point when they claim they get less attention than other siblings, this lack of attention is not always negative.

2. **Having a social life is good . . . mostly.**

   Although peer pressure is a concern with middles, peer skills and social success are also very important. (Parents should be sure to encourage these aspects in their other children, too.)

3. **Take a closer look at your middle.**

   Spending time alone with your middle child periodically will help you gain insight into how the child operates. Take him or her out for breakfast or book shopping, or drive him or her alone to a playdate.

4. **Ask questions to open up a quiet child.**

   Most often middles are not being secretive but are simply quiet. Make time to draw them out. Talk with your middle child about the experience of being a middle. Ask her how she feels.

5. **Reward your middleborn.**

   Middle children seek recognition for their efforts, yet feel they don't get adequate attention from their parents. When your middle child has achieved something, make a sign, plaque, or banner in his honor. Celebrate his achievement vocally and allow the child ownership over those achievements.

6. **Watch out for signs of danger.**

   Middles don't often seek to grab parental attention in dramatic or alarming ways. When your middle does this, be aware that it's a red flag.

7. **Make your middleborn the boss.**

   To even out inadvertent inequities in how you treat your children, give your middle the chance to take control and make decisions every now and then. *Where do you want to go for dinner? What movie would you like to see? Which card game do you want to play?*

8. **Compliments are key.**

   Middles often put a lot of pressure on themselves, and this can reveal itself in different ways—by overachieving or underachieving, for example. Once middle children understand that their tendency to be self-critical is not productive, they often come to recognize their unique qualities. Share positives with your middle child, and he or she will blossom.

CHAPTER NINE

Middle Children as Parents

When she died, she was mourned the world over—despite the fact that she could be polarizing, elitist, and fodder for the tabloids. She gave the world plenty to gossip about. But this middle child left an enduringly positive legacy in her two children and thereby ultimately became defined not so much by the drama of her life but by her warm and deeply personal parenting style.

What comes to mind when one hears the name Diana, Princess of Wales? A swoop of blond hair. A svelte figure. A disarming but at times uncertain smile. In a culture known for its buttoned-up style, she was a woman who wore her heart on her sleeve. When Diana Spencer, just twenty years old, married into the British royal family, she quickly became everyone's favorite princess.

Diana had two older sisters, Sarah and Jane. When her mother was pregnant for the third time, her parents desperately hoped for a boy and an heir, but it was not to be at that time. Her little brother, Charles, was finally born a few years after Diana. As the only boy in the family, Charles Althorp would inherit his family's fourteen-thousand-acre estate north of London. Diana was squeezed in the middle, not only as the third girl overshadowed by the sole heir, but also as a child of divorce. Initially shuttled between two households, she was sent away to boarding school at age nine.

Known as a stubborn yet kind girl, Diana became a stubborn yet kind parent, too. She defied royal convention by having her baby, William, accompany her on a state tour of Australia and New Zealand. Then she insisted on taking a lead role in making decisions regarding her children: She chose their nannies and decided on their clothing. Each day she adjusted her schedule around her children's needs rather than the other way around. Whenever she could, she took them to school in the morning and tucked them into bed at night. When it came time to send them to boarding school, she decided Gordonstoun was not appropriate for them, whereas Eton was. While all this angered the royal family, it endeared her to the British people because in matters of family life, she wasn't afraid to operate in her children's best interests.

We tend to think of the British royalty as somewhat coldhearted, but Diana defied that convention with her compassion and dedication to her two boys. At the tenth anniversary of her death, Prince Harry said of his mother: "She never once allowed her unfaltering love for us to go unspoken or undemonstrated." In spite of having questionable role models, this middleborn child made parenting a priority and left her children with a strong sense of familial love and security even though she died when they were still just young boys.

FAMILY TIES

While Diana was clearly no saint, she's an excellent example of how middle children enthusiastically embrace parenthood. She embodied many of the positive qualities that middles develop (sociability, dedication to causes, and the ability to relate to different types of people), while also exhibiting some of the negative ones (such as insecurity about her role in society). These core elements of a middle's character certainly impacted her parenting style and are a useful starting point in our exploration of a chronically underanalyzed aspect of the lives of middles in general—namely, how they parent their own children.

One of the very first popular books on birth order written in the 1970s, *The Birth Order Factor*, suggests that middles are flexible and confident parents compared to only children, who are often disinterested or ambivalent about having kids. It suggested that middles typically want to have children, and since they've had experience parenting younger siblings, they find parenting duties less onerous. As we'll investigate further, the unique characteristics that middles bring to the table often make them more relaxed and well balanced as parents— able to enjoy the ride without stressing every detail, and not so intent on their own needs that they resent those of their children. But new research has uncovered some unexpected facts as well, and we'll explore these in depth.

MIDDLES' CHOSEN FAMILIES

It's perhaps not surprising, given that middleborns tend to get short shrift, that so little is known about how they parent their own children. To date there has been virtually no research in this area. So in order to test my hypothesis that middles are eager to start their own families and are generally devoted parents, I recently conducted two groundbreaking studies.

Almost three hundred parents participated in the first study.

While the number of onlies represented was very small, about 30 percent of respondents were firsts, almost 40 percent were middles, and 20 percent were lasts. (It is worth noting, too, that many middles identified themselves in the "others" category before stipulating in the comments that they were child number three out of five or number four out of six, thereby revealing that, even in adulthood, middles often remain uncertain about exactly how to classify themselves.)

In order to get a more objective take on parenting styles, I asked individuals to fill out the questionnaire both for themselves and for the other parent (if there was one). Typically in surveys, when asked to assess one's own nature and actions, respondents tend to present themselves favorably; they are uncomfortable revealing behavior that is deemed socially undesirable. In spousal or peer reporting, there tends to be more truth telling, and this can make for more honest revelations.

In addition, participants were given the opportunity to add comments and qualifiers to each question. Middleborns left three times as many comments as lasts and almost twice as many as firsts. In and of itself, this was fascinating to me: Clearly middles are more interested in defending and explaining their parenting practices than other birth orders. A follow-up study was then conducted with *only* middle child participants, and this provided a wealth of valuable anecdotal detail to flesh out the data from the first survey.

Middles welcome parenthood

"I used to want to have twenty kids," wrote Susan. "I started babysitting in fifth grade. Always loved kids. Having kids was my ultimate goal in life." It is not surprising, then, that the majority of middleborns responding to my survey had three or more children. Forty percent had three children, 15 percent had four, and 8 percent had five or more children. One mom, Charlotte, explained: "I grew up in a family with three children, and our house was always filled with friends and lots of chaos. I had a friend who was an only child, and her house seemed so quiet and lonely." Meanwhile, Deanna began with a smaller family, only to realize while in the thick of child rearing that she would prefer a different model after all: "I started out thinking two would be plenty, but when it was just the four of us at a holiday dinner, I knew something was missing and convinced my husband we needed one more."

Since middles often come from families with lots of siblings, they seek to give a similar feeling of family warmth and liveliness to their own kids by having multiple children. If they harbored resentment of their own siblings, you'd certainly find more middles choosing to have smaller families. Yet many studies point to the fact that despite a somewhat distant relationship with their parents, middles form tight and long-lasting bonds with their brothers and sisters.

The answers to the question about whether these middles had always wanted their own families and how important they considered parenthood were overwhelmingly positive: 99 percent said they had always expected to have children when they grew up. "I wanted to be a mum ever since I can remember. It never crossed my mind that I'd never be a mother—it was only a case of when, as I was picky about who'd be their father," explained Lisa.

We've already established that middleborns typically don't feel very close to their own parents, so it's a bit unexpected that they become such enthusiastic parents themselves. According to counseling reports and life satisfaction studies, middles are devoted to their children, often desire to have large families, and report being very satisfied with being parents. Research also corroborates that middle children tend to welcome the responsibilities of parenthood with open arms.

Parenting is a worthy challenge

She commands up to $25 million per movie. Traveling around the world for her career, she loves nothing more than to snuggle up with her three children. She's a homebody who has avowed to reporters that she'd love to have nine little ones running around the house. Julia Roberts may have serious Hollywood clout, but this middle child is most comfortable in her sweatsuit, taking her kids to school in the mornings.

In my *Middles as Parents* survey, 90 percent of participants said that being a parent was very important to them, if not *the* most important work they could pursue.

During these last few decades, balancing work with family life has become a serious concern for many modern women. In the past, most women worked at home—and even back when they were hunters and gatherers, they carried their children with them. It's hardly surprising, therefore, that modern women are conflicted about the current home dynamic, because it's so heavily impacted by their outside work. Middleborn moms are no different.

On the other side of the gender coin, men love being fathers because they see it as an achievement in and of itself even if they're not hands-on at home. Increasingly, men are shifting *away* from a work-focused life in order to embrace the many aspects of family life more completely. But even so, male middles with children may be more involved in parenting than most. When asked about his priorities, Jonathan, a middle-age banker (and middleborn) said, "Fatherhood has been the crowning achievement of my life, along with a successful marriage." This is a feeling many middles share.

In my study I posed a question about what middles needed in order to feel personally fulfilled, and I saw an unexpected pattern in the answers. Many middleborns explained that they believe being in a healthy relationship is as crucial to their sense of success and happiness as parenting is. "I think that being a supportive partner to my husband is equally important as my role as a parent," wrote Jane. "I do frequently wonder how parenting decisions that I have made will affect my children when they are older. I feel a greater sense of 'personal fulfillment' when I am confident with parenting choices that I have made."

We've seen that middles make loyal friends and partners, and this comes through in their feelings about family life, too. Dedicated to their children, middles are aware that stable, happy partnerships make for good parenting; it's about providing strong role models for healthy relationships. "The coolest thing you can do for your children," Julia Roberts has said, "is to love each other in their presence. I'm the luckiest girl in town. I really am."

Although Lady Diana's marriage failed, in her case we see a historically neglected middle child determined not to neglect her own children. She made them a priority despite having other pressing responsibilities. The level of dedication she showed to her two boys was previously unknown in the British royal family—so much so that after Lady Diana's separation from Prince Charles, a nanny of Princes William and Harry commented disdainfully, "I give them [the children] what they need at this stage, fresh air, a rifle, and a horse. She [Diana] gives them a tennis racket and a bucket of popcorn at the movies."

But perhaps their mother was aware that for children in the spotlight, a quiet activity and food that represents comfort—and private time with their mother—was just what they needed to feel secure and well loved, no strings attached.

THE PENDULUM OF PARENTING STYLES

If middles embrace parenthood in theory, what kind of parents do they make in reality? Taking a close look at parenting style in general will help us see where middles, specifically, fit into the picture.

In the mid-1960s, clinical and developmental psychologist Diana Baumrind split parenting styles into three prototypical categories in an effort to understand the main differences in approach. These are the three basic styles:

1. Permissive
2. Authoritarian
3. Authoritative

To understand these better, let's look at Stacy and Phil, a couple from Massachusetts. It is midwinter, and Stacy's daughter, Phoebe, refuses to wear winter clothing. As stubborn as a mule, the seven-year-old insists on wearing summer dresses despite the fact that three feet of snow lie outside and every pathway is covered in inches-thick ice. According to the different parenting styles, Stacy and/or Phil could handle this situation in three quite distinct ways.

Scenario #1

Phoebe comes downstairs in her sunflower dress.

"Honey, aren't you going to be cold?" Stacy asks, frowning.

"But I don't get cold, Mommy," Phoebe answers.

"I've told you before: We don't dress in summer clothes in the winter, right? Look at what I'm wearing." Stacy points to her wool tights and thick sweater.

"But I don't like your dress," Phoebe says, sitting down at the kitchen table.

Phil brings his daughter a plate of scrambled eggs.

"Yuck, Daddy. Those eggs are runny."

He takes them back and returns them to the frying pan for a quick stir. "I think it's great that you have your own style, sweetie," he says. "But I don't want you to get cold."

"I don't get cold!" Phoebe practically shouts. "I *like* this dress!"

Stacy sighs and exchanges a look with her husband. They're going to be late for work. "I'll get you a doughnut on the way to school if you'll at least put on a sweater," she says.

Stacy and Phil are permissive parents. They don't believe in punishing Phoebe but are comfortable rewarding her. When they make policy decisions and family rules, they like to get Phoebe's agreement. It doesn't occur to them to ask their daughter to clean up after herself or help with breakfast because they see themselves as a resource for her to use as she pleases rather than as agents charged with shaping her behavior. In addition, they use both reason and manipulation to get their way but will easily cave in if this approach doesn't work.

In recent years the permissive parenting category has been further split into two groups to better reflect the underlying motivations at play: indulgent permissiveness and neglectful permissiveness. Neglectful permissiveness is the most harmful. It's when parents give children a lot of freedom but minimal supervision. They don't spend much time talking to their children and generally lack warm and nurturing interactions. Instead, their behavior suggests to their children that other activities are more important to the grown ups than parenting. It leads children to have a low sense of self-worth, and they end up exhibiting poor self-control and an inability to handle independence.

Indulgent permissiveness, in contrast, is when there's a low level of demand in the house but a high level of responsiveness from the parent. It actually leads to strong self-confidence, though in the long run children do report more problems with drug experimentation and general misconduct. Permissive indulgent parents display warmth and nurturing behavior, and they allow their children a great deal of freedom of behavior and choices. Many of today's parents tend toward a permissive style; they prefer to see themselves as their child's "friend" rather than an enforcer of rules and order. This is due in part to the mobility of our modern culture in which we rarely remain close to childhood friends and gravitate more to immediate family for that lost sense of camaraderie.

The children of permissive parents often:

- have trouble regulating their emotions;
- are quite self-confident;
- are free to make their own mistakes, which makes it easier for them to find out who they really are;
- become rebellious and defiant when their desires are challenged;
- are not persistent in the face of challenges.

Scenario #2

Phoebe comes downstairs in her sunflower dress.

"Honey, that dress is silly. It's the middle of winter outside!" Stacy says, frowning.

"I *like* this dress, Mommy," Phoebe answers.

"No one wears things like that in the winter. You don't want kids to think you're strange. Now, go and change into the wool dress we got last week. See, I'm wearing something like that, and it looks nice," Stacy points to her wool tights and thick sweater.

"But, I don't get cold, Mommy," Phoebe practically shouts.

Phil turns around and raps the table loudly with his wooden spoon. "Cut it out or no movie tonight."

"Sorry," Phoebe says quickly, "but that dress, it's *itchy*!"

"Go get the dishes and set the table. I don't want you going to school looking like a street person."

Phoebe steps on a chair to reach the dishes on the shelf above the dishwasher. Her dad goes back to stirring the eggs on the pan. "Mornings like this are exhausting," he says to his daughter irritably when she climbs down. "Can't you use some common sense when you get dressed?"

Stacy sighs and exchanges a look with her husband. They're going to be late for work. "We're a lot older than you," she says. "We know what's best."

In this instance, Stacy and Phil are being authoritarian. They have a set standard of conduct to which they hold their daughter. In all ways—whether academically or socially—they shape, control, and evaluate her behavior in comparison to this standard. Obedience is a virtue; when the child's actions or beliefs conflict with what the parents consider "appropriate" conduct, they curb self-will and autonomy by being punitive or forceful. They believe in responsibility, work, and order, and they do not appreciate or encourage verbal give and take.

The authoritarian style is rooted in tradition and is often motivated by the sense that children need to learn who's boss. It encourages respect and conformity while discouraging self-expression—if that conflicts with what adults value. Typically, authoritarian households exhibit low warmth and a greater tendency toward punishment than reward.

Children who grow up in authoritarian households often:

- get good grades in school;
- do not engage in antisocial behavior, such as drug and alcohol abuse;
- become anxious or withdrawn or exhibit aggressive behavior;
- lack social competence;
- have bad reactions to frustrating situations (girls tend to give up, whereas boys become hostile).

Scenario #3

Phoebe comes downstairs in her sunflower dress.

"Honey, have you looked outside? You're going to be cold," Stacy says, frowning.

"But I don't get cold, Mommy," Phoebe answers.

"Last week you came home wearing Sasha's sweater. Weren't you cold then?"

"Yes, but, it was different—"

"How was that different?" Stacy asks. "I just don't want you distracted in school because your lips are blue and you've got goose bumps all over! Look at what I'm wearing. I'm nice and warm." Stacy points to her wool tights and thick sweater.

"Well, I don't like your dress," Phoebe practically shouts, sitting down at the kitchen table.

"Listen, you don't have to like my dress, but you *do* have to be warm enough when there's snow outside."

Phil brings his daughter a plate of scrambled eggs.

"Yuck, Daddy, those eggs are runny."

"Then put them on the toast. That'll make it taste better. And don't forget to put the plate in the dishwasher after. You're going to get cold, you know. You need to change."

"I *like* this dress!" Phoebe says.

Stacy sighs and exchanges a look with her husband. They're going to be late for work. "It is a pretty dress. You can wear it in the summer," she says. "You can pick something else, as long as it covers your legs and arms. Or put on tights and a sweater."

This last style is considered the most effective: It shows an authoritative attitude that is neither entirely inflexible nor entirely permissive. In this case, the parents attempt to direct Phoebe's activities, but in an issue-oriented way. There is verbal give and take, and reasoning is explained. Autonomous self-will and disciplined compliance are both valued by authoritative parents. Stacy exerts control when there's a difference in opinion between the parent and child, but does not hem Phoebe in with too many restrictions. She and her husband affirm the child's qualities, but also set standards for conduct. They use logic and power to achieve their objectives—namely having Phoebe be warm enough—but are not basing decisions on group consensus, or on the individual child's desires.

Typically, children with authoritative parents have:

- lively and happy dispositions;
- self-confidence, believing they can master tasks;
- well-developed ability to regulate emotion;
- better social skills than children of permissive or authoritarian parents;
- less rigid ideas about gender-typed traits (for example, sensitivity in boys and independence in girls).

Where middles fit into the picture

Growing up, he was raised by a governess and a remote father, but when he himself had children, Charles Darwin embraced fatherhood actively. Unlike other men of the Victorian era, he was deeply involved in his children's lives, writing about them almost daily in his journals. A middle child himself, he had six boys and four girls (three of whom died in childhood). "He always made us feel that we were each of us creatures whose opinions and thoughts were valuable to him," his son, Francis, wrote, "so that whatever there was best in us came out in the sunshine of his presence."

Naturally, not all middles parent in the same way. But considering their core personality traits—how much they love their friends, their great negotiation skills, and their interest in justice and harmony—it makes sense that we would assume they're the most authoritative of the birth orders in their parenting styles. A parent like Darwin indulged his children with lots of time, attention, and love, giving them the right to express their own personalities. He did not follow the old adage that children must be seen and not heard. Clearly, as a middle he had to be considered more authoritative than authoritarian.

But my research shows this isn't the full story on how middle children parent.

Fascinatingly, middles were revealed as more permissive than both firsts *and* lasts. In the case of firsts, this wasn't a big surprise. From all we know about firstborn children, it's to be expected that they run households in which parents are the undisputed decision-makers. But in the case of lasts, it came as a shock that middles were significantly *more* permissive than they were. And this result held true whether the parents were reporting on themselves or on their partners.

One answer provided an interesting clue as to why. "Though we are strict (compared to many parents we know, though not compared to our own parents)," an anonymous respondent explained, "we have a very hard time with discipline. Not because we don't want to do it or because we don't see the value of it, but because kids are so dang confounding!" The ability that middles have to see both sides of an issue can lead them to waver when it comes to discipline in the household. Because middleborns tend to be antiauthoritarian and are the least likely to insist on getting their own way, this means their little ones sometimes get *their* own way too often.

Here it is important to remember the different kinds of permissiveness and that these have varied effects on families. Neglectful permissiveness is harmful to children, and there is no research to suggest that middles are neglectful. On the contrary, my data show that middleborns parent their children thoughtfully and with a great deal of passion. Middleborn parents are more indulgent than careless. This fits with their personalities: Despite having grown up in an environment where they did not always receive as much attention as they wanted, once they are parents, middles give their own children the attention they themselves sought.

This does have its drawbacks, however: Middleborns can pander to their children's needs or desires. So a middleborn parent might allow little Phoebe to wear her sunflower dress in the snow, not because they don't care whether or not she gets frostbite, but because they are overly influenced by the intensity of her arguments. They can't override her without feeling guilty. This would fall into the permissive parenting category as they concede their role as figures of authority and allow their seven-year-old to be the boss.

Nuances that are easily overlooked

Because no one is black and white in their approach to parenting, I designed my survey so that participants could rate the *degree* to which they follow different parenting styles. For instance, in response to a question like *When our child asks why he/she has to conform, I state: Because I said so, or I am your parent and I want you to,* respondents could convey how vigorously they agreed or disagreed with the statement. If they gave it a high score, that meant they leaned toward authoritarian (i.e. strict) parenting.

Other questions explored the degree to which one birth order is more or less authoritative or permissive than others (such as, *I explain to our child how we feel about the child's good and bad choices or actions,* and *I give in to our child when he/she causes a commotion about something).* Additionally, comments could be added to further expound on the answers. This proved to be especially useful when interpreting just how much more permissive middles were than other parents.

Four main parenting effects could be discerned as a result of this type of questioning:

1. **Firstborns are the most authoritarian of all birth orders, and middles the least.**

   Firsts put high value on order and security, and they look up to authority. Thus they are more likely to run a tight ship in their households than other birth orders. This is the least effective parenting style, however, because it doesn't allow children to accept responsibility for their own behavior and choices. Phoebe, for instance, may well have changed into the itchy wool dress as her authoritarian mother ordered in scenario #2, but she would not have understood or accepted *why.* Faced with this situation again, she wouldn't be able to figure out for herself what the smartest option is for her. Middles, in contrast, rated the lowest on this scale, both when reporting on themselves and when reporting on spouses. In other words, they are least likely to insist on their children doing something "because I told you so."

2. **Middles score higher than everyone else on permissive and *authoritative* scales.**

   While authoritativeness is a positive approach to parenting, permissive parenting can be quite harmful. This mixed result means that a middleborn parent would be more likely than firsts or lasts to let Phoebe have her own way with the summer clothing—or they might insist on an exchange of ideas with the child so as to assure themselves that she understood their reasoning and agreed.

Since it's impossible to get agreement on all things from a child, middles would rather give in than fight to the death over something they don't see as all that critical.

3. *But* . . . middles are more authoritative than they are permissive.

Because questions were rated on separate scales, we were able to see that for middles the authoritative impulse is greater than the permissive one. It's more likely that they'll get renegade Phoebe to accept the wisdom of dressing warmly in the winter than that they'll allow her to tromp off to school in arctic conditions wearing her cotton sundress.

4. Reporting on yourself skews the answers toward the positive.

No one likes admitting they're pushovers. As a consequence, when reporting on themselves, respondents tend to veer toward a more positive representation than is warranted. In this case, it means that for the questions with negative connotations the actual numbers are likely to be a little off. Who would willingly admit to letting their seven-year-old rule the roost and decide what's best? Firsts and lasts probably scored lower on the permissive scale than reality warrants—meaning that middles are perhaps not as permissive as the data make out.

Factors that can change the playing field

A family with four kids is sitting around the dinner table, enjoying an evening meal together. They're African American and live in Georgia. A fourteen-year-old girl, Suliah, runs in, chewing gum. She throws her bag on the floor and says, "Where's my plate? I'm starving."

Her mother gets up from the table and cuffs her on the head. "You spit out that gum right now," she says. "Where have you been? I told you to be back at six o'clock. You're not going out during the week anymore." In bed that night Suliah thinks about her mom. She's not happy about being grounded, but she does feel secure knowing that her mother keeps an eye on where she is at all times.

In another household, an Asian mother stands up at dinner time, her face flushed. Looking down at her fourteen-year-old son, Chul, she says, "It's simply not good enough. I expect you to do better on your next test." A polite kid with thick glasses and an earring in his left ear, the boy nods and looks down at his food. He feels bad for having disappointed his mother, but later when he goes upstairs to finish his homework, instead of feeling angry or defeated, he puts in a little extra time on his math.

The parents in these two families express concern for their children in very different ways. A 2008 study by Wake Forest University looked at how adolescents perceived maternal warmth. What makes teens recognize that their mothers care about them? Was it when they engaged in collaborative parenting, asking the child's opinion? Was it when they were authoritarian and made the child feel protected and safe? This is relevant because it reminds us that there are so many different factors that play into an individual's parenting style—and how it's perceived by the children.

In order to compare and contrast these kinds of family situations, researchers studied three hundred European, Asian, and African American teens. They discovered that parental styles are not perceived the same way in every household. Practices such as harsh discipline in African American households were seen as "no nonsense" and protective. Asian American kids had no expectations of collaborative decision making, and so were more comfortable with strict parental control practices. Although parenting philosophies differed quite radically, the perceived maternal warmth did not. There was no direct, positive relationship between authoritative parenting, for example, and how much warmth the kids felt from their mothers.

In Suliah's case, although her mother hit her, Suliah did not feel attacked or belittled. Rather, she interpreted this behavior as an indication of the level of her mother's concern. Consequently, even authoritarian parenting cannot always be interpreted negatively. In some groups for which this is the more common parenting style, it is perceived by the children as a loving approach. In these cases the *level* of investment is paramount, not the *type of* investment.

How important it is, therefore, to have a collaborative and child-centered parenting approach depends directly on what the group norms are, and this is often determined by ethnicity. Everyone parents differently, and culture makes a difference.

A warm parenting style is the defining characteristic of the authoritative and permissive parenting style, both of which middles represent. Since middle children come from all different ethnic backgrounds, however, their learned behaviors can trump their instinctive style, which is by no means always a negative thing. We see this in the case of Sven (the middle of three), who parents his four children with his wife, Anna, (the lastborn of two). When asked about his parenting style, Sven hesitates before launching into a long explanation. Having grown up in a Swedish household in California, he was accustomed to getting affection from his parents, but at arm's length. "We didn't say, *I love you* very often," he explained. "But we showed it all the time. And we spent a lot of time together as a family."

It is his instinct to be somewhat standoffish as far as public displays of affection are concerned. But as a middle, he's more inclined to give his kids a lot of attention (with homework, play time, and family routines) since he often felt "unseen" as a child. His wife, Anna, is a lastborn, so she tends to be very warm and somewhat indulgent with the kids. Consequently, Sven works harder than many parents to figure out how he wants to parent his children: What traditions does he want to carry over from his own childhood? How much does he want to balance out Anna's style? Is it okay for him to be loving and yet not so touchy-feely with his children?

The three parenting style dimensions we discussed using Phoebe as an example are helpful in highlighting the pros and cons of parenting in a certain way. There are limitations to such categorization, however, and for middles this is especially true. Middleborns are complex and often have competing impulses as a consequence of their upbringing. While they may feel inclined to overindulge their children, they usually know that this isn't an effective strategy.

Mom or dad? It makes a difference

What if you're a middle child father as opposed to a middle child mother? Does your parenting style—whether you're more authoritative or permissive, for instance—make more or less of a difference depending on your gender? In one study, three hundred students in grades 9 and 11 were questioned about family life, and their answers were related to their self-esteem, life satisfaction, and depression. The results showed that children thought much more positively about authoritative mothers than they did permissive mothers. Authoritative mothering led to high self-esteem, life satisfaction, and lower rates of depression, whereas permissive mothering had a negative impact on self-esteem and life satisfaction.

But the results were quite different for fathers. High school children who considered their fathers permissive saw it as far less negative than when their mothers were permissive. Why? "It is possible that since fathers play a more playful role in the lives of children," say the authors, "having a permissive father may complement the fatherhood role and hence may not interfere with a child's well-being as much as having a permissive mother."

In addition, a literature review of papers on adolescent substance abuse from 1996 to 2007 pointed out that "the parenting style of the parent of the same sex has the strongest relationship with self-regulation and substance use." In other words, a male middle child with all male children will exert a different influence on his family than a male middle with all females—and the same can be said for female middles and the level of influence they have over their children.

Many family households are run by two parents—most often a

mother and a father—and typically their different parenting styles balance out. (We saw this to some extent in Sven's case.) Furthermore, two middles married to each other may not both parent in an identical manner, nor do they need to in order to be successful. As we'll see in the next section, the qualities that make for good parenting can be expressed in many different ways. If two middles are parenting together, they may approach this responsibility differently even though their core principles are the same. Equally, a middle who parents with another birth order may find that the gender, ethnic, or birth order differences each parent exhibits can be used to the child's advantage. The key lies in being able to figure out what works best for your family, your relationship, and your children. For middles, assessing their baggage and determining what to leave behind and what to bring with them on the parenting journey is what will give them the power to be great parents to their children.

HOW WELL MIDDLES PROVIDE WHAT CHILDREN NEED

Even though he's one of the richest men on earth, this middle child often brought home Cs and Ds from school as a kid. Now, despite being worth over $40 billion, he still lives in the same five-bedroom house he bought for $31,000 in 1957, wears rumpled business suits, and admits to an addiction to cherry Coca-Cola. He has three grown children from his long marriage: Susan, Howard, and Peter.

Warren Buffett is a risk taker, a fabulous orator, a man of action and determination, a dreamer rooted in reality, and a practical, hardworking father. Known as the "Oracle of Omaha," he's a middleborn who brought his unique blend of qualities to bear on raising his children. Yet, unlike Lady Diana Spencer, Buffett isn't especially known for his personal warmth or his compassion. The public doesn't think of him as a terrific dad above and beyond all else; we think of him as a phenomenally successful businessman who is able to give his children unprecedented opportunities. By all accounts, his children have become happy, productive, and well-adjusted adults. Despite being born into unimaginable privilege, they seem to have their heads screwed on straight; that is quite a feat.

So what do Warren Buffett and Diana Spencer, two middle children, have in common in terms of their approach to parenting? Both managed to rise above their particular circumstances and instill in their children a sense of their strong personal values, keeping them grounded, productive, and apparently quite contented in spite of the extraordinary swirl of activity around them (in Lady Diana's case, navigating a dysfunctional yet high-profile private life, and in Buffett's case, being stupendously wealthy). It is astonishing that in spite of their iconic status in our modern culture, their limitless access to wealth and power, and their polar opposite lifestyles, these two middle children can both be seen as parental role models.

What, then, are the core elements that make for successful parenting? The top traits—some of which Buffett and Spencer exhibit—can be split into five vital components. We'll see how middles fulfill, and in some cases *fail* to fulfill, these important mandates.

Table 12. TOP FIVE PARENTING TRAITS

Positive	Negative
Giving unconditional love	Basing love and affection on how your child behaves or performs
Treating each child as an individual	Trying to recreate children in own image
Being empathetic without losing control of logic	Having a rigid point of view or losing control of emotions
Problem solving with creativity and flexibility	Being overly controlling and allowing negative "scripts" to pervade
Showing personal discipline and consistency	Lacking structure and discipline; being inconsistent

1. Giving children unconditional love

Harry grew up in a family of seven children in Louisiana. He was the second to last child, and one of two boys. When he started his own family and moved east, he was delighted to have three athletic boys. Harry had always loved sports, especially basketball and lacrosse, and savored weekends spent at his sons' games. He prided himself on being an active and loving father.

The spring that Harry's oldest son, Michael, turned fifteen, weekend lacrosse games started being a lot less fun. "Mike just wasn't trying anymore. I could tell by the way he ran—or rather, didn't run," Harry explained. Just weeks before the next lacrosse season was about to start, Michael dropped a bomb. He wanted to quit; he didn't like lacrosse and never had. It was a shock to his father who had put a lot of time, effort, and money into helping his son improve his skills. "When he said he didn't like it, it felt like a personal blow," Harry said. "But I realized pretty soon that it was actually for the best."

Thinking back over the previous year and Michael's lackluster attitude, Harry understood that without authentic internal motivation, his son would never grow to love the game or excel at it. They moved on pretty quickly, and although Harry certainly missed the weekend games, he was actually kind of proud of his son for turning his attention to something he found more fulfilling and productive: playing guitar in his band.

Harry's behavior is not unusual for a middle child. While he showed Mike lots of love when he excelled at lacrosse, he continued to show him love even when he failed to live up to his expectations. This is unconditional love.

Popular opinion is divided on the issue of whether unconditional love has an entirely positive effect on kids. In the last chapter we talked about the negative consequences of praising children too readily for achievement rather than effort. More authoritarian parents believe that withholding affection from younger children—for instance, during time-outs—is an invaluable tool in teaching civility and self-control. But beyond the toddler years, when children are no longer such an immediate danger to themselves (and a nuisance to others!), unconditional love forms the basis of healthy and positive parent-child relations. And parents who were middle children are inclined by their very natures to love and support their children, warts and all.

In 2004, two Israeli researchers and an American expert on the psychology of motivation wanted to find out the effects of using praise as a control mechanism—testing not whether it worked as a parental strategy, but what its lingering effects were. As expected, they discovered that children who were given *conditional* approval were somewhat more likely to behave as the parent wished. But this compliance was costly: These children resented their parents and said they didn't act based on "a real sense of choice." In addition, once they succeeded at something, their happiness was typically short-lived, and they often felt guilty about it.

In another study, researchers interviewed mothers of grown children to see what effects this conditional love had on multiple generations. The mothers who, as kids, felt loved only when living up to their parents' expectations also felt less worthy as adults and became controlling parents themselves. Moreover, their daughters recognized that these mothers had also treated them with conditional regard, and they resented that—thereby revealing that this negativity is transmitted from one generation to the next. Although conditional regard helps us socialize young children, it can have a negative effect on families, both psychologically to the individuals and in terms of family dynamics. Researchers argued strongly for the benefits of a more autonomous approach.

As a middle child from our survey put it, "Everyone needs to understand what's expected and why. I don't believe in blind obedience. It's not a good motivator. . . . [Kids] need to know why. They need to feel it inside themselves, or they won't in the end do it."

Middle children are less likely than other birth orders to attach strings to their love based on performance. Since they felt they had to work harder for affection and attention when they were children, they don't want their own kids to have to do the same. In addition, they tend to feel uncomfortable bowing to authority, and so they're uncomfortable being authoritarian in their own household. But as we'll see, this can come with its own set of issues.

Discipline can be dicey

Treating children with unconditional love is not the same as bowing to their every demand or allowing them to get away with bad behavior. Because middles are so apt to embrace their children wholeheartedly and are able to see everything from multiple perspectives, they can find it challenging to discipline their children.

When asked, "What have you found to be the biggest challenge in parenting and why?" the majority of respondents in my survey said facing fears about drugs, sex, media, and driving. But dealing with discipline came a close second. As one middle child mother explained, "My biggest challenge in parenting is being a disciplinarian, likely because I am a people pleaser and like everyone to be happy." Another wrote, "I am called 'the pushover' in our house."

But it's possible to assure children that you will love and support them no matter what, while also expressing disappointment when appropriate. Excessive praise or blind acceptance—especially when it's not truly warranted—can do more harm than good in the long run.

2. Treating each child as an individual

As a teenager she almost came to blows with her mother about their divergent opinions on her career dreams. At seventeen she left home to live in a dance studio. For years this middle child and her mother didn't even talk. Burning with the desire to become a star, Jennifer Lopez (middle daughter of three) insisted on doing things her way. Brought up Roman Catholic in a family that expected rules to be followed, she put her foot down when it came to building her career.

Middles don't usually resort to histrionics to get their own way, but they often insist on being treated as individuals and will go so far as to distance themselves from their families if their passions aren't respected. Because of this, when middles have their own children, they tend to respect them as individuals. This is something on which most pediatricians and childhood psychologists agree: No two children are alike, and so all children must be treated differently. "On every issue—rules, expectations, chores, responsibilities, rewards, and punishment—parents must individualize their parenting while trying to remain fair to all," declares the American Society of Pediatrics.

Having the same expectations for each child, regardless of their personalities, is bound to backfire. In Lopez's case, her family understood her love of dance and showmanship but were too fearful of the lifestyle to bring themselves to support their daughter in her choices. Ideally, each parent would assess the pros and cons of behavior chosen by the child in respect to the passions and talents that child exhibits. It is well documented that when children are motivated by their own desires and interests, they thrive. As child psychologist Madeline Levine says, "The self is born in the crucible of interaction between parent and child. Every time we encourage exploration, applaud independence, and require self-control, we help our children grow into their best selves."

One of the most unexpected findings in my survey of middles was that when they have three or more children, they do not treat their own middles any differently than their other children. A consistent theme in the answers was that middleborn parents work quite diligently to assess each individual child's personality but without spoiling their middles. Almost a full 100 percent of the answers showed a belief that each child is unique: "All three of my children are very different, and I have different relationships and expectations from each of them," wrote Danielle. "I expect more from my middle child and only daughter, because I feel she is more capable than my oldest son. I baby my oldest because he has always been very needy. My youngest is the goofball of the family, and I am always just trying to have fun with him." Middle parents learn, from their own childhood experiences, to simply take their children as they come.

3. Being empathic

Watching your child suffer is one of the hardest things a parent has to go through. Brad and his wife, Susan, were planning to move from their cottage in the country to an apartment closer to the city so Susan's commute was not so long. Their daughter, Lily, thirteen, thought this was the worst idea she'd ever heard.

Like many parents of teenagers, Brad and Susan have a strained relationship with their teen. But Susan, who was an only child, has a much harder time handling her daughter's mood swings than Brad, who's the third child in a family with five kids.

One Saturday, Susan and Lily had a huge blowup when they began discussing the possible move. Lily became so angry and defensive that she hurled insults at her mother and cried hysterically. Finally, Susan couldn't take it anymore and left the house. Later, just before dinner, their son came into the dining room as his parents were setting the table.

"I don't know what's wrong with Lily," he said, "but she's lying on the floor and not moving."

Lily had tired herself out so badly by crying all day and was feeling so overwhelmed by the idea of leaving her childhood home that she briefly lost consciousness. Susan was still furious with her, believing that Lily was being manipulative. In the two weeks since the argument began, Susan barely spoke to her daughter.

Brad, on the other hand, had a different approach. He understood Lily's angst, and while he didn't like the way she was treating her mother, he also knew it was not personal. He was highly empathetic while still assuming that his desires would prevail. That night he called the ambulance and sat by Lily's side, showing her sympathy and understanding—but, ultimately, his opinion on the matter of moving remained the same as his wife's. He and Lily began talking in private about what was going on. He told her that he knew what she was feeling, and this made her less defensive.

It's helpful to see how this middle child's emotional mind allowed him to bond with his daughter, despite their ups and downs, while his wife couldn't find a way to connect with her on an emotional level. While it's critical to be able to operate with a rational mind—making decisions, exercising self-control, completing tasks well—it's also important to recognize the value of emotional insights. In his book, *Emotional Intelligence: Why It Can Matter More Than IQ* (published fifteen years ago and now in its tenth printing), Daniel Goleman argued for the first time that "intellect cannot work at its best without emotional intelligence." Almost 95 percent of participants in my survey cited that the most important duty they had toward their children was to teach them to "give back," "have respect for others," "be good citizens," "be compassionate human beings," and "feel for others." Middles see the value of empathy.

Having the ability to be compassionate improves communication, validates a child's feelings, and helps avoid misunderstandings and overly quick judgments. When parents are empathic and open, and when they combine this with consistent discipline, children do well.

When you suffer along with every ache and pain

It's one thing to feel empathy for a youngster when he or she is frustrated or bored, but it's another to be drawn into the emotional dramas of a teenager. Parents today often want to protect their children from pain and failure, partly because they so closely identify with their offspring. They feel responsible for every bump in the road and want to fix or avoid every source of pain. It can be challenging for the empathic middle child parent to step away and recognize when it's time to loosen the reins or when it's time to lay down the law.

If you're too empathic, you can't get the job done. For instance, sometimes Brad will give in to his daughter's demands even though it doesn't benefit either of them.

Parents who are overly empathetic can suffer from anxiety, depression, and fatigue. But it is a necessary step for children to disentangle themselves from parental authority no matter how treacherous the road ahead may appear to be. Children learn from making mistakes and become resilient when they understand how to persist in the face of challenges or failure. If middle child parents who feel themselves drawn too deeply into their children's lives can remember this, then they will avoid suffering along with their children every time something goes wrong.

4. Problem solving with creativity and flexibility

In scenario #3, when Phoebe came downstairs in midwinter wearing her summer frock, her parents handled her with creativity and flexibility. Instead of belittling her, ordering her around, or getting angry, they explained what was wrong, brought her into the discussion, offered alternatives, but still lay down the law. This authoritative approach was successful because it validated the child's impulses (without pushing her into a defensive posture) while never giving up parental authority. Having a more flexible, open-minded approach to dealing with unexpected issues allows these parents to problem-solve each individual dilemma and come up with appropriate solutions that fit the particular circumstances.

In contrast, authoritarian parents are rigid and disinclined to talk things over with their children. They tend to apply blanket judgments to situations that may be quite different; they simply can't be flexible because they operate under a set of rules that doesn't allow for shades of gray. When their strict standards of conduct are not adhered to, they can be highly critical of their children. Children and adolescents from authoritarian families—in which demand is high but response and warmth is low—tend to perform quite well in school and be uninvolved in problematic behavior, but they also have poorer social skills, lower self-esteem, and higher levels of depression.

Well-known studies of American adolescents have reported that teens with authoritarian parents were less likely to feel socially accepted by their peers than those with parents who are more flexible. They were also rated as less self-reliant.

Authoritative and permissive parents, like middles, are much more likely to include their children in conversations when they're seeking solutions to problems. When parents are somewhat malleable, success is more likely. Entrenched attitudes and negative scripts ("I never behave," "I am bad," "I will never do well") are avoided, and mistakes are seen as an opportunity for learning. Also, and rather ironically, children of parents who have a more open approach to problem solving tend to rely more on their parents for moral guidance than children of authoritarian parents. In a 2003 study of undergraduates from the United States, researchers asked students who they turned to when faced with moral decisions. Undergraduates with authoritative parents said they were most likely to talk with their parents. Students with *authoritarian* parents and students from permissive families were more likely to reference their peers.

It has also been well documented that teens are wired to rebel and distance themselves from authority, and they will react with less compliance when ordered to conform, as opposed to when they're included in a discussion about it. In the end, these young adults will have to learn how to make good choices on their own, weighing for themselves the costs and benefits of various decisions. The middleborn parental approach bodes well for this dynamic.

One middle said, "I guess I have a more rebellious nature myself, so I appreciate it more in my children and try not be too despotic and always have a clever explanation rather than rely on age difference/power to win an argument." As we've seen, middles think outside the box and are not averse to changing their opinion if the situation calls for it. Their inclination is to talk, listen, weigh arguments, brainstorm options, and then make decisions. This is beneficial to children first and foremost because they feel heard and appreciated, even if they don't end up getting their own way. This is also helpful to them in the future when navigating work and love: They'll be more open to other people's opinions and not be so invested in always getting their own way. And, finally, it's critical for children to learn to how to disagree. Ultimately in life, we have to navigate disagreements with others on a daily basis, and having some experience in the give-and-take of healthy arguments is invaluable.

5. Showing personal discipline and consistency

It was splashed all over the papers and the airwaves. No one could quite believe it. The third richest man in the world was going to give away his fortune—and not to his children! Everyone wanted to know: How could a father turn his back on his kids? Were his three children bitter? What was he thinking?

"Our kids are great. But I would argue that when your kids have all the advantages anyway, in terms of how they grow up and the opportunities they have for education," said multibillionaire middle child Warren Buffett, "it's neither right nor rational to be flooding them with money."

All along, Buffet's children have been taught the value of good, honest work. Of course, parents without riches to disperse also have a variety of opportunities to model their self-possession and discipline to their children. Day-to-day activities reflect the parent's style, priorities, and values, and children are keen observers. The mode "do as I do" works best with children. A recent study of 430 teens was able to directly link children's behavior with their perception of their parents' behavior.

Children need and crave consistency. Discipline allows them to deal with the myriad responsibilities bestowed on them by adulthood. It encourages children to have self-worth as well as teaches them the value of dependability and work. It discourages the idea that we're all owed something by the world and that we deserve to reap our rewards instantaneously. In his book, *Positive Pushing*, James Taylor explains, "Children who learn to delay instant gratification are confident, assertive and capable of dealing constructively with frustration. They are also self-motivated, persist in the face of obstacles, and are less likely to crumble under the weight of stress."

Middle children parents are as human as any other parents. Operating with total control and discipline at all times is a virtual impossibility, and middles have to try as hard as other birth orders to model consistency and restraint. Kevin, the middle child of a big family, said he felt his primary duty to his four children was to "give them the reasoning skills to be able to make good choices throughout their lives. Starting at an early age they need to be able to figure things out on their own and either reap the rewards of those choices or suffer the consequences." To do this, he does his very best to model these behaviors in his own everyday interactions.

As one middle said, "If you don't walk the walk, don't even try and talk the talk."

MIDDLES ARE WORTH EMULATING

Romantic young men and women often have their parents to thank for their view of love and marriage. In the case of the future king of England, Prince William, he seems to have inherited his mother's sense of humor, her gregariousness, and her love of love. On a trip to Africa with his longtime girlfriend Catherine Middleton, William hid an engagement ring in his backpack, waiting for just the right moment to pop the question. The ring was the infamous sapphire and diamond ring that had belonged to his mother, Diana, the Princess of Wales (one she wore, by the way, even after her divorce). William explained that since she could not be with them in person, he wanted his mother to be there in spirit, as symbolized by her ring.

Lady Diana, a middle child with her fair share of personal challenges, will be remembered by her children and the general populace as a dedicated and loving mother. Not much was expected of her in terms of parenting, and she wildly surpassed those low expectations.

Many middleborns grow up to be nurturing adults, able to navigate family life with a mixture of flexibility and steadfastness. "Everyone has always said how laid-back I am," explained Kayla, a middle child with two children. "Compromise is always in the forefront of my mind. There has to be give and take from both my kids, and from us." The traits that stand middleborns in such good stead in other areas of their lives also make them parents who are worthy of imitation.

SECRETS BEHIND MIDDLES' PARENTING STYLES

1. **As parents, middles are mysterious.**
   Up until now, there has been very little research on how middle children parent. Two recent studies I conducted revealed that while middles are authoritarian parents, contrary to expectations, they are also more permissive than firsts or lasts.

2. **They are invested in the parenting game.**
   Middles not only like starting their own families, but they take their parenting duties seriously. Of all the birth orders, middleborn survey respondents offered far more comments explaining and defending their parenting practices than other birth orders.

3. **Middles like a busy household.**
   While middleborns are not that close emotionally to their parents, they're usually quite close to their siblings. They rarely choose to have only one child because they prefer to give their offspring the experience of having brothers and sisters.

4. **Partnerships are as critical as parenting.**
   Although most middles see parenting as their highest calling in life, many also highly rate working on having healthy partnerships; they find it almost as important and fulfilling as parenting.

5. **Middles' empathic natures can lead to inaction.**

   Middleborns relate well to their children but can sometimes have difficulty saying no to them. Too much sensitivity to their children's problems, moods, and behaviors can render middles inert.

6. **The playing field isn't always even.**

   Parenting styles and how children perceive them vary depending on both culture and gender. Consequently, there are some limitations to the practicality of defining mothers and fathers according to the three well-known parenting categories: permissive, authoritarian, and authoritative.

7. **Middles have a head start.**

   Of the five most important and healthy parenting traits, middles positively express all of them.

CHAPTER TEN

Looking to the Future

"From now on, I'll connect the dots my own way."

—*Bill Watterson,* Calvin & Hobbes

I'm always being asked why I study middleborns.

"Don't you know that family size is shrinking?"

"You're not even a middle—so why do you care?"

"Does anyone even *have* big families anymore?"

First and foremost, I find birth order fascinating. My father was a middle, I have friends who are middles, and, frankly, I feel there's not enough good information out there about what makes middles tick. There are millions of middleborns in the world, and there's just as much value in understanding how their birth order shaped them as there is value in studying firsts and lasts and onlies.

But I also feel a sense of urgency.

In the twenty years since I've been studying birth order, there are fewer and fewer middle children showing up in my classes or volunteering to participate in my studies. And future trends seem to be following suit: the average number of children per family in the United States hovers around two. While this isn't as low as Hong Kong's one child per family—or as high as Somalia's six—it's notable because if this trend continues, middles will essentially disappear from our population. And although these statistics are just averages, the overall drift toward smaller families is clear. In many Western countries, middles are slowly becoming an endangered species.

What about the "population explosion"?

From the beginning of recorded time until about two hundred years ago, population growth was stable and moderate. Every now and again there were bumps and dips—such as when world population was halved by the Black Plague in the 1300s—but the pattern was steady.

Until, in the 1800s, there was quite suddenly a veritable explosion of births.

The Industrial Revolution was beginning to impact every aspect of daily life: Mechanization was fundamentally changing production, commerce, and family life for the better. Medicine was more widely available, and work was plentiful. The trajectory of the population graph abruptly veered upward as parents in developing countries began producing more and more children. Having many children was no longer a liability but an asset. Larger families became critical: Children and siblings made steadfast allies, families offered shared childcare, and siblings worked in the factories, side by side. The social support networks that were made possible by families with multiple children became part of our social fabric. In 1800 the population was close to two billion. By 1970 it was close to double that. And now, only forty years later, it's about six billion.

Thus the term "population explosion" was coined, and economists predicted a massively overpopulated world in which children would starve to death for lack of food and resources. This rate of growth could not be sustained. Countries like China mandated a one-child-per-family maximum. Big families were no longer seen as viable.

Today the world we live in is heavily populated by middles, but in the next generation there's an unspoken bias against families of more than two children. Having "too many" kids exhibits a lack of respect for the environment. It's both show-offish and selfish. It's considered unhealthy: too much stress; too much sharing of time and resources; too many mouths to feed. My own recent history shows this dynamic at play: My mother grew up with seven siblings and lived a modest but comfortable and content life. Yet today my friend Carol *wishes* she could have had four children. She only had two because of concerns about money and lifestyle. How quickly mores have changed.

While the birthrate in developing nations is still high, population growth in developed nations is currently below two per family. This means that when the parents die, there are not enough children being born to replace them. In France, the government offers incentives to families that keep producing children. In Germany, young couples typically have only one or two children. And in Japan, population growth has dramatically tapered off.

So what does this mean? It means fewer and fewer middle children are being born.

For me, the fact that family size in the Western Hemisphere is shrinking is not a wholly positive trend (and not just because I have trouble populating my studies). If, increasingly, families have only one or two children, as a society I believe we'll be losing out in the long run. That's partly why I wrote this book: to herald the talents and inclinations of the middle child and to remind us all that these unrecognized skills are an integral part of what makes our world go 'round. Perhaps by focusing on these traits and recognizing why they're important for us as a civilization, we can continue to improve our society despite slowly losing our middles.

The modus operandi of Western society

A common complaint about our modern society is that people are too focused on themselves. After all, the current crop of young people in Western societies have been pegged as "The Me Generation." They're considered a bunch of navel gazers—*I deserve to get what I want, and I want it now!*—who expect instant gratification and compulsively put their needs and desires first. While I think this is an exaggeration (after all, a culture of mindfulness is being encouraged in classrooms; the next generation is being trained to be more generous and globally minded), there is a hint of truth to it.

On a larger scale, our entire culture's selfish modus operandi doesn't bode well for our ability to sacrifice for the greater good or for building strong communities. One could even argue that on a micro level some parents operate more from selfish impulses than those oriented toward the greater good. Helicopter parents (a term used to describe parents who are too involved in supervising their children's lives), for instance, are actually doing what they want rather than what's best for their children. They must know, inside, that developing a sense of independence and well-earned self-esteem is critical for their children, yet these parents can't help but hover. Why? Because helicoptering makes them feel satisfied that they're doing a good job.

But what I've addressed in this book points away from the notion that successful parenting is all about time and attention, and toward a healthier and more realistic approach to family life. In larger families, attention is shared, and while firsts—and sometimes lasts—may get the larger share, middleborns learn early on the hard yet important lesson that sometimes others come first.

Larger families, by definition, offer a different set of dynamics than smaller ones. When there are multiple children in a family, no one gets what they want all the time. It's simply not possible to please everyone simultaneously. Delayed gratification is the name of the game. Children have to pitch in and figure out how to get along. When you're not the sole focus of parental attention, you're unlikely to get an overinflated sense of self-importance. These kinds of behaviors are critical for conducting our lives outside the family, too.

As we now know, middles don't get as much attention as other birth orders, but in many ways they turn out better and stronger for it. While many middleborns perceive this lack of focus on them as unfair (especially when they're young), the fact is that it's excellent training for the future. After all, in the real world you rarely get exactly what you want when you want it. To live a full, successful, and happy life, one has to be able to negotiate, compromise, and sometimes even toil in the shadows. And one must often challenge the status quo in order to make progress.

In families where the focus is so carefully trained on just one or two children, these sorts of abilities tend to fall by the wayside. Yet many people believe that having fewer children represents an investment in quality over quantity. They think parents will be better able to concentrate their time and investment in one or two children and that this will ultimately benefit them. In certain instances this can certainly be the case. For a financially strapped family, for example, it's unwise to keep adding kids to the brood. Not all people are good parents, and in reality not everyone should have children. And, of course, there's a point at which family size does become unwieldy, and the children can't help but suffer from lack of attention and resources. But I believe that less is not always more.

Having spent this book looking at middles and how they influence our world, the positive dynamic they introduce into both their families and the larger culture is evident. What is it we might lose if we have no more middles in our population? It's worth taking a final look so we can absorb these lessons and apply them to our own lives and the lives of our children—and thereby continue working on making the world a better place.

Families of more than two children typically experience the following dynamics:

1. **There's more sharing and negotiating.**

Children from larger families learn from a very early age onward to share and to negotiate for what they want, and this is especially true for middle children. In terms of future life skills, these are perhaps the most critical of all. As Carl, the middle in a family of five children, explained, "I never had a new toy. I didn't mind. Actually, I really didn't even notice it. But after my first job, when I was a teenager, you can't imagine the joy when I bought myself a brand-new bike." Another middle, the third in a family of six, put it another way: "Now, as a grownup, I really understand that if I want something for myself, it's up to me to get it."

Imagine a world in which people simply don't understand the concept of sharing and yet are constantly being asked—or required—to share knowledge, ideas, and resources. Solving conflict and negotiating are skills we're usually not born with but develop over time. As children, socialization in the home and school leads us to become more intuitive about diplomacy. As adults, navigating the real world of love and work, this diplomacy becomes a vital skill. When should we introduce a radical idea, suggest unsettling change, or counter someone's point of view? How should we handle an opponent's defensiveness? Should we be quiet or forceful, generous or withholding? Hannah, an only child, admitted that she has trouble with her peers at work because they feel she's too direct. "Somehow, somewhere, I missed the lesson on how to be part of a successful give-and-take. I guess I was too used to always taking or getting." In bigger families you can't take anything for granted.

2. **Children enjoy the freedom to make mistakes.**

Today's parents are terrified of allowing their children to make mistakes because it seems that any misstep could affect their child's long-term success. As a result, parents feel responsible for their child's every action—such as when they get a D because they skipped math homework; amass four detentions because they can't get up when the alarm rings; or are rejected by a friend. All these experiences are painful for parents. The fear that their children's records will be impacted (what college will they get into?) or that they'll be emotionally scarred (how will they ever find a mate?) is hugely inhibiting.

What many parents don't quite want to accept—though I suspect that most do realize it—is that often the best way to learn is through your own mistakes. Middle children, by dint of their position in the family, are more likely to experience the freedom to make mistakes and learn from them. Pammy, the middle child in a family of four children (the youngest are twins), grew up having to fend for herself a lot. She enjoyed lively family dinners and vacations, but day-to-day life was pretty hectic. As soon as the twins were born, Pammy had to wake up and dress herself, catch the bus on time, do her own homework, and arrange her own rides to playdates. "You can't count the number of times I was late or missed handing in homework," she says. But now, as a senior in high school, she's more self-sufficient than most and is a top student with exceptional self-confidence.

Middles with the breathing space to make their own mistakes accept responsibility for their actions and are more apt to think ahead to the consequences rather than rely on luck (or a parent) to save the day. They become adults who are less likely to blame others for their own shortcomings and have a better grip on their unique strengths and weaknesses.

3. **Individual kids experience less pressure.**
By now we all know that the firstborn of every family re-

ceives more parental attention than the subsequent children. In a family of any size—whether there's one child or five—the firstborn will inevitably benefit (and suffer), at least for a while, from the effects of being the sole focus of his or her parents' attention. But in families with three or more children, the negative effects of parental pressure are minimized. The Hardy family is a great example of this.

The firstborn, Josh, and secondborn, Madison, are polar opposite personalities. Since Josh was a toddler, it was clear that he didn't see the point in expending excessive effort on pretty much anything. A kind, smart kid, he's an underachiever who frustrates his parents to no end. Madison, in contrast, is a full-of-energy self-starter, who crosses every *t* and dots every *i*. Were these the only children in the family, the comparisons between them would no doubt be harmful to them both. But then along came Sarah.

Sarah is the lastborn, a child with an entirely unique temperament. She likes to take things slowly and savors each moment intensely. School is not a priority for her. Because of her charm and optimism, she's great company. She softens the edges of both Josh and Madison, and her parents are incredibly grateful. "Without Sarah," her mother says, "I think the house would be a war zone. She takes some of the pressure off Josh and some of the glow off Madison. With her we have a much better balance."

Another benefit of not being under a spotlight is that children are freer to become themselves rather than adhere to their parents' image of who they should be. This is usually a good thing. Research and anecdotal evidence has proven time and time again that genuine motivation and desire, combined with a good grasp of personal abilities, lead to a greater and more authentic sense of well-being.

4. Parents get better with practice.

The Hardy family had its heart in the right place: When Josh was little, they signed him up for karate and piano. He played soccer early on, then switched to lacrosse. When Madison was born, they dragged her along to Josh's practices even though he was never that enthralled with any of his extracurricular experiences. Eventually, Madison became interested in sports. She was so gung-ho and driven by her own interests that it didn't take long for her parents to figure out that Josh didn't get nearly the same satisfaction from his activities as his sister did. When baby Sarah was old enough to enter the world of scheduled activities, she declined to get involved at all. "We tried our best with Josh and Madison, and it was *so* stressful for us all," said Catherine. "We thought it was the 'right' thing to do. Really, it wasn't till Sarah was about five that I felt I was beginning to understand how to be a good parent to all my kids. We had to learn that success and happiness come in very different forms."

By the time parents get to their third or fourth child, they have a much better understanding of their own parenting styles. Being exposed to children with very different personalities is both humbling and incredibly instructive. Parents learn to pick their battles and enjoy their successes. Most critically, they're able to better align their aspirations to their child's actual abilities and inclinations.

5. It's okay to be different.

In today's increasingly global world, where people change jobs a dozen times or more during their careers and juggle multiple roles in their personal lives, having a set world view or a rigid personality is in no way helpful.

Children from larger families—and middles in

particular—are more likely to be open to expressing themselves in different ways. They see themselves as part of the bigger picture. Since they haven't been the center of attention all their lives, they understand that they are not the center of the universe, either. As a consequence, they can put hurdles into perspective and develop a better sense of how to work in partnerships with others. They respect differences.

The ability of middleborns to diversify, to be open to new challenges and experiences, is a trait that's becoming increasingly valuable in the workplace. People must be flexible, often changing careers and domiciles many times in one lifetime. Jakob, the middle of three boys, is now a film editor. But first he trained as a journalist and then worked as an advertising executive before moving to the West Coast to become involved in the movie business. "It took me a while to figure out who I was supposed to be, but that was all right," he says. "I knew it was important to be open to a lot of options." Thus, the willingness to consider new opportunities and be flexible are vital traits.

What should we know after closing this book?

I've spent a lot of time online participating in discussions about the experience of being a middle, reading about their concerns, and seeing their perspectives played out in conversations and posts. That community reveals a largely negative view of being a middleborn. It doesn't take long to figure out that those middle children who take the time to vent online feel unfairly overlooked, and many of them feel worthless and despondent. In real life, middles I know personally or have interviewed seem less negative overall, but an undertow of resentment can still be detected.

It's my feeling that this is wholly unnecessary. I believe that when middles become aware that they've armed themselves with invaluable skills because of the strategies they employed growing up, they'll realize they have a lot going for them. And it's my hope that after reading this book, they'll feel confident about themselves and their abilities and will understand why getting less attention as a child was probably a plus for their future.

It is up to middles and their parents to recognize these advantages (and also the disadvantages) and put this knowledge to good use. Here are some important lessons for middleborns to take away with them:

- The amount of parental attention you receive as a child doesn't define how well you will turn out.
- Self-esteem is best when earned. It's a reminder that the world does not revolve around you.
- Sometimes you need to be able to walk away, especially when you're being taken advantage of.
- Sometimes you need to step up to the plate—such as when there's conflict you simply can't avoid.
- You'll be happiest if you continue to carve your own path through life—and take calculated risks.
- You are moderate and well-balanced by nature, so don't be afraid to rock the boat once in a while.

Friends and parents of middles need to recognize and respect middles' way of getting things done. Their desire to get along shouldn't be exploited. I hope this book will show everyone that their empathy and flexibility is a valuable skill, not a weakness to exploit. In the first chapter I talked about my friend Leslie, a middleborn who was so giving that she often found herself being taken advantage of. But once she matured, she was able to see that her kindness and generosity were gifts to be handled with care. She no longer allows people to take those gifts for granted, but first she had to recognize that these were precious traits.

Also, let's not assume middles aren't high achievers simply because they approach achievement differently than firsts. If there is one lesson to take away from this book, it's that we each have our own path to follow, and the first step on a smooth journey along that path is recognizing and encouraging individual potential.

Lastly, middles deserve the same amount of attention as other birth orders in terms of research. There is a lot more work to be done in the realm of birth order study. But before that can begin in earnest, researchers and counselors need to stop lumping middles with lastborns into the "laterborn" category. It is simply not accurate. We need more solid research that looks at middles as a separate category and also at the impact of gender. Some of my early work indicated that certain birth order effects are stronger in females, and others occur more frequently in males. As women continue to play larger roles in business and politics, it becomes increasingly important to determine whether these kinds of effects will have an impact on the society of the future.

Another notable change is that, despite the leveling off of population growth in developing nations, there's been an extraordinary increase in the number of multiple births. This also merits further study. Between 1980 and 1999, the overall multiple birth ratio increased almost 60 percent, with older mothers showing the biggest increases. This is likely to continue rising as the number of couples using reproductive technology increases. The effect on family dynamics and birth order is huge. Will the triplet born second automatically become the middle, or will birth order be determined by the individual personality of the children? In a family where multiple children are the same age (going through developmental milestones at the same time and requiring the same amount of attention), what strategies will children develop to grab their share of parental attention? Will the qualities that middles reveal continue to be in force in a household of multiples, or will it be more like having a family of all firsts or all lasts?

Or, who knows, perhaps it will be the best of all worlds, with each multiple ending up as a de facto middle child. I look forward to additional research in all these areas.

What the future looks like

We've all heard dire warnings about how, in the future, we'll no longer engage in real human contact. Sitting alone at our desks or in our virtual reality pods, we'll be able to experience everything we want or need without looking another person in the eye. So why does it matter in the long run that we recognize and learn from the positive traits that middles introduce into society? Won't these skills be obsolete soon?

But let's hold on a moment. If face-to-face interaction is no longer important and work can be done solely by email or webcasts—or whatever new method technology will offer us in the future—why is there such rapid growth in video conferencing technology? Even if people can't shake hands or react to intangible "vibes" in the air during meetings, we still want to have some sense of personal interaction with others when we're going about our daily business. It has been part of our DNA for tens of thousands of years and will likely continue to be.

Even if our mode of communication changes, I believe our work lives will always require the kinds of skills that middles embody. Whenever we are interacting with another human being, it will be crucial to show skill in negotiating, the ability to think outside the box, and an empathetic sensibility. And these will continue to be invaluable traits in our personal lives. Our definition of community may well change, but the ingredients for successful interactions will not.

Looking to the past, I often wonder about my dad. What would he think of my work in general, and especially this book? As a middle-born he achieved extraordinary balance between work and home life (and had the good sense to marry my well-organized, firstborn mom). He worked diligently so that his children could enjoy all the advantages he didn't have. And yet he was still a hands-on parent. Because of him I became much more independent than the average youngest child, and for that I will always be grateful. I like to think that in his own way he raised a first and lastborn to have a little of the best of middles.

We have a lot to learn from middle children. As negotiators they take the time to see things from other points of view. This give-and-take serves the best interests of both parties. As trailblazers, middles take considered risks and discover that the less trod path is often the best one. And our society will certainly continue to need justice seekers who understand that there is more to life than financial rewards. Middleborn independence and resilience are characteristics that I'd hate to see disappear in a future population of only small families—especially at a time when our world so needs these particular skills.

As parents and teachers we can take some of the lessons that middles reveal to us and apply them to the parenting and teaching of future generations. If we could all be a little more like middleborns, that would be a good thing.

Chapter One

Ansbacher, H. L., and Ansbacher, R. R. (1964). *The Individual Psychology of Alfred Adler.* New York: Harper.

Ernst, C., and Angst, J. (1983). *Birth Order: Its Influence on Personality.* Berlin: Springer-Verlag.

Galton, F. (1874). *English Men of Science: Their Nature and Murture.* New York: A. Appleton and Company.

Herrera, N. C.; Zajonc, R. B.; Wieczorkowska, G.; and Cichomski, B. (2003). "Beliefs about birth rank and their reflection in reality." *Journal of Personality and Social Psychology* 85, 142–150.

Leman, K. (2006, 5th print). *The Birth Order Book: Why You Are the Way You Are*. Grand Rapids, MI: Revell.

Lougheed, L. W., and Anderson, D. J. (1999). "Parent blue-footed boobies suppress siblicidal behavior of offspring." *Behavioral Ecology and Sociobiology* 45, 11–18.

Nyman, L. (2001). "The identification of birth order personality attributes." *The Journal of Psychology* 129, 51–59.

Salmon, C., and Daly, M. (1998). "The impact of birth order on familial sentiment: Middleborns are different." *Human Behavior and Evolution* 19, 229–312.

Sulloway, F. J. (1996). *Born to Rebel: Birth Order, Family Dynamics, and Creative Lives*. New York: Pantheon.

Trivers, R. L. (1974). "Parent-offspring conflict." *American Zoologist* 14, 249–64.

Chapter Two

Bereczkei, T., and Dunbar, R. I. M. (1997). "Female-biased reproductive strategies in a Hungarian Gypsy population." *Proceedings of the Royal Society, London, B,* 264, 17–22.

Bereczkei, T., and Dunbar, R. I. M. (2002). "Helping-at-the-nest and sex-biased parental investment in a Hungarian Gypsy population." *Current Anthropology* 43, 804–809.

Daly, M., and Wilson, M. (1988). *Homicide*. Hawthorne, NY: Aldine.

Daly, M., and Wilson, M. (1995). "Discriminative parental solicitude and the relevance of evolutionary models to the analysis of motivational systems." In *The Cognitive Neurosciences*, M. Gazzaniga, ed., pp. 1269–86. Cambridge, MA: MIT Press.

Dickemann, M. (1979). "Female infanticide, reproductive strategies, and social stratification: a preliminary model." In *Evolutionary Biology and*

Human Social Behavior, N.A. Chagnon and W. Irons, eds., pp. 321–367. North Scituate, MA: Duxbury Press.

Gaulin, S. J. C., and Robbins, C. J. (1991). "Trivers-Willard effect in contemporary North American society." *American Journal of Physical Anthropology* 85, 61–69.

Hamilton, W. D. (1964). "The genetical evolution of social behavior." *Journal of Theoretical Biology* 7, 1–16.

Koch, H. L. (1956). "Some emotional attitudes of the young child in relation to characteristics of his sibling." *Child Development* 27, 393–426.

Lee, B. J., and George, R. M. (1999). "Poverty, early childbearing and child maltreatment: A multinomial analysis." *Children and Youth Services Review* 21, 755–780.

Lindstrom, D. P., and Berhanu, B. (2000). "The effects of breastfeeding and birth spacing on infant and early childhood mortality in Ethiopia." *Social Biology* 47, 1–17.

Parker, G. A.; Mock, D. W.; and Lamey, T. C. (1989). "How selfish should stronger sibs be?" *American Naturalist* 133, 846–868.

Salmon, C. A., and Daly, M. (1998). "Birth order and familial sentiment: Middleborns are different." *Evolution and Human Behavior* 19, 299–312.

Segal, N. L. (1999). *Entwined Lives: Twins and What They Tell Us About Human Behavior.* New York: Dutton.

Sulloway, F. J. (1996). *Born to Rebel.* New York: Pantheon.

Sulloway, F. J. (1999). "Birth Order." In *Encyclopedia of Creativity 1,* M. A. Runco and S. Pritzker, eds., pp. 189–202. San Diego: Academic Press.

Trivers, R. L. (1974). "Parent-offspring conflict." *American Zoologist* 14, 249–264.

Trivers, R. L., and Willard, D. (1973). "Natural selection of parental ability to vary the sex-ratio of offspring." *Science* 179, 90–92.

Voland, E., and Gabler, S. (1994). "Differential twin mortality indicates a correlation between age and parental effort in humans." *Naturwissenschaften* 81, 224–225.

Reeves, R. (2007). *President Nixon: Alone in the White House.* New York: Simon and Schuster, p. 13.

Gannon, Frank: Feb 9, 1983. *Richard Nixon/ Frank Gannon Interviews.* Day 1, Tape 1, 01:12:41; Day 1, Tape 2, 01:17:09

http://www.brainyquote.com/quotes/authors/t/tom_cruise.html

Chapter Three

Bancroft, G. (1865). *Our Martyr President, Abraham Lincoln: Voices from the Pulpit of New York and Brooklyn.* New York: Tibbals and Whiting, p. 400.

Beck, E.; Burnet, K. L.; and Vosper, J. (2006). "Birth-order effects on facets of extraversion." *Personality and Individual Differences* 40, 953–59.

Bender, M. (1983). "The Empire and Ego of Donald Trump." *New York Times,* August 7.

Hall, A. (2002). "Curing a Sickness Called Success." *Sunday Times,* December 15.

Courtiol, A.; Raymond, M.; and Faurie, C. (2009). "Birth order affects behaviour in the investment game: Firstborns are less trustful and reciprocate less." *Animal Behaviour* 78, 1405–11.

Henshaw, L. (2002). "A study of self-esteem in middle children." Unpublished master's thesis, Rowan University.

Herndon, W. H., and Weik, J. W. (2009). "Herndon's Lincoln: A true story of a great life." New York: Cosimo Classics, 487–88.

Karrass, C. L. (1994). *The Negotiating Game*. New York: Harper Paperbacks.

Kidwell, J. S. (1982). "The neglected birth order: Middleborns." *Journal of Marriage and the Family* 44, 225–35.

Paulhus, D. L.; Trapnell, P. D.; and Chen, D. (1999). "Birth order effects on personality and achievement within families." *Psychological Science* 10, 482–88.

Saraglou, V., and Fiasse, L. (2003). "Birth order, personality, and religion: A study among young adults from a 3-sibling family." *Personality and Individual Differences* 35, 19–29.

Syed, M. U. (2004). "Birth order and personality: A methodological study." Unpublished master's thesis, San Francisco State University.

Trump, D. (2004). *Trump: The Art of the Deal*. New York: Ballantine Books, p. 50.

http://www.dattnerconsulting.com/presentations/birthorder.pdf

http://www.knesset.gov.il/process/docs/sadatspeech_eng.htm

Chapter Four

Bjerkedal, T.; Kristensen, P.; Skjeret, G.A.; and Brevik, J.I. (2007). "Intelligence test scores and birth order among young Norwegian men (conscripts) analyzed within and between families." *Intelligence* 35, 503–14.

Ernst, C., and Angst, J. (1983). *Birth Order: Its Influence on Personality*. New York: Springer, p. 240.

Gates, B. (1995). *The Road Ahead*. New York: Viking.

Eschelbach, M. (2009). "Crown princes and benjamins: Birth order and educational attainment in East and West Germany." BGPE Discussion Paper 85. University of Erlangen-Nuremberg.

Kalmuss, D., and Davidson, A. (1992). "Parenting expectations, experiences, and adjustment to parenthood: A test of the violated expectations framework." *Journal of Marriage and the Family* 54, 516–26.

Kennedy, G. E. (1989). "Middleborns' perceptions of family relation-ships." *Psychological Reports* 64, 755–60.

Marjoribanks, K. (1995). "Ethnicity, birth order, and family environ-ment." *Psychological Reports* 84, 758–60.

Musun-Miller, L. (1992). "Sibling status effects: Parents' perceptions of their own children." *Journal of Genetic Psychology* 154, 189–98.

Plomin, R., and Daniels, D. (1987). "Why are children in the same family so different from each other?" *Behavioral and Brain Sciences* 10, 1–16.

Plomin, R.; Asbury, K.; and Dunn, J. (2001). "Why are children in the same family so different from each other? Non-shared environment a decade later." *Canadian Journal of Psychiatry* 46, 225–33.

Rothbart, M. K. (1972). "Birth order and mother-child interaction in an achievement situation." In U. Bronfenbrenner (ed.), *Influences on Human Development*, 352–65. Hinsdale, Illinois: The Dryden Press Inc.

Saad, G.; Gill, T.; and Nataraajan, R. (2005). "Are laterborns more innovative and nonconforming consumers than firstborns? A Darwin-ian perspective." *Journal of Business Research* 58, 902–09.

Salmon, C. A., and Daly, M. (1998). "Birth order and familial sentiment: Middleborns are different." *Evolution and Human Behavior* 19, 299–312.

Salmon, C., and Janicki, M. "The impact of sex and birth order on parental investment and social exchange." Unpublished manuscript.

Sen, A., and Clemente, A. (2010). "Intergenerational correlations in educational attainment: Birth order and family size effects using Canadian data." *Economics of Education Review* 29, 147–55.

Suitor, J., and Pillemer, K. (2007). "Mothers' favoritism in later life." *Research on Aging* 29, 32–55.

Sulloway, F. J. (1996). *Born to Rebel*. New York: Pantheon.

Sulloway, F. J., and Zweigenhaft, R. L. "Birth order and risk taking in athletics: A meta-analysis and study of major league baseball players." *Personality and Social Psychology Review* 14, 402–16.

Syed, M. U. (2004). "Birth order and personality: A methodological study." Unpublished master's thesis, San Francisco State University.

Chapter Five

Adler, A. (1956). *The Individual Psychology of Alfred Adler*. H. L. Ansbacher and R. R. Ansbacher (eds.). New York: Harper Torchbooks, p. 380.

Douglass, W. O. (1949). Stare Decisis. *Columbia Law Review* 49, 735–58.

Grose, M. (2003). *Why Firstborns Rule the World, and Lastborns Want to Change It*. Sydney, Australia: Random House.

Healy, M. D. (2009). "Effects of birth order on personality: A within-family examination of sibling niche differentiation." Unpublished Ph.D. thesis. University of Canterbury.

Herrera, N. C.; Zajonc, R. B.; Wieczorkowska, G.; and Cichomski, B. (2003). "Beliefs about birth rank and their reflection in reality." *Journal of Personality and Social Psychology* 85, 142–50.

McGuire, K. T. (2008). *Justices and Their Birth Order: An Assessment of the Origins of Preferences on the U.S. Supreme Court*. Paper presented at the annual meeting of the Midwest Political Science Association, Chicago, April 3-6, 2008.

Sulloway, F. J. (1996). *Born to Rebel*. New York: Pantheon.

Pink, D. (2006). *A Whole New Mind: Why Right-Brainers Will Rule the Future*. New York: Riverhead Trade.

Plowman, I. C. (2005). "Birth order, motives, occupational role choice and organizational innovation: An evolutionary perspective." Unpublished Ph.D. thesis, University of Queensland.

Zweigenhaft, R. L., and Von Ammon, J. (2000). Birth order and civil disobedience: A test of Sulloway's 'Born to Rebel' hypothesis. *The Journal of Social Psychology* 140, 624–27.

http://www.unc.edu/~kmcguire/papers.html

http://www.time.com/time/magazine/article/0,9171,913732-1,00.html

http://www.anc.org.za/ancdocs/history/mandela/1990/release.html

http://www.afscme.org/about/1549.cfm

http://mlk-kpp01.stanford.edu/index.php/encyclopedia/documentsentry/doc_remaining_awake_through_a_great_revolution/

http://www.eliewieselfoundation.org/

http://www.dalailama.com/messages/compassion

Chapter Six

Barsade, S. G., and Gibson, D. E. (2007). "Why does affect matter in organizations?" *Academy of Management Perspectives*, February, 36–59.

Bhide, A. (1999). *How Entrepreneurs Craft Strategies That Work*. Boston: Harvard Business School Press, p. 83.

Bronson, P. (2005). *What Should I Do with My Life?: The True Story of People Who Answered the Ultimate Question*. New York: Ballantine Books.

Leong, F. T. L.; Hartung, P. J.; Goh, D.; and Gaylor, M. (2001). "Appraising birth order in career assessment: Linkages to Holland's and Super's models." *Journal of Career Assessment* 9(1), 25–39.

Levine, M. (2005). *Ready or Not, Here Life Comes*. New York: Simon and Schuster.

Moore, K. K., and Cox, J. A. (1990). "Doctor, lawyer . . . or Indian chief? The effects of birth order." *Baylor Business Review*, winter, 18–21.

Murawski, M.; Miederhoff, P.; and Rule, W. (1995). Birth order and communication skills of pharmacy students. *Perceptual and Motor Skills* 80, 891–95.

Palmer, P. (1999). *Let your Life Speak: Listening for the Voice of Vocation.* New York: Jossey-Bass, p. 15.

Plowman, I. C. (2005). "Birth order, motives, occupational role choice and organizational innovation: An evolutionary perspective." Unpublished Ph.D. thesis, University of Queensland.

Sulloway, F. J. (2010). "Why siblings are like Darwin's finches: Birth order, sibling competition, and adaptive divergence within the family." In *The Evolution of Personality and Individual Differences* D. M. Buss and P. H. Hawley (eds.), pp. 86–120. New York: Oxford University Press.

Steinbeck, J. (1958). *Once There Was a War.* New York: Bantam, p. 65.

http://www.achievement.org/autodoc/page/del0int-7

http://www.nytimes.com/2010/05/16/business/16corner.html?_r=1

http://www.bls.gov/news.release/pdf/nlsoy.pdf

http://www.leadershipnow.com/couragequotes.html

http://www.careerbuilder.com/share/aboutus/pressreleasesdetail.aspx?id=pr453&sd=8%2f20%2f2008&ed=12%2f31%2f2008

Chapter Seven

Cooper, A. (1997). "George Burns", *Playboy Magazine*: 26.

Draper, P., and Harpending, H. (1982). Father absence and reproductive strategy: An evolutionary perspective. *Journal of Anthropological Research* 38, 255–73.

Gottfried, M. (1996). *George Burns: The Hundred-Year Dash.* New York: Macmillan Publishing Company.

Henshaw, L. (2002). "A study of self-esteem in middle children." Unpublished master's thesis." Rowan University.

Herrera, N. C.; Zajonc, R. B.; Wieczorkowska, G.; and Cichomski, B. (2003). "Beliefs about birth rank and their reflection in reality." *"Journal of Personality and Social Psychology* 85, 142–50.

Kidwell, J. S. (1982). "The neglected birth order: Middleborns." *Journal of Marriage and the Family* 44, 225–35.

Miller, N., and Maruyama, G. (1976). "Ordinal position and peer popularity." *Journal of Social and Personality Psychology* 33, 123–31.

Mysterud, I.; Drevon, T.; and Slagsvold, T. (2006). "An evolutionary interpretation of gift-giving behavior in modern Norwegian society." *Evolutionary Psychology* 4, 406–25.

Parker, J. G.; and Asher, S. R. (1987). "Peer relations and later personal adjustment: Are low-accepted children at risk?" *Psychological Bulletin* 102, 357–89.

Roff, M., and Sells, S. B. (1970). "Juvenile delinquency in relation to peer acceptance-rejection and socioeconomic status." *Psychology in the Schools* 5, 3–18.

Rutherford, Megan, Nov. 13, 2000. "Pal Power" *Time*, http://www.time.com/time/magazine/article/0,9171,998457,00.html.

Salmon, C. A. (2010). "The impact of birth order on sexual attitudes and behaviour." Presentation at Human Evolution and Behavior annual meeting in Eugene, Oregon.

Salmon, C. A. (2003). "Birth order and relationships: Family, friends and sexual partners." *Human Nature* 14, 73–88.

Salmon, C. A., and Daly, M. (1998). "The impact of birth order on familial sentiment: Middleborns are different." *Evolution and Human Behavior* 19, 299–312.

Sells, S. B., and Roff, M. (1964). "Peer acceptance-rejection and birth order." *Psychology in the Schools* 1, 156-62.

Sulloway, F. J. (1996). *Born to Rebel: Birth Order, Family Dynamics, and Creative Lives*. New York: Oxford University Press.

Usher, Shaun (March 11, 1996) *The Daily Mail* 32.

Weller, L.; Natan, O.; and Hazi, O. (1974). "Birth order and marital bliss in Israel." *Journal of Marriage and the Family* 36, 794–97.

Zecher, Henry (1996). "Goodnight, George! The world's best-loved cigar smoker takes his final bow." *The Pipe Smoker's Ephemeris*, Dunn, T. (ed.), Winter/Summer 1996, 7.

Chapter Eight

Andrews, P. W. (2005). "Parent-offspring conflict and cost-benefit analysis of adolescent suicidal behavior." *Human Nature* 17, 190–211.

Argys, L. M.; Rees, D. I.; Averett, S. L.; and Witoonchart, B. (2006). "Birth order and risky adolescent behavior." *Journal of Economic Inquiry* 44, 215–33.

Brandon, N. (2001). *The Psychology of Self-Esteem*. Hoboken, N. J.: Jossey-Bass.

Bronson, P., and Merryman, A. (2009). *NurtureShock: New Thinking About Children*. New York: Twelve.

Harris, J. R. (1998). *The Nurture Assumption: Why Children Turn Out the Way They Do*. New York: Free Press, p. 349.

Johnson, E., and Novack, W. (1993). *My Life*. Greenwich, Conn.: Fawcett.

Kennedy, G. E. (1989). "Middleborns' perceptions of family relationships." *Psychological Reports* 64, 755–60.

Kidwell, J. S. (1982). "The neglected birth order: Middleborns." *Journal of Marriage and the Family* 44, 225–35.

Kidwell, J. S. (1981). "Number of siblings, sibling spacing, sex, and birth order: Their effects on perceived parent-adolescent relationships." *Journal of Marriage and the Family* 43, 315–32.

Lampi, E., and Nordblom, K. (2010). "Money and success: Sibling and birth order effects on positional concerns." *Journal of Economic Psychology* 31, 131–42.

Levin, M. (2008). *The Price of Privilege: How Parental Pressure and Material Advantage Are Creating a Generation of Disconnected and Unhappy Kids*. New York: Harper Paperbacks.

Levine, M. (2005). *Ready or Not, Here Life Comes*. New York: Simon and Schuster.

Salmon, C.A. (1998). "The evocative impact of kin terminology in political rhetoric." *Politics and the Life Sciences* 17(1), 51–57.

Salmon, C. A., and Daly, M. (1998). "The impact of birth order on familial sentiment: Middleborns are different." *Evolution and Human Behavior* 19, 299–312.

Sells, S. B., and Roff, M. (1968). "Juvenile delinquency in relation to peer acceptance-rejection and socioeconomic status." *Psychology in the Schools* 5, 3–18.

Sells, S. B., and Roff, M. (1964). "Peer acceptance-rejection and birth order." *Psychology in the Schools* 1, 156–62.

Taylor, J. (2003). *Positive Pushing: How to Raise a Successful and Happy Child*. New York: Hyperion.

Thirteen (2003). Movie cowritten by Catherine Hardwicke and Nikki Reed and directed by Catherine Hardwicke.

Watkins, Jr., C. (1992). "Birth order research and Adler's theory: A critical review." *Individual Psychology* 48, 357–68.

http://www.usatoday.com/money/companies/management/entre/2008-12-07-magic-johnson-urban-business_N.htm.

Chapter Nine

Assor, A.; Roth, G.; and Deci, E. L. (2004). "The emotional costs of parents' conditional regard: A self determination theory analysis." *Journal of Personality* 72, 47–89.

Baumrind, D. (1966). "Effects of authoritative parental control on child behavior." *Child Development 37*, 887–907.

Baumrind, D. (1967). "Child care practices anteceding three patterns of preschool behavior." *Genetic Psychology Monographs* 74, 43–88.

Beauregard, M.; Courtemanche, J.; Paquette, V.; and St.-Pierre, E. L. (2009). "The neural basis of unconditional love." *Psychiatry Research: Neuroimaging* 172, 93–98.

Bednar, D. E., and Fisher, T. D. (2003). "Peer referencing in adolescent decision making as a function of perceived parenting style." *Adolescence* 38, 607–21.

Brooks, R., and Goldstein, S. (2002). *Raising Resilient Children*. New York: McGraw Hill, p. 7.

Darwin, C. (1992). *Autobiography of Charles Darwin and Selected Letters*. F. Darwin (ed). New York: Dover Publications, pp. 90–92.

Dogan, S. J.; Conger, R. D.; Kim, K. J.; and Masyn, K. E. (2007). "Cognitive and parenting pathways in the transmission of antisocial behavior from parents to adolescents." *Child Development* 78, 335–49.

Forer, L. K., and Still, H. (1977). *The Birth Order Factor*. New York: Pocket Books.

Goleman, D. (1997). *Emotional Intelligence: Why It Can Matter More Than IQ*. New York: Bantam Publishers, p. 28.

Kohn, A. (2009). "When a parent's 'I love you' means 'do as I say,'" *New York Times*, NY Edition, Sept. 15, D5.

Levin, M. (2008). *The Price of Privilege: How Parental Pressure and Material Advantage Are Creating a Generation of Disconnected and Unhappy Kids*. New York: Harper Paperbacks, p. 94.

Loomis, C. L. (2006). "A conversation with Warren Buffett," *Fortune Magazine*, June 25.

Rothrauff, T. C.; Cooney, T. M.; and An, J. S. (2009). "Remembered parenting styles and adjustment in middle and late adulthood." *Journal of Gerontology B Psychological Sciences* 64, 137–46.

Shor, E. L. (2004). *Caring for Your School-Age Child*. New York: Bantam, p. 53.

Steinberg, L.; Lamborn, S. D.; Dornbusch, S. M.; and Darling, N. (1992). "Impact of parenting practices on adolescent achievement: Authoritative parenting, school involvement, and encouragement to succeed." *Child Development* 63, 1266–81.

http://www.americanrhetoric.com/speeches/princeharrydianaeulogy.htm

http://www.time.com/time/business/article/0,8599,1843839,00.html

http://www.time.com/time/specials/2007/article/
0,28804,1595326_1615754_1616304,00.html

http://www.guardian.co.uk/uk/1999/oct/13/monarchy.features11

http://www.nytimes.com/2009/09/15/health/15mind.html

INDEX